Emotions in the Law School

Law schools are failing both their staff and students by requiring them to prize reason and rationality and to suppress or ignore emotions. Despite innovations in terms of both content and teaching techniques, there is little evidence that emotions are effectively acknowledged or utilised within legal education. Instead law schools are clinging to an outdated and erroneous perception of emotions as at best, irrational, and at worst dangerous. In contrast to this, educational and scientific developments have demonstrated that emotions are a fundamental, inescapable part of learning, teaching and skills development. Harnessing these emotions will therefore have a transformative effect on legal education and enable it to adapt to the needs and demands of the twenty-first century.

This book provides a theoretical overview of the role played by emotions in all aspects of the life of the law school. It explores the relationship emotions have with key traditional and contemporary approaches to legal education, the ways in which emotions can be conceptualised, their interaction with the politics and policies of legal education and their role within teaching and learning. The book also considers the importance of emotional wellbeing for both law students and legal academics.

Overall, this book argues for a more holistic form of legal education in which emotions play a valuable (and valued) role. This requires a new vision for law schools, in which emotions are acknowledged and embedded at all levels, institutional and personal.

Dr Emma Jones is Senior Lecturer in Law and Teaching Director at The Open University Law School. Her research focuses on the role of emotions and wellbeing in legal education and the legal profession.

Legal Pedagogy

Series Editor Kris Gledhill

Auckland University of Technology, New Zealand

This series consists of high-quality monographs, each of which explores best practice in an aspect of the law school curriculum. Books cover teaching methods and curriculum design in the main areas of law, how to integrate themes and areas of jurisprudential thought, and wider questions about legal education more generally. With contributions from around the world, this series explores innovative thinking and practice within the context of a generally conservative branch of academia, with the aim of promoting discussion as to how best to teach the various aspects of the law degree and ensure the ongoing validity of the law degree as a whole. Typical topics addressed include the value of variety in teaching methods and curriculum design, how best to incorporate educational research, the role for more practical courses, and the need to ensure that law schools provide degrees of relevance to the needs of students and of society.

The books in this series will be of great interest to academics, researchers and postgraduates in the fields of law and education, as well as teachers of law who may be interested in revising curricula and need guidance in doing so. In addition, the legal profession, and in particular those who regulate entry into the profession, will find much to interest them within the series.

Books in this series:

The Teaching of Criminal Law
The pedagogical imperatives
Edited by Kris Gledhill and Ben Livings

Re-thinking Legal Education under the Civil and Common Law
A road map for constructive change
Edited by Richard Grimes

Reimagining Contract Law Pedagogy
A New Agenda for Teaching
Edited by Warren Swain and David Campbell

For more information about books in this series, please visit www.routledge.com/law/series/LEGPED

Emotions in the Law School

Transforming Legal Education Through the Passions

Emma Jones

Routledge
Taylor & Francis Group
LONDON AND NEW YORK

First published 2020
by Routledge
2 Park Square, Milton Park, Abingdon, Oxon OX14 4RN

and by Routledge
605 Third Avenue, New York, NY 10017

First issued in paperback 2021

Routledge is an imprint of the Taylor & Francis Group, an informa business

British Library Cataloguing-in-Publication Data
A catalogue record for this book is available from the British Library

Library of Congress Cataloging-in-Publication Data
A catalog record for this book has been requested

Typeset in Galliard
by Apex CoVantage, LLC

ISBN 13: 978-1-03-224051-0 (pbk)
ISBN 13: 978-1-138-55521-1 (hbk)

DOI: 10.4324/9781315149370

This book is dedicated to my children, William, Annie and Huey, who I love more than words can say. It is also in memory of my grandmother, Margaret Lomas (née Stubbs), who is always loved and missed.

Contents

Acknowledgements viii

Introduction: passions and prejudices in the law school 1

1 Enmity and exclusion within legal education 12

2 A broadening scope, or reason revisited? 36

3 Emotions as a transformative force 58

4 Situating emotions within the politics and policies of academia 80

5 Embracing emotions within learning 104

6 Healthy, wealthy and wise? Law student wellbeing 125

7 Creating an emotionally engaged legal academy 147

Conclusion: feeling our way towards transformation 167

Index 186

Acknowledgements

I was incredibly fortunate to have Professor Fiona Cownie and Professor Anthony Bradney (both of Keele University) as my Phd supervisors. I am even more fortunate that they have continued to offer their support and guidance since that time. This book would not exist without their insight and understanding.

During the writing of this book, I was also grateful to be in the supportive and collegiate atmosphere of The Open University Law School. My thanks to the Head of the Law School, Paul Catley, for allowing me sabbatical time in which to complete the work.

My colleague, Rajvinder Samra, Lecturer in Health at The Open University, provided valuable comments on Chapter 3 of this book. Her standard of work is inspirational.

I also appreciate the support from the team at Routledge throughout my work on this book, together with that of Kris Gledhill, series editor for Legal Pedagogy.

My parents, Mervyn and Margaret Lomas, provided much practical and emotional support during the period in which this book was written (and the forty-two years prior to that), not least somewhere to live during a difficult house move. I am not sure I ever adequately show them how much I love and appreciate them.

Finally, my husband, David Jones, has provided endless love, support and patience throughout the time spent writing this book. I hope he knows how very much he means to me.

Introduction

Passions and prejudices in the law school

The law is uncomfortable with emotions.[1] It largely seeks to disregard them as irrelevant and irreverent, or it attempts to suppress them as difficult, damaging and even dangerous. This is despite (or perhaps even because of) the law's lifeblood being crimes of passion, angry disputes, jealous rivalries and bitter fallings-out. This is despite it regularly dealing with the full spectrum of emotions from shame, disgust, suspicion and hate to lust, love, happiness and joy. This is despite it being questionable whether the law would even exist, or what form it would take, if it were not for the need to regulate the reality of humanity's emotional existence. Perhaps the most obvious manifestations of this emotional maelstrom are in relation to the dark passions and motives abounding within criminal law. However, emotions are also inherent within the civil law. Even a minor breach of contract can generate emotions such as anger, misery, shame or indignation. Consulting a legal professional is accompanied by a range of emotions, be it anger or injustice, sadness or bitterness, or a desire for revenge. Even the concept of the law itself engenders an emotional response for many, be it pride, contempt or frustration. There is, therefore, a paradox at the heart of legal matters as the law attempts to ignore or quash the very part of human existence which necessitates its own existence. It seeks to discard or denigrate the inescapable, and the essential, presence of emotions in human affairs (Bailey and Knight, 2017; Maroney, 2016; Grossi, 2015; Bandes and Blumenthal, 2012).

> The notion that reason and emotion are cleanly separable-and that law rightly privileges and admits only of the former-is deeply engrained.
>
> (Maroney, 2006, p. 119)

For the law, emotions represent the messy, the subjective, the irrational and the dangerous. In contrast, the law imposes order, objectivity, rationality and reason (or so it says). It seeks to disregard emotions and, when it cannot do so, it works hard to suppress them (Bandes, 2013; Schlag, 1998). Where emotions have to be admitted into the legal arena (for example, with the loss of control defence for manslaughter in the United Kingdom (UK))[2] they are regularised, contained and (as far as possible) sanitised. A circumscribed display of so-called emotions may even, on occasion, be encouraged in contemporary neo-liberal society. Take, for example, the case of the convicted defendant in a criminal matter who during sentencing must show remorse or be labelled a "hardened criminal", even if it is later discovered they had the integrity to continue correctly maintaining their innocence (Sanger, 2001, p. 111; see also Weisman, 2014). The particular emotion involved in such a display often becomes a shallow, inauthentic and tame replica of its real self. Bandes (2013, pp. 927–928) encapsulates this well when recalling a New Yorker cartoon in which a lawyer advises their client "Make eye contact with the jury, but not homicidal maniac eye contact". This demonstrates that any such encouragement and acknowledgement of emotions is within strictly prescribed limits, reinforcing legal boundaries that are themselves designed to reinforce the contrast between the human frailty of the law's accused and the invulnerability of the law itself.

This disregard and suppression (or at best mistreatment) of emotions is not an approach to law that is tied to one philosophical or legal tradition and it is not one perspective amongst many. Instead, it is the dominant, overriding, mainstream approach taken by law to emotions within Western society. At least traditionally, it has been an approach that has persisted with relatively little sustained challenge. Although alternative viewpoints and narratives have been proffered throughout history, from Aristotle's discussion of judgement in his *Rhetoric* to the critique provided by the early twentieth-century legal realists in the United States of America (USA), the impact of these has been, at best, limited and, at worst, easily ignored (Bailey and Knight, 2017; Maroney, 2011). As feminist, critical and law and emotions scholars aim arrows and darts at its assumptions, biases and prejudices, the law remains steadfast and, seemingly, imperturbable in its retention of an outdated, and often demonizing, characterisation of emotions. Abrams and Keren (2010) suggest that the law has found it far easier to embrace recent developments relating law to behaviour and economics and neuroscience than the law and emotions movement because those movements seek to correct legal decision-making in a way which makes it more rational, whereas incorporating and utilising emotions within law challenge the law's notion of rationality itself. Whatever the reasons, the relatively small pinpricks created by personal narrative, empirical accounts and ideological excavations have not, to date, created a long-lasting and deep impression.

In taking this approach, the law draws comfort, even support, from the western tradition of Cartesianism, in particular Cartesian dualism, based on the work of the philosopher Rene Descartes (1596–1650) who believed there was a division in human functions between the body and the mind (which he referred to as the soul). Within the body, he argued, there are tiny particles carried by the blood which send messages from the heart to the brain and from there to the muscles. In other words, what we would now call emotions are bodily sensations which travel to, and excite, the mind. The mind itself is viewed as the site of reason and rationality. Although it cannot prevent the emotions from occurring, it does regulate the person's response to them by exercising wisdom and sound moral judgement. The mind perceives the dangers of such "animal spirits" and seeks to control its response to them, something requiring an almost Pavlovian training in those with weaker minds (Descartes, 1989, p. 24). Descartes does emphasise that emotions can be beneficial and good so long as they are not excessive in nature, or misused. However, he draws a clear distinction between the rationality and wisdom of reason and the tempestuous excitations of emotions. It is this split, or dualism, which is in turn mirrored in the perceived split between the cognitive and affective domains that has traditionally been accepted by scientists.[3]

Such a Cartesian dualism suggests that reason is required to discern and obtain knowledge. This formulates the concept of knowledge as a separate, objective entity which exists to be discovered by a person through their use of reason. This means that the individual:

> Must restrain his emotions, so that they do not cloud his reason, and he must reduce his particularities-as a judge, for example, assumes an institutional role that distances him from personal experiences that might affect his view of the issue before him-so that he can reach a more neutral or universally valid answer.
>
> (Williams, 1993, p. 67)

This enduring view of emotions can be also characterised using a master and slave metaphor with the wisdom of reason as the master who must control the irrationality and dangers of emotions by suppressing, channelling or harmonising them in accordance with the dictates of reason (Solomon, 2000, p. 3).

Therefore, the split between mind and body which Descartes postulated is mirrored in the perceived divide between reason and emotions. Reason is associated with the mind and the higher functions of humanity. Emotions are associated with the body and its animal impulses. Hence the former is prized and exulted and the latter may be despised and disregarded. This tradition does not only persist within law, rather it can often be seen within other facets of society, including education more generally (Hyland, 2014). However, it appears to feed particularly well into law's seemingly innate prejudices and its fascination with being seen as a form of science, with all the accompanying notions of objectivity, neutrality and intellectual status (Nussbaum, 2003). The "enchantment of reason" well and truly has law under its spell (Schlag, 1998, p. 1).

An argument for fundamental change

The purpose of this book is to explore how law's disregard for, and suppression of, emotions has manifested itself within legal education. In particular, it will consider how this approach moulds law students, the legal academy and the law curriculum in its image. The way it prizes the rigid, analytical, unemotional ability to "think like a lawyer" whilst devaluing the traits and abilities that shape our humanity. Its requirement of steadfast and single-minded devotion from its disciples, often at the expense of wellbeing, balance and all those other watch-words of contemporary society. It will emphasise how, at present, legal education does not even seek to sanitise emotions, but instead wholly rejects or ignores them, or at best characterises them as a form of individual weakness to be overcome. It is the law school, the creator of new generations of legal actors, whose mainstream traditions largely still unquestioningly accept and perpetuate the prejudices of law and ignore the passions running through its students and academics, its teaching and learning, its structure and conventions. It seeks to deny the lifeblood of law itself and the genesis of its very own existence. In doing so, it perpetuates a wider legal culture that is narrow, shallow and unexamined in terms of values, feelings and, most particularly, emotions.

This book will argue that such an approach is fundamentally and irrevocably wrong – misguided, misconceived, damaging and foolish. Emotions are inescapable and ever-present within legal education, as within all facets of life. Trying to avoid or ignore this cannot and will not work. Instead, acknowledging and utilising the role of emotions would have a powerful, transformative effect on the law school. In essence, this book argues that emotions can and should be the driver for a more holistic form of law school, one which is beneficial to all involved within it. One in which law students and legal academics can accept and explore emotions and consider when and how they should be regulated and utilised. One in which emotions and wellbeing are integral within the curriculum itself, rather than occasional adjuncts. One in which the law school as an institution appreciates and values the role of emotions in teaching and learning and seeks to nurture and develop this role as a core policy tenet and integral institutional value. One in which emotional wellbeing is not relegated to a pastoral matter targeted at specific individuals, or emotional distress given a medical label, but where instead law schools see it as part of their duty to ensure all their staff and students do not merely survive, but also thrive (Baron, 2007, p. 28).

To this end, the term "transformative" is used here to represent a fundamental change or shift. Unusually (shamefully? Embarrassingly?) for a law book, in this instance it is the simplest definitions that encapsulate this best. Standard dictionary definitions commonly define "transform" as a verb which relates to something changing its form, shape or substance and it is these definitions which encapsulate the fundamental shift this book calls for. It is worth pausing here and acknowledging a debt to transformative learning theory, the concept that learning can contribute to individual change and transformation, allowing each learner to construct a new form of meaning (Taylor and Cranton, 2012). However, the definition of transformation in this book encompasses more than simply the individual as a learner. It is also about the individual as a student, with all the implications of consumerism and employability that entails. Most importantly, it is about the wider conceptualisation of the law school – its staff, culture, curriculum and standing. Personal transformation is vital within legal education, but insufficient on its own. Emotions pervade all structures, hierarchies and aspects of the law school and thus needs to be acknowledged at all levels.

Is emotion inexcusable or inescapable?

Of course, such transformation and change is not intrinsically a beneficial or positive experience. It can equally be divisive, controversial, and even damaging, as exemplified by the introduction of critical legal studies into USA law schools (Hutchinson and Monahan, 1984). In the case of emotions, there are real dangers lurking in the form of neo-liberal, skills-based policy agendas, the medicalisation of wellbeing and the potential, unintended consequences of therapeutic interventions, all of which will be explored within this book. However, there are also imagined, fevered notions that spring from the most basic form of Cartesian dualism and appeal to years of legal tradition, and which need exposing, examining and dispelling at the very start of this book's journey.

For some, when the idea of emotions in the law school is raised, this is viewed as akin to a Woodstock revolution. There are perhaps images of lecture rooms of students crying inconsolably at the ubiquitous Mrs Donoghue and her traumatic discovery of the decomposed snail or Mrs Carlill and her unexpected bout of influenza (plus her reported eventual, strangely fitting demise from, yes, influenza at the age of 96). Or the offices of the law school being congested with queues of students, waiting to spill out their existential angst to a (possibly) sympathetic academic ear. There are strange echoes of Twining's description of the undergraduate law school offering "a primary or even a nursery school for the profession" (Twining, 1997, p. 306) in the idea of time, resources and energy being devoted to a metaphorical mopping up of emotional and childish crises and squabbles. This illustrates well the particular view of emotions that pervades the law and legal education – characterising them as messy, chaotic and irrational. It also represents a fundamental misunderstanding. Acknowledging and utilising the role of emotions in the law school should not be equated with some form of all-encompassing emotional free-for-all. Instead, it will give those involved, particularly students and legal academics, the vocabulary and tools to understand, interpret, appreciate, regulate and utilise emotions in a way which is appropriate, constructive and ultimately enriching both academically and personally. In fact, it is the individual or institution who allows emotions to remain unacknowledged and unexamined that will both create, and struggle to deal with, such heightened emotional responses and reactions by failing to allow emotions their natural and healthy role, and thus not equipping those involved with the ability to respond in an emotionally mature manner (Boran and Delany, 2011).

For other potential critics, there is a perception that the research and foundations of work on emotions in the law school must be purely phenomenological – based on personal, direct experience. However, in another irony, the evidence for the role of emotions is, in fact, based on reason and rationality. The argument for the transformative power of emotions is based on a wide range of evidence drawn from science, education and, indeed, the limited forms of qualitative and quantitative work on law schools that is currently available (most notably in relation to law student wellbeing). For those who adhere to law as a science or quasi-science in the footsteps of Langdell and many others, there is, it is suggested, ample evidence to satisfy their quest for logic and objectivity.

Having said that, if emotions are to be acknowledged and examined, it would be wrong to solely rely on such analytical arguments. The lived experience and narratives of those involved within legal education are also valuable and relevant. As a lawyer myself, my inclination is to write using the objectivity of the third person, focusing on synthesising and evaluating the evidence and perpetuating the veneration of a so-called scientific approach. Writing this paragraph in the first person is a conscious and not altogether easy act, which in itself says something about the socialisation into legal culture and norms within legal education. Nevertheless, I would not be writing this book at all if it were not for my own personal experiences both inside and outside of the law – as a law student, as a solicitor, as a trainee teacher, as a mature Phd student, as a legal academic and as a wife and mother. These have shaped my research interests and my fundamental beliefs around legal education. The fact that I live in the UK and work in a UK-based university also means that my perspective on law schools, and many of the examples I draw upon, are UK-based and focused on legal education as it is characterised within UK higher education, although I believe my arguments and examples have relevance and currency elsewhere. Such context and experiences are integral to my work, as is my own emotional investment in this topic and in the transformation I am arguing for. I am perhaps fortunate in that I do not have to justify any divergence between my personal experiences and beliefs and the analytical arguments in favour of emotions in the law school. Both point to its importance and value and it would be wrong of me to leave either to be unacknowledged and unexamined (Etherington, 2004).

Another, related assumption (not necessarily always a criticism) is that discussion of emotions in the law school is actually a discussion of emotional intelligence. This ranks along wellbeing as a theme that has emerged in contemporary society, with a simple internet search for the term generating over 12 million hits. In some ways, such popularity has been beneficial, introducing the idea of the importance of emotions to many and perhaps going some way to challenge the ubiquitous Cartesian dualism in Western society. Indeed, one of its best-known proponents has claimed that emotional intelligence "can be as powerful, and at times more powerful, than IQ" (Goleman, 1996, p. 34). However, emotional intelligence is only one construct (and a highly contested one) that has emerged to explain the importance of emotions. It is not sufficient (or even necessary) to use this construct to support the integration of emotions into the law school. Instead, a wider view of emotions must be taken which considers not only emotional intelligence (in itself a construct with a variety of models, drawing on wider research into emotions) but also broader, humanist, feminist and critical conceptions which add a richness and philosophical depth to the debate.

A final notion to dispel is, in itself, a form of academic Cartesian dualism (Descartes, 1989). This is the idea that there is a schism between the theoretical and practical. A sense of "it's all very well saying that, but in reality . . .". The first issue this raises is whether emotions can, in practice, form a part of the law school. The simple answer is: they already do. They are inescapably present in all of its aspects and thus, in reality, form part of what institutions and individuals are already dealing with. The more nuanced answer is that emotions can be acknowledged and utilised in many ways. There is no "one size fits all" solution, but there are many practical ways in which this can be done – from revamping the week-one induction provided for first year students to developing students' awareness through experiential learning (in particular, via clinical legal education).

The second issue this notion of "well yes, in theory . . .", raises is how much time and how many resources will be required to implement such practical suggestions. This is perhaps unsurprising at a point where the general consensus is that legal academics are over-worked and facing ever-increasing pressures from all angles (and initials – REF and TEF in particular) (Strevens and Wilson, 2018).[4] This leads to a sense that, whilst emotions can perhaps be theoretically acknowledged as relevant, in reality there are more important practical considerations which over-ride and effectively extinguish their relevance. Does transformation equate to additional pressure, more targets, diverted funds and bureaucratic wrangles? The honest answer is "maybe". Any form of fundamental change is unlikely to be straightforward or without some trauma. At a personal level, a legal academic may be able to make a real difference through simple and (relatively) easy changes to their teaching style or approach to students. However, to embed consistent, long-lasting transformation throughout legal education the change must be at a broader, wider, collective level. This is challenging, but the results are worth it. There is an apt quotation which states:

> You never change things by fighting against the existing reality. To change something, build a new model that makes the old model obsolete.
>
> (Buckminster Fuller, 1982 cited in Ratcliffe and Lebkowsky, 2005, p. 101)

If the power and benefits of emotions within legal education can be demonstrated, then it is arguable that this renders the existing model obsolete. It becomes about creating a new model in which emotions play a fully integrated role, one which works at both theoretical and practical levels.

Of course, offering up these potential criticisms and reflections on allowing emotions into the law school assumes that people will be interested in the topic. It is, quite possibly, more likely that a significant number of stakeholders in the legal academy will view discussion of emotions as a distraction. To borrow the title of Fish's 2008 book, don't just "save the world in your own time" but also "have feelings in your own time". In other words, emotions are part of your personal life, not something to bring into your work. This is perhaps the most fundamental misconception of all within law, one which ignores swathes of scientific evidence that emotions simply do not work like that. We are not robots, we cannot flick a switch and turn our emotions on and off. They are far more fundamental and integrated into our being than that. Emotions are a part of the law school, whether we want them to be or not, whether we acknowledge them or not. They are there and, left unacknowledged and unexamined, they are damaging and potentially corrosive. That is not to say there are not dangers with exposing the role of emotions and potentially blurring a well-established public/private distinction. As hinted earlier, emotions can be appropriated and refashioned for ideological and inauthentic purposes. They can be manipulated and exploited. However, this danger is ever-present in any event. Wherever emotions exist, so does the potential for Machiavellian calculation. Enhancing emotional awareness and understanding arguably reduces, not increases, the potential for this to occur. Brought out into the open and examined, emotions can become a part of health and wisdom, removing them further from unexamined or twisted machinations.

Potential and pitfalls for the law school

To provide the foundations for a new model which draws on the transformative power of emotions, this book considers the core ways in which emotions permeate and influence legal education. It begins, in Chapter 1, by tracing the philosophical and historical shaping of legal education and its view of emotions, drawing particularly on the way the doctrinal and liberal traditions within the contemporary law school both uphold the supremacy of reason and seek to disregard or suppress emotions. Chapter 2 continues this survey of the existing place (or, rather, non-existent place) of emotions within legal education. It will consider the increasing pluralism within legal education, with the growing importance of socio-legal and other legal perspectives. These offer academic breadth, but have done little to widen the fetishisation of reason and intellect that remains the overwhelmingly dominant paradigm within the law school. Less mainstream, more alternative approaches to law and legal education are explored, including the comprehensive and integrative law movements, to assess not only their current status within the law school, but also their potential. This will enable a consideration of whether, and if so how, key underpinnings of these alternative paths can be translated into educational pedagogy and practice within the law school.

To answer some of the criticisms this introduction has already speculated upon, to move even further forward from the existing, enduring portrait of legal education, and to incorporate such alternative approaches, it is necessary to demonstrate that emotions can and do have a transformative role to play. Therefore Chapter 3 considers what emotions actually are, drawing on rich philosophical and scientific evidence on their role and purpose and, perhaps most significantly, establishing their intertwined, inseparable relationship with cognition. Chapter 4 will then consider the wider policies and politics of academia, considering how the shift towards employability and the skills agenda within higher education is gradually emphasising specific emotional competencies, whilst at the same time demonstrating the dangers of ideological manipulation and reductivism.

Having established the importance and value of emotions, and contrasted this with their treatment within legal education, the remainder of the book explores particular facets of the law school experience as lived by its key stakeholders. In relation to students, Chapter 5 considers the vital role that emotions play within learning, siting this within key learning theories (in particular, constructivist and humanist perspectives) as well as drawing on the broad array of literature that demonstrates the intimate relationship between the emotions of the individual, the learning environment and the educational setting.

The role of emotional wellbeing in relation to students is then explored in Chapter 6. This is perhaps the area where most empirical and practical work has been undertaken, providing valuable data from which to extract key themes and critically address the impact of disregarding and suppressing emotions. Indeed, this chapter could easily be called "We messed things up, now we need to fix it". As a companion to this, the emotional wellbeing of legal academics is considered in Chapter 7, for how can the legal academy promote transformation through the emotions if they themselves are struggling with unacknowledged emotional labour and failing to model the healthy and open relationship with emotions that is essential for transformation at individual, collective and institutional levels?

In some ways, flagrantly (cheekily? merrily?) flouting advice to generations of essay-writing law students, this Introduction serves as a conclusion for the key theoretical arguments within this book. This is justified because of the vast bodies of literature that already exist within philosophy, psychology and educational literature on these topics – what is being said is not new, it is simply being synthesised and applied to a different (and somewhat challenging) environment, that of the law school. The actual conclusion of this book will then seek to begin the development of a vision for how legal education should look, sketching out the end point should such a transformation be engendered. This final vision will not be entirely complete or cohesive or determinative. This is simply because legal education itself is none of those things – it is pluralistic, diverse and evolving. Therefore, it is only right that an examination of the role of emotions leaves room for development, change, reflection and surprise. If the law school is to embrace the vivid, exciting and myriad role of emotions, it must be prepared to be brave and courageous in accepting some uncertainty whilst at the same time transforming itself into the holistic experience that reflects law's true role and calling within society.

Notes

1 The terminology used within discourse on emotions can be both challenging and contested. In this book, the term 'emotions' will be used to encapsulate the whole range of emotions that may be experienced within legal education (or elsewhere), in accordance with one of its common usages in relevant literature (see, for example, Goldie, 2002). The term 'emotion' will be used to denote a particular "emotional episode" (for example, sadness or love) appropriate to the context of its usage (Oatley et al., 2006). The term 'emotional' will be used to refer to the presence or application of emotion within a specific situation or experience.

2 Section 54 of the Coroners and Justice Act 2009 c.25.

3 Although the term "affective domain" has been used in a variety of ways (and will be referred to again in Chapter 3) for the purposes of this book it is used to encompass both emotions and also longer-lived feelings, moods and attitudes. The "cognitive domain" is used to refer to those processes and mechanisms commonly (if not always accurately) associated with thought, reason and intelligence. For example, Bloom's 1956 taxonomy of the cognitive domain refers to

lower-order skills of knowledge, comprehension and application and higher-order skills of analysis, synthesis and evaluation. It is perhaps telling that Bloom's taxonomy of the affective domain has received significantly less interest within legal (and other forms) of education.

4 The Research Excellence Framework and Teaching Excellence Framework.

References

Abrams, K. and Keren, H. (2010) "Who's Afraid of Law and the Emotions?", *Minnesota Law Review*, 94(6), 1997–2074.

Bailey, M. L. and Knight, K. J. (2017) "Writing Histories of Law and Emotion", *The Journal of Legal History*, 38(2), 117–129.

Bandes, S. A. and Blumenthal, J. A. (2012) "Emotion and the Law", *Annual Review of Law and Social Science*, 8(1), 161–181.

Bandes, S. A. (2013) "Centennial Address: Emotion, Reason, and the Progress of Law", *DePaul Law Review*, 62(4), 921–929.

Baron, P. (2007) "Thriving in the Legal Academy", *Legal Education Review*, 17(1–2), 27–52.

Bloom, B. (1956) *Taxonomy of Educational Objectives: The Classification of Educational Goals.* Handbook 1, Cognitive Domain, London, Longman.

Boran, L. and Delany, D. (2011) "Enhancing Self-control: Insights from Neuroscience", in Maharg, P. and Maughan, C. (eds), *Affect and Legal Education: Emotion in Learning and Teaching the Law*, London and New York, Routledge.

Coroners and Justice Act 2009 c. 25.

Descartes, R. (Translator Voss, S. H.) (1989) *The Passions of the Soul*, Indianapolis, Hackett Publishing.

Etherington, K. (2004) *Becoming a Reflexive Researcher – Using Our Selves in Research*, London and Philadelphia, Jessica Kingsley Publishers.

Fish, S. (2008) *Save the World on your Own Time*, New York, Oxford University Press.

Goldie, P. (2002) *The Emotions. A Philosophical Exploration*, Oxford, Clarendon Press.

Goleman, D. (1996) *Emotional Intelligence*, London, Bloomsbury.

Grossi, R. (2015) "Understanding Law and Emotion", *Emotion Review*, 7(1), 55–60.

Hutchinson, A. C. and Monahan, P. J. (1984) "Politics, and the Critical Legal Scholars: The Unfolding Drama of American Legal Thought", *Stanford Law Review*, 36(1/2), 199–245.

Hyland, T. (2014) "Mindfulness-based Interventions and the Affective Domain of Education", *Educational Studies*, 40(3), 277–291.

Maroney, T. A. (2006) "Law and Emotion: A Proposed Taxonomy of an Emerging Field", *Law and Human Behaviour*, 13(2), 119–142.

Maroney, T. A. (2011) "The Persistent Cultural Script of Judicial Dispassion", *California Law Review*, 99(2), 629–1683.

Maroney, T. A. (2016) "A Field Evolves: Introduction to the Special Section on Law and Emotion", *Emotion Review*, 8(1), 3–7.

Nussbaum, M. (2003) "Cultivating Humanity in Legal Education", *The University of Chicago Law Journal*, 70(1), 265–279.

Oatley, K., Keltner, D. and Jenkins, J. M. (2006) *Understanding Emotions*, 2nd edn, London, Blackwell Publishing.

Oxford English Dictionary, www.oed.com.libezproxy.open.ac.uk/view/Entry/204738 (accessed 22 July 2017).

Ratcliffe, M. and Lebkowsky, J. (2005) *Extreme Democracy*, LuLu.com.

Sanger, C. (2001) "The Role and Reality of Emotions in Law", *William & Mary Journal of Women and the Law*, 8(1), 107–113.

Schlag, P. (1998) *The Enchantment of Reason*, Durham, Duke University Press.

Solomon, R. C. (2000) "The Philosophy of Emotions", in Lewis, M. and Haviland-Jones, J. M. (eds), *Handbook of Emotions*, 2nd edn, New York and London, The Guilford Press.

Strevens, C. and Wilson, C. J. (2018) "Perceptions of Psychological Well-being in UK Legal Academics", *The Law Teacher*, 52(3), 335–349.

Taylor, E. W. and Cranton, P. (2012) *The Handbook of Transformative Learning: Theory, Research and Practice*, San Francisco, John Wiley & Sons.

Twining, W. (1997) *Law in Context: Enlarging a Discipline*, Oxford, Oxford University Press.

Weisman, R. (2014) *Showing Remorse. Law and the Social Control of Emotion*, Farnham, Surrey and Burlington, VT, Ashgate Publishing.

Williams, S. H. (1993) "Feminist Legal Epistemology", *Berkeley Women's Law Journal*, 8, 63–105.

1 Enmity and exclusion within legal education

Introduction: emotion and reason dichotomised

The law largely views emotions as the enemy of reason and thus it seeks to disregard or suppress them. In doing so, the law is following well-trodden societal conventions and drawing on the dominant Western philosophical tradition of Cartesianism (Descartes, 1989; Williams, 1993). As such, it applies forms of Cartesian dualism which distinguish between reason and emotions, mind and body, objective and subjective, and male and female, separating and dichotomising these concepts. For law, it is reason that becomes its supreme driving force, representing rationality and enlightenment. Emotions become portrayed as irrational, messy and embodied, representing the antithesis of legal aspirations.

The initial focus of this chapter is on illustrating the disregard for, and suppression of, emotions which characterises much of legal history (for a more detailed exploration see Bailey and Knight, 2017). The emphasis of the historically dominant philosophical traditions in legal thought on containing and devaluing emotions has helped to construct the dominant paradigms within which legal education has traditionally operated – the doctrinal and liberal traditions. The practical applications of the law and the stance of legal actors has further perpetuated this approach to emotions and thus reinforced these paradigms. Providing this form of broad-brush overview situates the chapter's subsequent discussion of legal education within the wider context of law as a discipline. The way in which the doctrinal and liberal paradigms approach emotions, and the extent to which these paradigms are still dominant, will arguably play a significant role in determining the potential future role of emotions within legal education. Their influence can be discerned in both the view of emotions, and the perception of how they interact with law, that is held by key stakeholders within the law school.

Philosophical paradigms and practical applications

A key argument of this book is that a disregard for, and suppression of, emotions characterises much of legal history and that this is reflected within the dominant paradigms of legal education. This approach to the emotions is illustrated by the two key philosophical traditions in legal thought – natural law theory and legal positivism.

Natural law theory has its origins within a certain scientific conception of the world (science being a theme which is also writ large within the doctrinal tradition of legal education even today). The theory posits the idea of enduring and stable principles which both underlie legal doctrine and which can be discerned by a careful study of it. As such, classical legal thinkers treated their studies as a branch of the natural sciences (chemistry, biology, physics) and focused on constructing taxonomic categories based on previous legal precedents to identify and perpetuate these foundational principles (Feldman, 2009). In previous centuries, these principles were often shaped around religious belief. In its modern form, natural law is usually secular in approach, but it retains the focus on a higher form of morality and/or ethics which laws must be derived from and appertain to (Bix, 2010).

In characterising this moral and ethical framework as an objective, discoverable reality, there are clear overlaps with the Cartesian conception of knowledge. There has been little discussion which suggests that emotions have a role to play within the discovery of such a legal framework. Indeed, attitudes, values and emotions were traditionally not viewed as part of such a voyage of scientific discovery (Feldman, 2000). A tentative connection to emotions can be made when considering some of the bases of these frameworks, for example, the Aristotelian concept of *Eudaimonia*, linked to appraisal theories of emotion, embraces concepts such as flourishing which have a significant emotional resonance (Nussbaum, 2001). However, such potential links appear to have been left largely disregarded and unexplored when set against the quest for scientific reason.

In more recent iterations of natural law, theorists tend to assume a more relativistic, less dualistic approach, and accept there is no longer one single set of absolute morals or ethics which the law is to be tested against (although each theorist may perceive their own adopted set to be absolute). It can be argued that emotions will play (and always have played) a part in the formation of each individual's ethical or moral principles and framework. However, there is nothing to suggest that any role for emotions has been explicitly acknowledged within the development of such frameworks, or their underlying values (Marske et al., 2017).

The second key philosophical tradition in law is legal positivism. Coleman and Leiter (2008) suggest that there are two fundamental premises underlying different theories of legal positivism. Firstly, the belief that what constitutes law is determined by the conventions and demands of society; secondly, the belief that morality and law can be considered separately, without being interconnected. Conaghan argues that a key component of the positivists' approach is the distinction between descriptive and normative analysis. In other words, between describing what the law is and what the law ought to be. She suggests that legal positivism sees it as possible to identify what the law actually is as a "neutral, non-evaluative exercise" (Conaghan, 2013, p. 161). These concepts of objectivity and neutrality, together with the focus on law as a science, have a strong resonance within the historical development of both the doctrinal and liberal traditions of legal education. Overall, the positivistic outlook has played a key role in the development of a modern academic framework in which law is associated with particular notions of objectivity, rationality and science at the expense of the emotions.

Although natural legal theory and legal positivism are generally perceived as opposing philosophical traditions, there is arguably a common theme when relating them to the law and emotions. Neither demonstrates any significant engagement with emotions and both appear to largely disregard them. Indeed, Bandes and Blumenthal, discussing the term "emotion", suggest that:

> In the legal realm, the term has long functioned as a catchall category for much of what law aspires to avoid or counteract: that which is subjective, irrational, prejudicial, intangible, partial, and impervious to reason.
>
> (Bandes and Blumenthal, 2012, p. 161)

Perhaps unsurprisingly, therefore, the law in its practical application has only acknowledged emotions in a marginal and limited manner. On occasion, the law has been required to recognise that emotions are present in a real-life situation. However, the relationship is a difficult one. The master and slave metaphor referred to in this book's Introduction once again applies, with law viewing emotions as a separate sphere which requires stringent control to ensure it does not infringe on the rationality of the legal realm (Solomon, 2000, p. 3; Maroney, 2006).

Within practical applications of the law, it is easiest to identify instances of where law has acknowledged the existence or strength of a particular emotion in relation to the criminal law. In the example of the loss of control defence under section 54 of the Coroners and Justice Act 2009 it applies where "the killing resulted from D's lack of self control" (provided there was a qualifying trigger). Such a concept of "loss of control" arguably implies an emotion such as anger or fear. However, the instances where such an acknowledgement of emotion occurs in the criminal law generally are still relatively narrow. As an illustration, Stannard (2010) refers to the principle that the English criminal law will only take account of emotional harm if accompanied by a diagnosis of psychiatric injury. Based on this, he argues that the law fails to acknowledge the seriousness of emotional harm. The overall lack of recognition of emotions in criminal law has also been emphasised. Spain argues that emotions such as disgust, anger and repulsion have helped shape the criminal law and underpin theories of punishment. However, despite this "the law has consistently attempted to remove emotion from consideration" (2011, p. 6).

It has also been suggested that those attempts which have been made to find a place for emotions in the criminal law have not always been positive. Sanger (2001) points to the use of victim impact statements (in a USA context, but they are also used in the UK) and asks whether their use to help families achieve closure actually furthers the interests of justice. She suggests that there are significant difficulties when the law is able to select which emotions it chooses to acknowledge and integrate into its decisions. Her argument is that, where an emotion begins to be required by law, the danger is it will lose the very authenticity which made it worthy of note in the first place and instead become scripted. This is a salutary warning that, although the incorporation of emotions is an important first step, it is neither sufficient nor wholly positive without a sound theoretical and philosophical basis.

In relation to civil law, there is a lack of literature explicitly engaging with the role (or potential role) of emotions. The lack of acknowledgement of emotional harm referred to in the criminal context is mirrored in tort cases, where only certain categories of pure psychiatric harm are recognised, which must involve medically-recognised conditions (Mulheron, 2012). There are occasional (and perhaps unexpected) glimpses of the relevance of emotions to other areas of substantive civil law, for example, in the use of unrequited love to evoke the equitable doctrine of unconscionability in Australia (Grossi, 2018). Areas such as asylum and family law have also garnered an increasing body of research both relating to the emotional impact on legal actors involved in their practice (Baillot et al., 2013; Melville and Laing, 2007) and discussing the influence on emotions and wellbeing which applications of these laws can or could have on those involved (see, for example, Huntington (2008) in relation to family law). However, despite these instances of emotions being acknowledged, the overall examples available to discuss are pretty sparse, therefore indicating that the civil law, as a body of legal rules and doctrines, has relatively little explicit engagement with emotions.

While the preceding examples are not an exhaustive survey of instances where emotions are present or acknowledged within the law, they are representative of the overall approach the law takes to emotions. Indeed, it appears that on most of the occasions when the law does specifically acknowledge emotions, the intention is to suppress or exclude them by doing so. For example, Posner (2001) refers to the exclusion of gruesome crime scene photographs where they are likely to provoke extreme outrage or disgust in the USA. He uses this as a demonstration of the significant role emotions play within law. However, the intended consequence of this would appear to be to prevent a jury from becoming emotionally involved in a case in a way which once again separates the perceived irrationality of emotions from the reason and rationality of the law. There is little to disturb the view of the law as imposing normative order and reason on the messy emotions of human life, although it does demonstrate the law acknowledging (at least in part) that the subject matter it must deal with is emotive.

Legal actors and emotions

Those who are involved within the practical application of the law, legal actors, similarly tend to disregard or ignore emotions. With regard to the judiciary, the judicial oath itself in the UK appears to reflect the perceived separation between reason and emotions, requiring the judiciary to "do right to all manner of people after the laws and usages of this realm, without fear or favour, affection or ill will" (HM Courts and Tribunals Judiciary, 2015, n.p.). While it is understandable that objectivity and impartiality are required, the difficulty arises because of the underlying assumption that a judge can simply choose to effectively shut off their emotions and remove them from the courtroom. This is captured well by Anleu et al. (2015) when discussing their research into the role of emotions in the Australian and Swedish courtrooms. They identify the paradox that emotions are viewed as inappropriate within the courtroom, but at the same time the judicial role requires involvement with emotions to a significant degree, whether displaying, managing or experiencing them.

A number of explanations have been provided for the judicial lack of regard for emotions. Perhaps the most obvious, and compelling, is that it follows the form of dualism that is riven deep within law itself drawing on its wellspring of disregard and the Cartesian notions that have shaped so much of Western philosophy and science. A striking UK example of how this Cartesian dualism translates in practice is given in the case of *R v Konzani* [2005] 2 Cr App R 198 in which the judge, in summing up for the jury, states "Make sure that emotion does not enter into your judgment in this exercise that you must embark upon. There is an old saying that, 'When emotion comes in, sense moves out'. Emotion has its place, of course, but it can mislead judgment" (*Konzani* cited in Weait, 2012, p. 175).

Abrams and Keren argue that the conventional view is that:

> Emotion floods careful, stagewise reasoning in a tidal wave of affect; its association with particulars sweeps decisionmakers from their impersonal, Archimedean pedestal.
>
> (Abrams and Keren, 2010, p. 2004)

They suggest that this need for detachment and rationality has also been historically emphasised to deflect political pressures and undue sympathy with any of the parties involved. However, it is equally arguable that assuming emotions are, and can be, excluded, obscures and devalues the emotional experience of the courtroom.

With regard to the legal profession more generally, there is a lack of literature identifying the role of emotions in the work of solicitors and barristers in the UK. There has been a small amount of work done on emotional labour in these professions, but generally those studies which do touch upon emotions tend to focus solely on a relatively limited, specific group, such as asylum or family law practitioners (as discussed previously). There is little sense from this literature of the wider ways in which emotions interact with all aspects of legal practice, in all fields, across all stages of involvement. In the USA context, there appears to be more interest in issues relating to emotions, stemming (at least partly) from movements such as preventative law and comprehensive law and growing concerns over lawyer wellbeing (see, for example, Silver, 2017; Wright, 2016). These will be considered in more detail in Chapter 2, but suffice to say here, their key thrust is to both identify and critique conventional approaches to legal practice which still focus on disregarding or suppressing emotions. However, despite the valuable role these movements play, they do not (yet) represent mainstream legal practice. It is very easy to understand why a lack of acknowledgement or respect for emotions remains the *status quo* for so many legal practitioners when considering the dominant paradigms in legal education in which so many of them have been immersed and socialised, in particular the doctrinal and liberal traditions.

The doctrinal tradition

> The conception of legal education that still dominates the legal academy today is a conception borrowed from the sciences
>
> (Nussbaum, 1993, p. 1629)

The focus on law as a form of scholarly science seeking to categorise, order and dissect legal principles is an enduring one whose origins can be traced most clearly back to the development of the doctrinal tradition in the law school (Sugarman, 1986). This is the tradition which held sway during the twentieth century and which still holds a central, if evolving, place within legal education today (Bartie, 2010). At its core is the attempt to achieve objectivity, precision and order through the idea of law as a scientific body of principles. It therefore echoes the focus of both the natural law and positivistic philosophical legal traditions and their emphasis on such qualities. This is an emphasis which is perpetuated by the practical applications of the law and the conventional roles of legal actors. Most importantly, for the purposes of this book, it is an emphasis which seeks to ignore or suppress the role of emotions.

Sugarman (1986) discusses the nineteenth century development of the doctrinal tradition in the UK[1] and argues it sought to carve out an identity for university law schools by focusing on the development of a set of coherent, orderly legal principles which would demonstrate law to be a coherent and ordered body of doctrines. In contrast, the potentially more problematic and messy ways in which law intersected with everyday life were left to the legal practitioners, largely in the form of the courtroom. This separation was mirrored in the structure of legal education itself, with the Inns of Court holding responsibility for the highly practical, vocational forms of training whilst the universities concentrated on law's academic development as a form of science. Their role was perceived as creating the scientific form of harmony within the law that would then determine its practical applications by legal practitioners (from a benign distance), inculcate students into the mysteries of this new science and develop the law in a logical and orderly fashion in keeping with the advancements of society (Bartie, 2010).

The reasons for the development of this doctrinal tradition were partly ideological and partly practical (Sugarman, 1986; Collini, 1991). The ideological impetus derives from the nineteenth-century development of libertarianism, particularly as espoused by J. S. Mills (1999). The focus on preserving an individual's autonomy and protecting an individual's rights required the law to act as an arbiter in delineating the boundary between an individual's rights, and that behaviour which would infringe on the rights of others. This is supported by the view of law espoused by Greenleaf (a Harvard Professor in the 1840s) who described this new science as:

> A *liberal science* – an harmonious arrangement of *principles* essential to the well-being of society – not as a *trade* – or a mere instrument of litigation – or of political advancement – but as the department of labor in which we are to discharge our duty to our contemporaries."
>
> (Greenleaf, 1838, p. 1)

This reflects the idea that, although classical legal thinkers viewed emotions as irrelevant to the taxonomies they created, in fact these categories were underpinned by a specific, libertarian conception of human nature which revolved around rights, ownership and free market concepts (Feldman, 2000).

The pragmatic impetus for the doctrinal tradition resulted from the need to improve the quality and stature of legal education in England and Wales. This is a need encapsulated well by the Report of the Commons' Select Committee on Legal Education in 1846 which stated "It is apparent from the foregoing statements that nothing sufficiently appropriate, systematic, or comprehensive, has up to this hour been accomplished to meet the demands, professional or unprofessional, for Legal Education" (Select Committee on Legal Education, 1846, p. 44). It drew the conclusion:

> That it may therefore be asserted, as a general fact to which there are very few exceptions, that the student, professional and unprofessional, is left almost solely to his own individual exertions, industry, arid opportunities, and that no Legal Education, worthy of the name, of a public nature, is at this moment to be had in either country.
>
> (Select Committee on Legal Education, 1846, p. 56)

One of the witnesses in particular (a Mr Empson) argued that the focus by the legal professions on the practicalities and procedures of law had discouraged writers and thinkers and deprived legal studies of its scientific nature. In their conclusions, the Select Committee appeared to endorse this by referring to the methods by which solicitors and barristers had sought to remedy defects in legal education and suggesting that this minute knowledge of particular forms could not "be considered as a substitute for that systematic and comprehensive information, and philosophic spirit, which are the highest qualities of the Lawyer" (1846, p. 56). The Select Committee suggested that the lack of "scientific" legal education had led to the absence of a class of jurists and legalist who were able to "apply themselves exclusively to Law as to a science" (1846, p. 57).

In many ways, this was a call to action for legal education within the UK. It demonstrated the need for legal academics to carve out their own niche within the law, with many (such as Dicey and Anson) beginning the production of the type of student texts which have become synonymous with doctrinal, black-letter law (Leighton, 2017). By clearly indicating the value of a scientific, systematic approach with which to take law schools forward it also unwittingly contributed to the development of a paradigm in which emotions are disregarded and suppressed and reason deified. In moving away from the human experiences and emotions of law in practice, it also distanced law ever further from the affective domain.

In repositioning university legal education as a science, rather than a trade, these jurists were drawing on similar developments within law schools in the USA. In particular, the innovation introduced by Harvard and disseminated to law schools throughout the USA and beyond commonly known as the "case method" (Garner, 2000, p. 307). In this method, students are asked to focus upon picking apart a case to determine the reasoning and the resulting legal principles, mirroring in many ways a form of science laboratory experiment or dissection. In addition (and closely aligned) the "Socratic method" also developed.

This involves an academic focusing on one student and asking them a series of questions to "lead the student down a chain of reasoning" to apply the legal rules to a set of facts in an ordered and analytical manner (Williams, 1993, p. 1573). These methods are commonly attributed to the work of Christopher Columbus Langdell (1823–1906), Dean of the Harvard Law School from 1870 to 1895, who argued that law should be taught, not only as a doctrine of thought, but as a process of scientific thinking:

> Law, considered as a science, consists of certain principles or doctrines. To have such a mastery of these as to be able to apply them with constant facility and certainty to the evertangled skein of human affairs, is what constitutes a true lawyer; and hence to acquire that mastery should be the business of every earnest student of law.
>
> (Langdell, 1871, p. viii)

Hoeflich (1987) emphasises the influence of Harvard and USA legal education on legal education in England and Wales during this period (and earlier), arguing it played a significant part in transforming it from the deterioration of the early nineteenth century into its modern form. He suggests that contemporaries at that time saw the key attribute in the success of USA law schools as their scientific nature, re-emphasising this as the core of the developing doctrinal tradition.

The preceding discussion has emphasised that, for both ideological and pragmatic reasons, legal education in England and Wales in the nineteenth century developed and prized the idea of law as a neutral, cohesive whole which could be identified and analysed scientifically and which did not include any acknowledgement of emotions. In doing so, it drew heavily on the influence of both the positivist approach to law and developments in USA legal education. As Thomas puts it, referring to his own time as a student, "The quiet certainty of law was held out to those who were diligent and enthralled by the seamless web of the common law" (Thomas, 2000, p. 2). Of course, it is somewhat simplistic to refer to the entire doctrinal tradition as a wholly homogenous approach. There were also some challenges to the dominance of this paradigm, as encapsulated by Holmes's often-quoted statement that:

> For the rational study of the law the black-letter man may be the man of the present, but the man of the future is the man of statistics and the master of economics.
>
> (Holmes, 1897, p. 457)

However, overall, a view of the law as a scientific body of unemotional, neutral, autonomous rules that could be learnt and applied was developed. This demonstrates the desire of the law to preserve reason in its purest form without attempting to sully it with the messy and complicated tapestry of emotions to which it perceives itself as bringing order and rationality. The perceived neutrality and objectivity involved appears to leave no room for emotions within the doctrinal tradition.

This therefore brings law schools to a point where, if the doctrinal tradition alone is sufficient and appropriate for the education of law students, there is an argument that emotions are unnecessary and irrelevant, at least to the content of the degree (wider issues of learning and teaching will be explored further on). However, as many legal academics are no doubt shouting at this page, this is not the case. The doctrinal tradition has been heavily and extensively critiqued. Perhaps most damaging amongst these, given the doctrinal tradition's development as a purportedly scientific approach, is the suggestion that it is based on a form of flawed science (see, for example, Krannitch et al., 2009 and McCrudden, 2006). The doctrinal tradition's claim to be based on a scientific approach has been challenged by arguments that the assumptions behind the body of legal principles it identifies have not been adequately tested and may be irrational or incomplete. In other words, law students are encouraged to analyse and interpret legal authorities, but cannot question the doctrine's inherent logic and reason. Questions have also been raised about the claim that it is possible to develop a coherent and logical argument from the common law. The area of contractual mistake springs to mind as one in which there is a lack of clear conceptual overview given the somewhat tortuous development of the doctrine, but no doubt the reader will be able to think of other examples. Perhaps Wilson expresses these doubts most evocatively, with his statement that:

> The words "English legal scholarship" though high sounding have a similar function to the words "disposable plastic cup". Each adjective strengthens the message that one cannot expect much in terms of quality or long-term utility from it.
>
> (Wilson, 1987, p. 819)

As well as its scientific validity, the doctrinal tradition's positivist perception of the law as neutral and objective has also been challenged, with commentators pointing to the policy considerations and ideological biases which can affect its formation and application (see, for example, Conaghan, 2013; Cotterrell, 2002). By portraying law as scientific, the doctrinal tradition seems to disregard the power struggles, politics and human influences that are inherent within its creation and implementation. Indeed, the ideological origins of the tradition themselves demonstrate this bias as the black-letter law more often than not adheres to libertarian tenets which support the "man of law", a middle-class, monied and educated individual who thrives in the competitive market place (Naffine, 1990, p. 44). The proclaimed objectivity of the law can therefore be seen as obscuring the wider social, political and human content and values inherent in the law and legal processes.

> A world of owners, producers, and consumers is different than a world of, say, hedonists, thrill seekers, and adventurers; or a world of saints, ascetics,

> and dreamers. What matters to these different personalities varies, and so should the law, insofar as it seeks to promote what matters to the people it serves.
>
> (Feldman, 2000, p. 1425)

At present, it is arguable that the law cannot easily shift the values and tenets it implicitly ascribes to, partly because of its refusal to acknowledge them, but also because of its inward-looking nature (McCrudden, 2006). In analysing legal principles (as created by cases and legislation) to extrapolate logical conclusions, doctrinalists are seeking to fit these principles within the existing framework of the law, moulding them into a cohesive and logical whole. As Bradney describes it, legal doctrine then becomes reduced to a series of "advertising slogans" which do not allow for wider reflection or the understanding of underlying philosophies and political issues (Bradney, 1998, p. 79). This insularity, traditionally at least, involved treating law as if it exists in a vacuum, standing apart from any political, economic or social forces. As James puts it

> The doctrinal curriculum allows no place for the chaos, context and uncertainty of real life; it treats law as already justice, instead of an attempt to achieve it, as if there is one correct and identifiable answer in every case.
>
> (James, 2008, p. 92)

The preceding paragraphs have cherry-picked arguably the most compelling and germane criticisms of the doctrinal tradition, particularly when seeking to consider the potential role of emotions in legal education. However, they are not the only criticisms. Indeed, Salter and Mason (cited in Van Gestel and Micklitz, 2011, p. 6) refer to over forty-two "main objections" to it. We have therefore reached the point in this narrative where the doctrinal tradition faces a heavy and sustained critique. However, it is also the stage where there emerges one of a number of paradoxes in the development of legal education since the nineteenth century. Although the doctrinal tradition developed partly as a result of the ideology of liberalism, and partly as a way of carving out a separate niche from that of the legal profession, more recently its role has shifted. The doctrinal tradition now portrays itself as vital in the development of legal professionals (see, for example, Edwards, 1992). Its ability to inculcate law students into "thinking like a lawyer" means it is often at the core of more vocational approaches to the law degree. Perhaps this current synchronicity can be partially attributed to the practical impetus for its development. By focusing on bringing a form of scientific order to the law, its scholars had defined law as a discipline by its relationship with the legal profession, which arguably eventually steered legal education towards a more vocational form designed to equip law students with the ability to perceive and apply the relevant principles to real-life scenarios. Certainly today a key contention (particularly in the USA context) appears to be that the doctrinal tradition is required to prepare students for a career as a legal professional (see, for example, Stropus, 1996). Whilst this in part reflects the postgraduate nature of the USA law degree, it can be seen that vocationalism also has strong roots within the UK law degree, particularly within post-1992 universities. It is telling that law school websites are heavily populated with pictures of legal professionals and mooting (Broadbent and Sellman, 2013). In a time of neo-liberal marketisation with the accompanying emphasis on employability and the creation of skilled knowledge workers, such roots are arguably more entrenched than ever.

Perhaps unsurprisingly, in light of the extensive critique of the doctrinal tradition and its re-evaluation in relation to vocational legal education, the focus of its contemporary proponents increasingly appears to be on redefining or repositioning it as being the core foundation for legal teaching and research, whilst acknowledging that external insights, such as those offered by a socio-legal approach, can then add layers of meaning on top of this basis to counter accusations of insularity and intractability (van Gestel et al., 2017; Hutchinson and Duncan, 2012). The doctrinal tradition is reinvigorated and remoulded as the foundational method that distinguishes legal scholarship from all other disciplines and socialises students into a particular form of intellectual mind-set required for the production of future legal professionals. Thus it can still be characterised as key to legal study and research, despite the challenge of a range of other approaches (which will be explored in Chapter 2). Its latest regeneration particularly emphasises its academic rigour, suggesting it is necessary to develop a higher level of analytical skills and intellectual ability within law. There is a sense of it providing law students and legal academics with a form of academic status and separateness from the remainder of the academy, as the chosen ones who have mastered this intricate knowledge and language and the accompanying legal skills (see, for example, Van Hoecke, 2013). The Council of Australian Law Deans encapsulates this view well in their statement that:

> If doctrinal research is a distinctive part of legal research, that distinctiveness permeates every other aspect of legal research for which the identification, analysis and evaluation of legal doctrine is a basis, starting point, platform or underpinning.
>
> (Council of Australian Law Deans, 2005)

It is worth pausing here to note that this quotation refers to "legal research" alone, not legal teaching as well. There has been an interesting tendency amongst the literature on legal education to assume that shifts in the legal research conducted by academics are mirrored by changes in teaching content. It would be a worthwhile research project to ascertain whether the two do correlate. However, for the present purposes, the key point to emphasise is the continued importance of the doctrinal tradition, with all its scientific and intellectual trappings and pretentions.

So we arrive at the contemporary position where the doctrinal tradition has undoubtedly developed and evolved in response to sustained critique, but has not withered or disintegrated along the way. It is now most commonly characterised as a distinctive intellectual core from which to weave in wider insights and interdisciplinary approaches around its periphery. What does this mean for the incorporation of emotions into the law school? In some ways, this is a positive shift. If even the doctrinal tradition's proponents do not now see it as standing alone as a coherent and wholly adequate approach to the law and legal education, then it can be seen that there are opportunities to bring philosophical and scientific insights on emotions into the sphere of the law degree. However, at the same time, the tradition's persistence and centrality also pose significant challenges. If the core of legal education is a rigid, (quasi-)scientific form of analysis, this still leaves precious little room for emotions to become truly embedded within the curriculum and the wide law school. The doctrinal tradition has been critiqued for its narrowness in intellectual terms alone, with Bradney describing it as a form of "intellectual straitjacket" which forces law students to focus on a narrow set of rules which preclude broader reflections (1998, p. 78), a comment which appears particular pertinent to the purer forms of doctrinal analysis. If such a criticism can be levelled against it within the cognitive domain of rationality and reason where law is most at home, then how much harder will it be to widen its scope to the affective domain and the embrace of emotions? The legal norms and cultures the doctrinal tradition perpetuates also suggest a wider resistance to more holistic approaches to the law school in general. Why would such different approaches be required if the fundamental requirement that students "think like a lawyer" is already satisfied? At present, there is certainly little (if anything) to suggest that emotions have a role to play within the doctrinal tradition, despite (or perhaps because of) its longevity and ability to adapt within legal education.

Nevertheless, before sounding the death knell for the role of emotions in the law school, it is necessary to examine the other core paradigm which has developed within legal education from the nineteenth century, the liberal tradition.

The liberal tradition

> A liberal legal education is one which does not focus on education for a particular purpose other than education itself. It is not aimed at preparing students for a particular job or profession and is not concerned with notions such as employability. It is, however, concerned with pursuing knowledge for knowledge's sake and developing skills of knowledge acquisition through research, critical thought and debate.
>
> (Guth and Ashford, 2014, p. 6)

Alongside the doctrinal tradition and the vocationalism aspects of the law degree, liberal legal education has always retained a firm place in the hearts of legal academics, if not always in their daily work. This approach encapsulates the idea that law should stand independently of the legal profession as an intellectual discipline (see, for example, Guth and Ashford, 2014 and Bradney, 2003). In another of the paradoxes that litter this book, at the very time legal education's focus was narrowing into the rigidity of the doctrinal tradition, it was the writings of figures such as John Henry Newman (1801–1890) which began to develop the modern concept of a liberal university education, a concept which is still drawn on by supporters of a liberal legal education today. However, it would be wrong to attribute the origins of liberal legal education to these writings alone. Liberal education more generally has its origins in the notion of a university as a type of "finishing school" for young gentlemen who had the means and status to enjoy education as a form of "preparation for society" received and enjoyed for its own sake, rather than being required as preparation for work or any other more specific object (Corson, 2000, p. 111).

It has been argued that, nowadays, many law schools and individuals pay lip service to the ideal of a liberal education without a clear vision of what it entails (Bradney, 2003). This may, at least in part, stem from the wide diffusion in strands of liberal thought generally, varying from the "traditional" liberalism of J. S. Mills to the far more constraining form of social contract envisaged by Hobbes (to give just two examples out of many). This is a diversity which has led Rothblatt (1976) to suggest that it can effectively mean whatever the individual using the term requires it to mean! Such a lack of theoretical clarity may also stem from a more general traditional lack of interest in educational theories amongst the legal academy (Cownie, 1999). For the purposes of undergraduate university education generally, a concise and perhaps relatively uncontroversial description of the liberal position is encapsulated by Newman when he states "Knowledge is capable of being its own end" (1994, p. 103). As the key proponent of this approach in the legal academy, Bradney himself echoes this, drawing a comparison with an art gallery – something that is, quite simply, a good in itself (Bradney, 1995).

Nevertheless, some qualification is still required. Within liberal thought, it is not knowledge as a set of facts which is truly valued. Instead, it is the experience of learning and the manner in which this contributes to the development of a person's cognitive faculties – notably reason and rationality. In other words, what is prized is the acquisition of knowledge to enable an individual to be able to more clearly see, analyse and respond to the world around them. For Newman, as a Catholic Cardinal, seeing more clearly would enable the individual to discern certain absolute truths. For today's proponents of the liberal approach, in a pluralistic postmodern society, the emphasis is not on using knowledge to divine broader truths, abiding or otherwise, but on giving students the understanding and capabilities to make rational, reasoned choices (or perhaps to knowingly choose not to do so) (Bradney, 2003). Knowledge in the form of dry facts as insufficient; it must instead be used by the student as an illuminating, enriching tool – shaping their understanding, reasoning and intellect. In other words, their "qualities of mind" (Quality Assurance Agency, 2015, p. 7).

Drawing on these overarching principles of liberal education, many of liberal legal education's proponents have added to the aforementioned critiques of the doctrinal tradition for its narrow and rigid approach. This does appear to point to an interesting paradox in legal education in the way that the liberal paradigm, with its focus on reason and rationality, tends to reject the "scientific" approach of the doctrinal position. However, the liberal position is that such an overriding focus on doctrine allows the law to become a self-validating body of rules which lack actual logic and coherence. In other words, it could be said they are arguing that the doctrinal tradition is not scientific or intellectual enough. In fact, many supporters of the liberal tradition do appear to see the doctrinal tradition as having a role within legal education, but one which is more limited and which requires rigorous critical examination to enable the legal academy to retain an appropriate distance from it, whilst at the same time providing different ways to participate in legal scholarship. Burridge and Webb suggest that:

> However imprecise and incomplete, liberal legal education has provided the platform from which to expose the narrowness of the traditional law school with its concentration on doctrinal mastery to the exclusion of social function or ethical implications.
>
> (2009, p. 264)

This wider liberal vision also tends to involve a less enmeshed and symbiotic relationship with the legal profession. If legal practice is not the end purpose of a law degree, then the profession becomes simply one more element of the law to be explored in academic terms. However, for many liberal commentators some form of relationship is still important, as a strategic alliance to protect mutual financial and institutional interests, to provide insights into legal practice and, possibly, to provide a united focus in terms of the development and reforms of law. As Duncanson suggests:

> It is possible to provide an understanding of what the various kinds of Christians believe, what the world seems like to them and what they consider appropriate to do in this world, without sharing their religion. One may do the same with lawyers and the law.
>
> (Duncanson, 1997, p. 81)

This form of strategic or intellectual interest in lawyering does not involve the formation of legal professionals, or indeed the cultivation of any form of professionalism as one of its key aims. Jakab (2007) suggests that legal education can be seen as having three ends – the training of legal practitioners, the training of legal academics and the training of cultivated men and women. He argues that it is the latter of these which represents a true liberal education. A law degree may well impart knowledge and skills which will be useful in the legal professions, but that is a lucky by-product, not its aim. Similarly, it may well impart knowledge and skills that can be used to produce the next generation of the legal academy, but that is also not its aim. More broadly, it may develop in students the ability to make wise and appropriate choices in their working lives (in law or otherwise), but again that is not its aim. The value of a liberal legal education lies within the wider form of learning and intellectual development it engenders, notwithstanding these possible side-effects. For liberal commentators, there is a sense that a liberal education is a precursor to any vocational training required. Newman (1994) likens this to the need to have a healthy body – a good in itself – before the body undertakes manual labour. It is arguable that this form of liberal education does, by its very nature, assist with any future profession or vocation an individual may choose. By developing a deeper understanding of the world around them, they have a sense of themselves and their role within the world which is in and of itself precious in many settings, including potentially the world of work. However, there is a note of caution to add in that, by providing such an understanding, a liberal education may in some circumstances be anti-vocational. It does not produce "docile employees" but "sceptical citizens" who may view some forms of employment as incompatible with liberal values (Bradney, 2009, p. 300).

The longstanding debate around liberal education and vocationalism is perhaps best characterised within legal education by a form of uneasy co-existence, one which is arguably forcibly imposed by the financial pressures and employability agenda within higher education (which will be explored in Chapter 4).[2] For some, co-existing in this manner is beneficial and appropriate; for example, Twining (1997) argues that a false dichotomy has been created between the two stances and that it is unnecessary for there to be conflict between a good liberal education in law and a sound preparation for practice. Instead, he sees both as being part of a more general form of liberal legal education. However, others have suggested that the differing epistemologies, methodologies and ideologies involved are fundamentally incompatible (Arthurs, 1997). There are also suggestions that where there is such a conflict, overtly at least, it is vocational, and thus more doctrinal, approaches that are triumphing (Sanders, 2015; Guth and Ashford, 2014).

In terms of the acknowledgement and incorporation of emotions, it could be argued that, despite potential conflicts, a legal education freed from the (perceived at least) demands and requirements of the legal profession offers huge scope for different approaches and methodologies, including the acknowledgement and incorporation of emotions. However, to date, it is difficult to identify any instances where this has occurred. To analyse why, it is necessary to consider what the end-result of a liberal legal education is intended to be. As discussed earlier, the idea is that it will produce a law graduate who is not simply adept at "thinking like a lawyer" or academically prepared for legal practice. Instead, it is a broader conception of a law graduate who is equipped, at least intellectually, for all spheres of life. Many liberal commentators have characterised such a graduate as either a good citizen, or a better person, or possibly both (Brownsword, 1999; Bradney, 1995)! There is arguably a lack of conceptual clarity amongst writers on liberal legal education in how and if such concepts should be defined and whether they are interchangeable. For example, Burridge and Webb define both as involving "rational participants in the life of the community" (2009. p. 264). However, it is possible to identify certain defining characteristics amongst each school of thought.

The idea of a good citizen is encapsulated by Johnston (1999), who views undergraduate legal education as preparing students for a role as useful members of society. It implies some form of contribution – economic or, more likely, political or social – which adds to (and by doing so supports) the societal structure in which they find themselves. Similarly, Brownsword (1999) puts forth a vision of a law school which prepares its graduates for involvement in the legal and political aspects of community life. This is a conceptualisation which is key to a certain strand of liberal thinking, notably found in the USA, which links the concept of good citizenship inextricably to support for a model of Western liberal democracy and the values it upholds (Pue, 2008). Whilst this concept of liberal legal education is broader than doctrinal and purely vocationalist approaches, it still appears to offer relatively little in terms of the incorporation of emotions. The emphasis appears to be on the wider intellectual benefit to society of such informed, even enlightened, contributions. A potential link to emotions is implied through Nussbaum's characterisation of the "world citizen" whom she sees as the desired end product of university education – one who has the ability to examine oneself and one's traditions, understand ways in which common needs and aims are differently realised in different circumstances and develop the narrative imagination (1997, p. 59). The notion of the narrative imagination is characterised as involving empathy and a sympathetic responsiveness to others' needs (although at the same time retaining the ability to objectively scrutinise the situation), which suggests both cognitive and affective elements (Westaby and Jones, 2018). However, it appears to be the cognitive element of perspective-taking which dominates in the vision of citizenship held by Nussbaum (perhaps also influenced by her cognitivist conceptualisation of emotions, which will be discussed in Chapter 3). For other commentators within the liberal tradition it is difficult to find even this implicit link with emotions in their discussions of law graduates and good citizenship.

At first glance, it may seem that the concept of a better person is more attuned to the role of emotions than that of a good citizen, assuming it is accepted that emotions do have a link to individual behaviour and morality (Kristjánsson, 2018). The notion of a better person is most clearly articulated by Bradney, who indicates that, although law graduates may contribute usefully to society and to a particular profession, equally they may well take a reasoned decision not to contribute to or support these concepts at all, providing the decision to do so will "adhere to the principles of sceptical enquiry and individual responsibility" (2003, p. 56). Indeed, he has suggested that the key focus of the university "lies in allowing the student to explore their humanity" (1995, n.p.) and "the pursuit of human flourishing" (Bradney, 2011, p. 68). This richer, broader conceptualisation of a graduate as a better, or even good, person appear to be in stark contrast to the more homogenised and vocational "product" created by the doctrinal tradition (Stanley, 1988, p. 85). However, once again, it contains little (if any) explicit engagement with emotions – the individual exploration envisaged appears to be intellectual and driven by the concepts of reason and rationality which are so well embedded within law and legal education. Indeed, it could be argued that implicitly this vision retains the Cartesian dualism of the doctrinal tradition by failing to explore the potential role of emotions within intellectual and personal growth.

So far, in describing liberal legal education, a number of the words used to describe it have pertained to its width and breadth. This is certainly correct when compared to the doctrinal tradition in its purist forms. However, the preceding discussion demonstrates that there is an important caveat to be made, namely that the form of freedom that the liberal approach has focused on providing to date is a purely cognitive, intellectual form. It does not seek to develop the whole person, it does not look to the emotions, feelings and personality traits of individuals. Instead, the emphasis remains on reason and rationality: a reason and rationality that is characterised in a manner which focuses on the intellect and is largely free of emotions. Hence, largely unknowingly, the liberal tradition shares a key similarity with the doctrinal tradition in prizing existing legal conceptions of reason and rationality at the expense of all else (including emotions). Overall, liberal legal education has failed to recognise the role emotions play within both relationships and actions. It fails to appreciate the importance of relationality within individual lives and society as a whole (Hyland, 2014; Grummell et al., 2009).

This lack of regard for emotions is reflected in a number of the critiques of liberal legal education. In particular, commentators have argued that a liberal education by its very nature inculcates liberal values into its recipients, as this is a necessity for liberalism to survive and flourish. Based on this view, it would appear that a liberal education, if successful, will inevitably lead to students performing their societal and civic duties to protect and maintain a liberal state (Pue, 2008). A number of key feminist critiques suggest this form of liberalism within law as privileging a certain "man of law" who encapsulates liberal values and attitudes (Naffine, 1990, p. 44). This is the property-owning individual who merely requires the law to regulate the boundaries of interactions within the public sphere. The thrust of this argument (although, of course, there are many variations and themes) is that liberal values which support and facilitate male dominance are hidden behind the supposed neutrality of the rule of law (Munro, 2007). This suggests a parallel with the doctrinal tradition in the way in which the value placed on objectivity, rationality and reason has (at the least) the potential to obscure subjectivities and partiality. It also demonstrates, at least in part, why emotions are disregarded or suppressed in the liberal approach. It is because they are viewed as inimical to such objectivity, rationality and reasoning and thus to the persona of the "man of law". In terms of liberal education generally, it is argued that these notions have manifested themselves through a focus on the development of an ideal citizen who will be able to contribute in the public sphere, whilst the private domain has remained largely disregarded. Thus contemporary educational thought:

> Has inherited from classical liberalism an indifference to the affective domain and an allegiance to the education of the rational autonomous subject.
>
> (Lynch, 2010, p. 62)

Nevertheless, it is important not to create a false dichotomy in this regard between liberal and feminist legal traditions. It has already been emphasised that there are a range of liberal traditions and approaches and this is equally clear within legal education. For example, Bradney's work (1998) expressly decries the effect of the doctrinal tradition on law students' social and emotional habits, suggesting it distances their psyche from their academic persona by forcing them to focus on a narrow set of rules which preclude broader reflections. He also shows a concern with the social and emotional when he discusses the need for a work-life balance among the legal academy itself (Bradney, 2003). His implication appears to be that the broader vision of the liberal tradition will resolve tensions between the psyche and academic persona of law students and integrate work and personal life for the legal academic. The habits of reason and rationality should integrate all spheres of life into a commonality of approach that avoids artificial distinctions being made. However, although this approach holds promise for the acknowledgement of emotions, once again, the focus appears to be on reason and rationality, using these as tools to manage the potential irrationality of an individual's emotions. There remains a lack of recognition that emotions could form a part of reason or rationality, simply an imperative to apply these concepts to tame and control emotions.

The liberal commentator who appears to move closest to offering an overview of how the process of legal education could potentially acknowledge and incorporate emotions is Webb when he talks about the "care-why" as a neglected part of the law degree (2006, p. 149). In other words, the traditional focus on objectivity has prevented law students from a healthy introspection that would enable them to assess their own feelings, motivations and values in a way which allows them to tailor their education to their own needs and engage in deeper forms of learning. Without this, they are lacking (amongst other things) the "sort of motivational 'juice' which converts, for example, a moral thought into a consistent moral action" (2006, p. 148). Webb goes on to propose a constructivist, emotionally-engaged approach to learning to develop these neglected aspects of the law degree. However, he offers only a brief summary of this approach. Webb's greater focus appears to be on the role of values within legal education. In later articles, he calls for a form of post-liberalism: one in which there is a "permissive neutrality" (as opposed to a "persuasive neutrality") which values experience and enables students to explore the ethical and moral dimensions of law (Burridge and Webb, 2007, p. 85). Within liberalism generally, there does not appear to be anything to preclude the exploration of these issues. Indeed, the requirement for sceptical enquiry and rationality in all decisions appears to assume an exploration and analysis of values as a precursor to making fully reasoned life choices. However, for this book, the importance of Burridge and Webb's argument lies in their suggestion of a broader vision which could arguably include a greater recognition of emotions as an influence within such experience, values and ethics. Unfortunately, in the years following their call, marginal (if any) headway has been made with this picture. Liberalism still deifies reason and rationality. Emotions remain largely ignored or suppressed.

Conclusion: the supremacy of reason

As the law itself largely disregards and suppresses emotions, it is perhaps therefore unsurprising that the doctrinal tradition views emotions in the same way. Its approach to law and legal education is one which prizes what it perceives to be objective, rational, scientific analysis in a way which does not acknowledge or value emotions, rendering them irrelevant. However, perhaps most damningly, it also seemingly encourages the active suppression of emotions, rather than simply disregarding them. In his classic USA polemic, Kennedy argues that law students' natural sympathies in more contentious cases are quashed by reference to established case law, which demonstrates in a seemingly objective and rational manner that their first reaction was wrong. He vividly describes how you are taught to repress emotions in this setting. For example, students may be given a "hot" case which will engender sympathy, but then having this contrasted with "cold" cases to show them that this reaction is wrong and that a cold, objective approach must be taken (Kennedy, 1982, p. 595). Thus "it will appear that emoting will only isolate and incapacitate you" (Kennedy, 1982, p. 595). More recently, in the context of Australian legal education, James (2008) has echoed this in criticising the narrow concept of "thinking like a lawyer" which dominates and portrays itself as a superior way of thinking rather than a more limited legal tool. Such an approach prizes perceived reason and rationality at the expense of emotions. How often are law students praised for their analysis and evaluation? When (if ever) are they praised for showing sympathy, anger, happiness or joy? In the UK, this appears to be an accepted wisdom, rarely written about or discussed as a result; instead law students are simply socialised into the reproduction of existing legal norms and culture (Stanley, 1988). Somewhat ironically, this very socialisation which purports to suppress emotions can have its own (potentially severe) emotional consequences in relation to both learning and wellbeing.

The idea that emotions aid and assist reasoning (and are therefore very much the concern of the law school and the law degree itself) is one of the key themes of this book. There is a significant body of evidence demonstrating that the doctrinal tradition's disregard for, and suppression of, emotions has a number of detrimental effects on law students, including impacting on their learning, wellbeing and professional and personal development, and this will be explored in depth in subsequent chapters. At present, it is suffice to illustrate this with a simple quotation:

> The polarization of reason and emotion prevents either from enriching the other, resulting in emotion that is undisciplined, unexamined, and unowned, as well as thinking that is hard and shallow.
>
> (Harris and Schultz, 1993, p. 1779)

Therefore, at the end of this chapter, we have reached a point where the two traditionally dominant paradigms in legal education both largely contrive, intentionally or unintentionally, to ignore and suppress emotions in their characterisation of the law school. Despite hints that emotions may not be wholly incompatible with their tenets, neither has chosen to encompass them within their key principles or narratives. Given this common flaw, it is necessary to move on to consider how other, alternative conceptions of legal education treat emotions to ascertain whether a holistic, integrated vision of the law school is within grasp.

Notes

1 Sugarman refers to this as the "textbook tradition" (1986, p. 34).
2 At the time of writing, it is unclear how the proposed introduction of the Solicitors Qualifying Examination will impact on the role and purpose of the law degree.

References

Abrams, K. and Keren, H. (2010) "Who's Afraid of Law and the Emotions?", *Minnesota Law Review*, 94(6), 1997–2074.

Anleu, S. R., Blix, S. B. and Mack, K. (2015) "Researching Emotion in Courts and the Judiciary: A Tale of Two Projects", *Emotion Review*, 7(2), 145–150.

Arthurs, H. W. (1997) "Half a League Onward: The Report of the Lord Chancellor's Advisory Committee on Legal Education and Conduct", *The Law Teacher*, 31(1), 1–12.

Bailey, M. L. and Knight, K. J. (2017) "Writing Histories of Law and Emotion", *The Journal of Legal History*, 38(2), 117–129.

Baillot, H, Cowan, S. and Munro, V. E. (2013) "Second-hand Emotion? Exploring the Contagion and Impact of Trauma and Distress in the Asylum Law Context", *Journal of Law and Society*, 40(4), 509–540.

Bandes, S. A. and Blumenthal, J. A. (2012) "Emotion and the Law", *Annual Review of Law and Social Science*, 8(1), 161–181.

Bartie, S. (2010) "The Lingering Core of Legal Scholarship", *Legal Studies*, 30(3), 345–369.

Bix, B. (2010) "Natural Law Theory", in Paterson, D. (ed), *A Companion to the Philosophy of Law and Legal Theory*, 2nd edn, Oxford, Blackwell.

Bradney, A. (1995) "Raising the Drawbridge: Defending University Law Schools", *Web Journal of Current Legal Issues*, 1.

Bradney, A. (1998) "Law as a Parasitic Discipline", *Journal of Law and Society*, 25(1), 71–84.

Bradney, A. (2003) *Conversations Choices and Chances the Liberal Law School in the Twenty-First Century*, Oxford and Portland, Oregon, Hart Publishing.

Bradney, A. (2009) "Elite Values in Twenty-First Century, United Kingdom Law Schools", *The Law Teacher*, 43(2), 291–299.

Bradney, A. (2011) "English University Law Schools, the Age of Austerity and Human Flourishing", *International Journal of the Legal Profession*, 18(1–2), 59–71.

Broadbent, G. and Sellman, P. (2013) "Images of Law and Legal Education: Law School Websites and the Provision of Information", *European Journal of Law and Technology*, 4(1).

Brownsword, R. (1999) "Law Schools for Lawyers, Citizens and People", in Cownie, F. (ed), *The Law School: Global Issues, Local Questions*, Aldershot, Ashgate Publishing.

Burridge, R. and Webb, J. (2007) "The Values of Common Law Legal Education: Rethinking Rules, Responsibilities, Relationships and Roles in the Law School", *Legal Ethics*, 10(1), 72–97.

Burridge, R. and Webb, J. (2009) "The Values of Common Law Legal Education Reprised", *The Law Teacher*, 43(2), 263–269.

Coleman, L. J. and Leiter, B. (2008) "Legal positivism", in Cane, P. and Conaghan, J. (eds), *The Oxford Companion to Law*, [online], Oxford, Oxford University Press.

Collini, S. (1991) *Public Moralists. Political and Intellectual Life in Britain 1850–1930*, Oxford, Clarendon Press.

Conaghan, J. (2013) *Law and Gender*, Oxford, Oxford University Press.

Coroners and Justice Act. (2009) c. 25.

Corson, D (2000) "The Eclipse of Liberal Education in the Twenty-First Century", *Educational Review*, 52(2), 111–123.

Cotterrell, R. (2002) "Subverting Orthodoxy, Making Law Central: A View of Socio-legal Studies", *Journal of Law and Society*, 29(4), 632–644.

Council of Australian Law Deans (2005) *Statement on the Nature of Legal Research*, https://cald.asn.au/wp-content/uploads/2017/11/cald-statement-on-the-nature-of-legal-research-20051.pdf (accessed 1 July 2018).

Cownie, F. (1999) "Searching for Theory in Teaching Law", in Cownie, F. (ed), *The Law School – Global Issues, Local Questions*, Aldershot, Dartmouth Publishing.

Descartes, R. (Translator Voss, S. H.) (1989) *The Passions of the Soul*, Indianapolis, Hackett Publishing.

Duncanson, I. (1997) "The Ends of Legal Studies", *Web Journal of Current Legal Issues*, 3.

Edwards, H. (1992) "The Growing Disjuncture Between Legal Education and the Legal Profession", *Michegan Law Review*, 91(1), 34–78.

Feldman, H. L. (2000) "Foreword: Law, Psychology and the Emotions", *Chicago-Kent Law Review*, 74, 1423–1430.

Feldman, R. (2009a) *The Role of Science in Law*, Oxford, Oxford University Press.

Garner, D. (2000) "The Continuing Vitality of the Case Method in the Twenty-First Century", *Brigham Young University Education & Law Journal*, 2000, 307–345.

Greenleaf, S. (1838) "'The Law Reporter' in Hoeflich (1987). The Americanization of British Legal Education in the Nineteenth Century", *The Journal of Legal History*, 8(3), 244–259.

Grossi, R. (2018) "Love as a Disadvantage in Law", *Journal of Law and Society*, 45(2), 205–225.

Grummell, B., Devine, D. and Lynch, K. (2009) "The Care-less Manager: Gender, Care and New Managerialism in Higher Education", *Gender and Education*, 21(2), 191–208.

Guth, J. and Ashford, C. (2014) "The Legal Education and Training Review: Regulating Socio-legal and Liberal Legal Education", *The Law Teacher*, 48(1), 5–19.

Harris, A. P. and Schultz, M. M. (1993) ""A(nother) Critique of Pure Reason": Toward Civic Virtue in Legal Education", *Stanford Law Review*, 45(6), 1773–1805.

Hoeflich (1987) "The Americanization of British Legal Education in the Nineteenth Century", *The Journal of Legal History*, 8(3), 244–259.

Holmes, O. W. (1897) "The Path of the Law", *Harvard Law Review*, 10, www.constitution.org/lrev/owh/path_law.htm (accessed 1 July 2018).

Huntington, C. (2008) "Repairing Family Law", *Duke Law Journal*, 57(5), 1245–1319.

Hutchinson, T. and Duncan, N. (2012) "Defining and Describing What We Do: Doctrinal Legal Research", *Deakin Law Review*, 17(1), 83–119.

Hyland, T. (2014) "Mindfulness-based Interventions and the Affective Domain of Education", *Educational Studies*, 40(3), 277–291.

Jakab, A. (2007) "Dilemmas of Legal Education: A Comparative Overview", *Journal of Legal Education*, 57(3), 253–265.

James, C. (2008) "'Lawyers' Wellbeing and Professional Legal Education", *The Law Teacher*, 42(1), 85–97.

Johnstone, G. (1999) "Liberal Ideals and Vocational Aims in University Legal Education", Web *Journal of Current Legal Issues*, 3.

Kennedy, D. (1982) "Legal Education and the Reproduction of Hierarchy", *Journal of Legal Education*, 32(4), 591–615.

Krannitch, J. M., Holbrook, J. R. and McAdams, J. J. (2009) "Beyond "Thinking Like a Lawyer" and the Traditional Legal Paradigm: Towards a Comprehensive View of Legal Education", *Denver University Law Review*, 86(2), 381–404.

Kristjánsson, K. (2018) *Virtuous Emotions*, Oxford, Oxford University Press.

Langdell, C. C. (1871) *A Selection of Cases on the Law of Contracts*, 2nd edn, Boston, Little Brown.

Leighton, P. (2017) "The LLB as a Liberal Degree? A Reassessment from a Historical Perspective", in Sherr, A., Moorhead, R. and Sommerlad, H. (eds), *Legal Education at the Crossroads. Legal Education and the Legal Profession*, Abingdon, Oxon and New York, Routledge.

Lynch, K. (2010) "Carelessness: A Hidden Doxa in Higher Education", *Arts & Humanities in Higher Education*, 9(1), 54–67.

Maroney, T. A. (2006) "Law and Emotion: A Proposed Taxonomy of an Emerging Field", *Law and Human Behaviour*, 13(2), 119–142.

Marske, C. E., Kofron, C. P. and Vago, S. (2017) "The Significance of Natural Law in Contemporary Legal Thought", *The Catholic Lawyer*, 24(1), https://scholarship.law.stjohns.edu/cgi/viewcontent.cgi?article=2015&context=tcl (accessed 29 June 2018).

McCrudden, C. (2006) "Legal Research and the Social Sciences", *Law Quarterly Review*, 122, 632–650.

Melville, A. and Laing, K. (2007) ""I Just Drifted Into It": Constraints Faced by Publically Funded Family Lawyers", *International Journal of the Legal Profession*, 14(3), 281–300.

Mills, J. S. (1999) *On Liberty*, Hadleigh, Broadview Press.

Mulheron, R. (2012) "Rewriting the Requirement for a 'Recognized Psychiatric Injury' in Negligence Claims", *Oxford Journal of Legal Studies*, 32(1), 77–112.

Munro, V. (2007) *Law and Politics at the Perimeter Re-Evaluating Key Debates in Feminist Theory*, Oxford and Portland, Oregon, Hart Publishing.

Naffine, N. (1990) *Law and the Sexes Explorations in Feminist Jurisprudence*, London, Allen & Unwin.

Newman, J. H. (1994) *The Idea of a University Defined & Illustrated I. In Nine Discourses Delivered to the Catholics of Dublin II. In Occasional Lectures and Essays addressed to the Members of the Catholic University*, London, Routledge.

Nussbaum, M. (1993) "Use and Abuse of Philosophy in Legal Education", *Stanford Law Review*, 45(6), 1647–1666.

Nussbaum, M. (1997) *Cultivating Humanity: A Classical Defense of Reform in Liberal Education*, Cambridge, Massachusetts, Harvard University Press.

Nussbaum, M. (2001) *Upheavals of Thought: The Intelligence of Emotions*, Cambridge, Cambridge University Press.

Posner, E. A. (2001) "Law and the Emotions", *The Georgetown Law Journal*, 89(6), 1977–2012.

Pue, P. (2008) "Legal Education's Mission", *The Law Teacher*, 43(2), 270–289.

Quality Assurance Agency (2015) *Subject Benchmark Statement Law*, www.qaa.ac.uk/docs/qaa/subject-benchmark-statements/sbs-law-15.pdf?sfvrsn=ff99f781_8 (accessed 5 July 2018).

Rothblatt, S. (1976) *Tradition and Change in English Legal Education. An Essay in History and Culture*, London, Faber and Faber.

R v Konzani [2005] 2 Cr App R 198 in Weait, M. (2012) "Criminal Law: Thinking about Criminal Law from a Trial Perspective", in Hunter, C. (ed), *Integrating Socio-Legal Studies into the Law Curriculum*, Basingstoke and New York, Palgrave Macmillan, 161–183.

Sanders, A. (2015) "Poor Thinking, Poor Outcome? The Future of the Law Degree after the Legal Education and Training Review and the Case for Socio-Legalism", in Sommerlad, H., Harris-Short, S., Vaughan, S. and Young, R. (2015) *The Futures of Legal Education and the Legal Profession*, Oxford and Portland, Oregon, Hart Publishing, 139–168.

Sanger, C. (2001) "The Role and Reality of Emotions in Law", *William & Mary Journal of Women and the Law*, 8(1), 107–113.

Select Committee on Legal Education (1846) *Report from the Select Committee on Legal Education, together with the Minutes of Evidence, Appendix and Index*, The House of Commons.

Silver, M. A. (2017) *Transforming Justice, Lawyers and the Practice of Law*, Durham, Carolina Academic Press.

Solomon, R. C. (2000) "The Philosophy of Emotions", in Lewis, M. and Haviland-Jones, J. M. (eds), *Handbook of Emotions*, 2nd edn, New York and London, The Guilford Press.

Spain, E. (2011) *The Role of Emotion in Criminal Law Defences: Duress, Necessity and Lesser Evils*, Cambridge, Cambridge University Press.

Stanley, C. (1988) "Training for the Hierarchy? Reflections on the British Experience of Legal Education", *The Law Teacher*, 22(2), 78–86.

Stannard, J. E. (2010) "Sticks, Stones and Words: Emotional Harm and the English Criminal Law", *Journal of Criminal Law*, 74(6), 533–556.

Stropus, R. K. (1996) "Mend It, Bend It, and Extend It: The Fate of Traditional Law School Methodology in the 21st Century", *Loyola University of Chicago Law Journal*, 27(3), 449–489.

Sugarman, D. (1986) "Legal Theory, the Common Law Mind and the Making of the Textbook Tradition", in Twining, W. (ed), *Legal Theory and Common Law*, Oxford, Basil Blackwell.

Thomas, P. (2000) *Learning about Law Lecturing*, Warwick, National Centre for Legal Education.

Twining, W. (1997) "What are Law Schools for?", in Twining, W. (ed), *Law in Context: Enlarging a Discipline*, Oxford, Oxford University Press, 292–311.

van Gestel, R. and Micklitz, H. W. (2011) *Revitalizing Doctrinal Legal Research in Europe: What about Methodology?* European University Institute Working Papers Law 2011/05.

van Gestel, R., Micklitz, H. W. and Rubin, E. L. (2017) *Rethinking Legal Scholarship: A Transatlantic Dialogue*, New York, Cambridge University Press.

Van Hoecke, M. (2013) "Legal Doctrine: Which Method(s) for What Kind of Discipline?", in Van Hoecke, M. (ed), *Methodologies of Legal Research. Which Kind of Method for What Kind of Discipline?* Oxford, Hart Publishing, 1–18.

Webb, J. (2006) "The "Ambitious Modesty" of Harold Arthur's Humane Professionalism", *Osgoode Hall Law Journal*, 44(1), 119–155.

Westaby, C. and Jones, E. (2018) "Empathy: An Essential Element of Legal Practice or 'Never the Twain Shall Meet'?", *International Journal of the Legal Profession*, 25(1), 107–124.

Williams, S. H. (1993) "Feminist Legal Epistemology", *Berkeley Women's Law Journal*, 8, 63–105.

Wilson, G. (1987) "English Legal Scholarship", *Modern Law Review*, 50(6), 818–854.

Wright, J. K. (2016) *Lawyers as Changemakers: The Global Integrative Law Movement*, Chicago, American Bar Association.

2 A broadening scope, or reason revisited?

Introduction: changes and challenges

Chapter 1 ended in a somewhat pessimistic vein. Despite glimpses of potential for emotions to be recognised in both, it was evident that the doctrinal and liberal traditions of legal education have largely perpetuated the form of Cartesian dualism which dichotomises reason and emotions, devaluing the latter. However, those are not the only traditions or paradigms within law schools. A variety of different approaches to law, including socio-legal studies, critical legal studies, feminist legal studies, law and emotions scholarship and integrative or comprehensive law, have emerged as influences (or potential influences) on legal education, both in the UK and elsewhere. It is important to analyse the impact on law schools of these different approaches to law and the law degree to consider what this demonstrates about the current and potential role of emotions in legal education. This allows an exploration of whether shifts in approach which have already occurred have significantly altered the role of emotions within the law school (or whether they have the potential to do so in the future). The movement which has had the most longevity and influence internationally has been that of socio-legal studies (also known as Law and Society in the USA) and therefore this chapter will begin by exploring both its development and its significant impact on law schools.

The impact of socio-legal studies

> Many younger academic lawyers became dissatisfied with the traditional type of legal scholarship, which concentrated on the internal consistency of the law and the inter-relationship of different legal rules. . . . They accepted the view that law was only one social phenomenon amongst many others, and that the working of the law could be properly understood only as part of the total social context.
>
> (Harris, 1983, p. 315)

The preceding quotation encapsulates the development, during the latter half of the twentieth century, of a socio-legal approach to law. This is a gradual shift, so although its emergence was particularly marked in the 1960s and 1970s, its roots can be traced back much further. The exact definition of socio-legal studies has been disputed throughout its development, but overall it has evolved from a specific focus on the application of sociological principles to law, into a much broader pluralistic approach. This contemporary usage both acknowledges and examines the social, economic, political and cultural influences which form and shape the law, drawing on and applying insights from a range of disciplines. This arguably constitutes both its key strength and main potential weakness. On the one hand, it has led to socio-legal studies being portrayed as vibrant and intellectually diverse. However, it has also led to it being critiqued as a form of catch-all whose very breadth prevents it from providing a cohesive alternative to scholars. Its scope is captured by the UK Economic and Social Research Council's reference to the term socio-legal studies being used as a form of umbrella for an excitingly diverse and broad range of legal research interests (ERSC, 1993, p. 1). Such a definition offers the tantalising potential for insights from psychology, sociology, neuroscience and philosophy (to name but a few) to be drawn upon in a way which challenges the disregard and suppression of emotions within the traditionally dominant doctrinal and liberal paradigms of legal education. However, for this potential to be realised it requires socio-legal studies to both influence (or even challenge) these paradigms and also to build a body of research and shared understanding on emotions which breaks free from the Cartesian dualism still displayed within both the doctrinal and liberal traditions.

In fact, there is an on-going debate within legal education over the extent to which socio-legal studies has either supplanted the doctrinal tradition, learnt to co-exist with it, or even been assimilated within it. In Cownie's 2004 survey of legal academics, she reports that half of all respondents unequivocally described themselves as taking a socio-legal or critical legal studies approach to teaching and researching law, while the other half saw themselves as taking a black-letter (doctrinal) approach. However, of the half who described themselves as black letter, only a fifth described themselves as black letter without qualification. Around a third gave the immediate qualification that they did not concentrate solely on legal rules and thought it important to introduce contextual issues. Cownie argues from this data that a focus on "pure doctrinal law" is no longer dominant amongst legal academics; instead its role has been diluted by its use alongside wider (socio-legal) analysis (2004, pp. 54, 56). She raises issues of perception by pointing to a number of respondents who associated socio-legal studies with purely empirical work or who were uncomfortable about the label in terms of their perceived academic image. She argues that, in reality, the concepts themselves are fluid and that the majority of the legal academy actually occupy a middle ground between the two (Cownie, 2004).

Cownie's interpretation does appear to presuppose that a doctrinal and socio-legal approach can actually be combined or co-exist comfortably. It has instead been argued that Cownie's data supports the idea that the doctrinal tradition has succeeded in largely absorbing (and therefore neutralising) newer interdisciplinary approaches to remain the default position in university law schools (Webb, 2006). Bartie suggests that socio-legal studies has built upon the traditional core of legal scholarship, diluting its purest form, but not seeking to reinvent it as a whole. She argues that the "essence of the old orthodoxy has survived the repeated attacks" due to its ability to adapt its features and the fact that not all scholars are influenced or impacted by newer movements (2010, p. 349). More recently, Sanders has also argued that the doctrinal tradition remains dominant within undergraduate teaching in England and Wales, suggesting that the self-assessment of academics in this regard should not be accepted too unquestioningly (2015, p. 144; see also Twining, 2014).

Bartie and Sander's comments reflect Vick's earlier discussion of interdisciplinarity and the doctrinal tradition where he argues that the doctrinal tradition will emerge relatively unscathed from the variety of interdisciplinary approaches now being undertaken. He suggests that this is partly because of legal education's continued links with the legal profession and partly because the very diversity of interdisciplinary work prevents one particular form of it from displacing the doctrinal tradition. Instead of being challenged, he suggests that the doctrinal tradition has become a "benchmark" against which different forms of legal scholarship are measured (Vick, 2004, p. 166). Conaghan also emphasises the appeal of the view of law as a "discrete, unified and coherent whole" which gives it the credibility to present itself as a neutral bystander untouched by the chaos of society. She suggests that this is a perception of law which is easily welcomed and absorbed by students as it aligns with their expectation of law. In contrast, she argues that students find "unruliness in law" (which could equally be defined as uncertainty) harder to comprehend and accept. Therefore, while acknowledging the scepticism, and trends away from, the doctrinal tradition she concludes that the notion of the law as imposing certainty and order upon human conduct still has considerable attraction for those studying, teaching and researching it (Conaghan, 2013, pp. 10–12). As demonstrated in Chapter 1, such a sense of scientific order and certainty has traditionally militated against the inclusion of emotions within legal education, relegating emotions to the realm of messy disorder which the law must control.

The suggestion that the doctrinal tradition is assimilating the socio-legal (and other) approaches, together with the lure of science and certainty, both suggest emotions will remain largely disregarded or suppressed within the law school. This is arguably a greater threat because of the more recent attempts to rejuvenate or re-conceptualise this tradition as the core of a distinctive and rigorous (and still unemotional) intellectual culture in law, which were touched upon in Chapter 1. Several commentators have recently emphasised the need to explicitly identify (and by implication defend) the elements of the doctrinal tradition to ensure its value continues to be recognised. For example, Hutchinson and Duncan, in the context of Australia and the UK, argue that it must be clearly defined so that it has an accepted meaning within the legal academy and can be explained to those outside the legal academy. They suggest that this will meet the criteria of funders who require an explicit research methodology and thus enable doctrinal researchers to compete in a competitive climate where empirical and interdisciplinary research is prized and non-lawyers are often contributing to research bids:

> It is when lawyers step or are pushed into wider interdisciplinary work, or find themselves competing for grants with researchers from other disciplines that the articulation of method becomes of paramount importance.
>
> (Hutchinson and Duncan, 2012, p. 99)

They conclude that doctrinal research is a separate methodology in its own right, but one that needs further examination and elaboration to demonstrate its particular distinctiveness as a method of research that is specific only to law.

van Gestel and Micklitz (2011) also discuss the current status of the doctrinal tradition, but in relation to European legal scholarship. They point to the various criticisms of the doctrinal approach (including those raised in Chapter 1). However, they argue that much of the criticism of the doctrinal tradition is based on an out-of-date conception of it. They suggest that its core features are that it derives its arguments from authoritative sources, that it views law as a coherent system and that it sees decisions in cases as maintaining the coherency of that system. They do suggest that it no longer needs to take an internal approach, arguing that it should view the law in context with "added value in the introduction of multidisciplinary law and . . . approaches on top of a tradition of sophisticated doctrinal research" (Van Gestel and Micklitz, 2011, pp. 23–24). This suggested approach echoes Bartie's analysis of the doctrinal tradition as essentially surviving intact, but with adaptations made to incorporate an additional layer of contextual research. If, as many commentators appear to believe, socio-legal studies has become this additional (but important) layer on top of the core doctrinal tradition, it can be argued that this does open up the possibility of a greater acknowledgement, and even utilisation, of emotions within legal education. At the same time, if the essentials of the doctrinal tradition have remained largely unscathed, it is questionable whether a notion that has been portrayed as so antithetical to the reason and rationality of doctrine will be able to flourish in a law school environment where the siren call of scientific certainty, combined with practical imperatives, seem to militate against its inclusion.

However, an alternative interpretation of the contemporary position suggests that socio-legal studies is now in ascendancy in the UK and beyond and is effectively forcing a gradual shift by all scholars, however avowedly black letter, an argument which seems to be supported through Cownie's research (2004). More recently, Siems and Mac Sithigh have attempted to map the current position of legal research using the classifications "law as a practical discipline", "law as humanities" and "law as social sciences". The concept of "law as a practical discipline" is referred to as a "comparatively value-free analysis of legal rules" with law as an "applied discipline" (Siems and Mac Sithigh, 2012, p. 653). Leaving aside the question of whether it is indeed possible for legal analysis to be value free, it can be seen that this concept encompasses at least parts of the doctrinal tradition. The second concept, "law as humanities" relates to law in relation to "interpretive disciplines" such as history and literature. The third "law as social sciences" is perhaps not as clearly defined, but is described as helping challenge legal rules through an "external and often empirical perspective" (Siems and Mac Sithigh, 2012, p. 655), thus appears to correlate most closely with a socio-legal approach.

Siems and Mac Sithigh refer to Cownie's UK study (2004) as well as similar studies in the USA and the Netherlands. They argue that an issue with these studies is the fact that many academics actually take a mixed approach (although in fact this is clearly acknowledged by Cownie). They construct a ternary plot (a diagram more commonly used for scientific observations) to construct the balance between the three classifications discussed. By doing this they conclude that "most" UK legal academics actually use mixed research methods, falling between the three categories (Siems and Mac Sithigh, 2012, p. 670). In support of this, they cite McCrudden's comment that "today, academic law is pluralistic, involving a bewildering diversity of subject-matters, perspectives, objectives and methods" (2006, p. 642). In effect, their findings seem to indicate there has been no radical shift in UK legal scholarship since Cownie's 2004 findings. This is a position which is supported by Murphy and McGee in the Australian context when they suggest that it is now common for researchers to use a "hybrid" of methods. However, Murphy and McGee do suggest that "the distinguishing feature of legal research is that the data and conclusions are usually synthesised with legal doctrine" (2015, p. 3). This indicates that there remains a clear place of the doctrinal tradition in this hybrid, despite an increasingly pluralistic approach. Such an approach makes it is possible to speculate that the greater breadth and diversity in legal research could encourage portions of the legal academy to increasingly acknowledge the role of emotions within the law school, whilst other (more doctrinal) elements retain a cautious distance. Of course, it can be argued that some such acknowledgement is better than the wholescale lack of recognition currently afforded to emotions in the law school. However, if emotions are truly as integral and fundamental to legal education as this book argues, then this is, at best, an uneasy compromise.

The preceding discussion suggests that the doctrinal tradition still has a core role, but that it has, at the least, been significantly diluted by the socio-legal approach. Whether this is part of a lasting shift or whether the doctrinal tradition will continue to reinvent and reassert itself is open to question. Feldman suggests:

> The notion of what constitutes science and what it would take to make law more scientific varies across time. What does not vary is our constant return to the well. We are constantly seduced into believing that some new science will provide answers to law's dilemmas, and we are constantly disappointed.
>
> (Feldman, 2009, p. 95)

It could be argued that the doctrinal tradition still has the lure of providing a coherency and consistency that appeals to scholars whose own background reflects this "scientific" approach. Alternatively, it could be argued that the use of social sciences has introduced a new form of "science" for those returning to the well to draw on. On that point, Siems and Mac Sithigh (2012) demonstrate an optimism that the use of social sciences could engender a long-lasting paradigmatic shift in law. However, they sound a number of notes of caution as well, identifying several possible dangers. The first is that concerns could arise about the usefulness of legal research to practising lawyers, potentially causing a shift towards practical legal scholarship. The second is if the existing approaches become viewed as stagnant, causing a shift to the humanities. The third is if concerns are raised that the research is insufficiently "scientific" in nature. Each of these cautions appears to have both potential benefits and detriments for the acknowledgment of emotions, for example, a more "scientific" approach could lead to the inclusion of findings from neuro-science on the role of emotions, but at the same time could lead to a retreat into the forms of rigid quasi-scientific thinking often promoted by the doctrinal approach. At present, there is no clear evidence that these cautions have been realised, but they do indicate the complexities, and potential dangers, which still exist when considering the contemporary status of socio-legal studies.

In addition to these threats, within England and Wales, at the time of writing there is also the potential impact of the Solicitors Regulation Authority's proposed new Solicitors Qualifying Examination (SQE) to be considered. This will remove the requirement for students wishing to qualify as solicitors to study for a law degree at all, let alone specifying particular core subjects that must be included. There are fears that this will result in financial and reputational pressure on Law Schools to remain competitive by revising their curriculum so that they produce graduates who are "SQE ready". Given the SQE Part 1 focuses on specific areas deemed most relevant for practice, such as dispute resolution in contract and tort, the suspicion would be that this will add further impetus to a more doctrinal approach. Alternatively, it may be that some Law Schools will embrace the new freedom of liberation from the core subjects and seek to provide a much broader (dare it be said, more exciting) range of topics for students to choose from. Anecdotally, it appears some of the more research-intensive institutes may be moving towards this, but for many providers the perceived requirements in terms of student numbers, student satisfaction and student fees seem to militate against this.

One final note of caution when considering the status of the socio-legal approach is that the majority of the preceding research into the position of the doctrinal tradition and socio-legal approach has focused on legal research and scholarship by academics (with the exception of Cownie (2004)). There is no contemporary research to indicate whether or not those involved are applying the same approach to their teaching of undergraduates where their focus may be influenced by a wide range of different factors, as discussed in later chapters. However, it appears likely that the increasing importance of socio-legal research will impact on teaching as well.

Although there are clearly challenges and pitfalls, contemporary writing on the status of socio-legal studies in the undergraduate law degree still sounds a note of reserved optimism as to its growth and influence. Whilst this may well be a good in its own right, for the purposes of this book, the questions are, firstly, to what extent has and could this involve the greater acknowledgement and inclusion of emotions within legal education and, secondly, to what extent has or could this have any impact on the traditional dualism of the doctrinal and liberal traditions in relation to reason and emotions.

The place of emotions in socio-legal studies

Taking a narrow definition of "socio-legal", focused on the application of principles from social science, suggests that there has been little relatively socio-legal engagement with the emotions. Such an approach would appear to have an impact in terms of content and breadth of curriculum by requiring legal researchers and students to draw upon sociological data, leading to empirical research methods more usually associated with the social sciences becoming far more common amongst researchers. However, while this change in content and breadth may bring such researchers (and perhaps even students) some benefit in terms of intellectual freedom, there is little within this to indicate any significant shift towards the acknowledgement of emotions. The focus would seem to be more on the gathering of empirical, sociological data to support theoretical conclusions in a way which makes them more reasoned and rational and less open to being accused of intuition or feeling. As Cotterrell explains:

> legal analysis focuses most readily on what it takes to be rational – especially instrumentally driven – action. And it has particular difficulties in dealing with matters of affect (that is, the emotion that lies behind or gives rise to action). Social theory has often seemed to have a similar emphasis. The sociology of emotions is a relatively undeveloped field. Yet both law and social theory need to recognize and address the non-rational or perhaps differently rational aspects of social life.
>
> (Cotterrell, 2006, p. 2)

It is arguable that there may be a greater indirect acknowledgement of emotions as legal academics increasingly incorporate empirical work. This is particularly the case where the researcher is dealing with difficult or sensitive subject-matters or applying a more intensive, qualitative research method (such as ethnography). For example, it seems difficult to imagine that a researcher could conduct research into an area such as child sexual exploitation without experiencing some form of emotional response to the content and the participants. Dickson-Swift et al. (2009) emphasise the importance of emotion within qualitative research in particular, arguing that it is an embodied experience which has both intellectual and emotional aspects. However, as they indicate, this form of emotional effort and engagement has not been widely acknowledged in academia. It is more commonly referred to in terms of acknowledging and examining subjectivities, rather than emotions being expressly referred to. It often appears that a key aim of any discussion of emotional (or "subjective") aspects is to eliminate such subjectivities from the research in question, once again mirroring the law's focus on reason and rationality.

In addition, the extent to which such research methods have permeated the law school can also be questioned. While emphasizing the importance of empirical research, the Nuffield Inquiry's report on empirical legal research, Law in the Real World, suggested that the lack of capacity for UK universities to undertake such research was leading to an emerging crisis (Genn et al., 2006, p. 36). Interestingly, in light of practical constraints on universities generally, the shortfall was not found to be due to a lack of intellectual or funding opportunities but rather that there were insufficient researchers to utilise the opportunities available. From a survey of 189 potential empirical legal researchers it was found that almost no institutions had more than five or six empirical legal researchers in place (Genn et al., 2006, p. 14).

Of course, the preceding numbers could equally be re-construed as demonstrating the extent to which such researchers have become integrated into the legal academy, moving away from the desk-based theoretical focus of doctrinal work. The Nuffield report's concerns also focused solely on empirical research in civil law and justice, only one of many areas of socio-legal interest. Adler and Simon in their discussion of the possible future of empirical legal research expressly avoid resolving the debate over the Nuffield report's findings. However, they do point to critics of the Nuffield Inquiry's findings who highlight the vitality of the Socio-Legal Studies Association (representing socio-legal researchers in the UK). Nevertheless, they acknowledge that there is "a sense of uncertainty and perhaps even decline in the United Kingdom" (2014, p. 174). Therefore, although perhaps a more remote possibility than suggested by the Nuffield Inquiry, such a capacity shortage could impinge on the potential for the acknowledgement of emotions within empirical work. If those who are conducting empirical work lack prior skills or training it also seems unlikely they will have the awareness and understanding to examine the role of emotions in their work when they have been largely taught to ignore and suppress it.

If a narrower definition of socio-legal studies is taken, its impact appears to largely be in terms of content and breadth of curriculum, rather than in terms of a wider acknowledgement of the role of emotions. Indeed, the focus appears to be on making the law more rational and objective, rejecting false or flawed logic in a continuing quest for the scientific "right" answer, whether it be through empirical data or developing a theoretical framework. However, taking a relatively broad definition of "socio-legal", the emerging body of scholarship on law and emotions could also be attributed to it. Indeed, Guth and Ashford suggest that it could be seen as encompassing "a limitless range of legal topics, analysed through a "law in context" lens" (2014, p. 11).

The existing body of law and emotions scholarship developed, at least partially, from the work of feminists and critical legal scholars who challenged (and arguably undermined) the positivist claims of law as neutral and objective. Some scholars would include such critical jurisprudence within the socio-legal approach, whereas others see them as separate bodies of scholarship, but in many ways this is an issue of semantics rather than a debate with notable theoretical or practical consequences. Overall, it is true to say that the feminist and critical approaches have more clearly and directly influenced law and emotions scholarship than the mainstream thrust of the socio-legal approach.

Critical legal studies

The mainstream epistemology in Western society is one of Cartesianism (Howson, 2013), creating and preserving dichotomies between reason and emotions, mind and body, objective and subjective, and male and female; in other words, generating the form of Cartesian dualism which permeates legal education. This not only distinguishes between reason and emotions, but also suggests that reason is required to discern and interpret an objective, detached reality which is there to be discovered and understood by those who apply themselves to the task. In other words, individuals are able to obtain this knowledge through their use of reason. For law students, that involves "thinking like a lawyer", putting aside emotions and applying themselves to the task of ordering the mass of legal knowledge which is there to be assimilated and refined. For those of a more socio-legal bent it may also involve adding to this legal depositary through the gathering of empirical data to further shore-up the structure of this metaphorical mass.

Williams (1993) suggests that this Cartesianism is based on four assumptions. Firstly, that there is an objective reality which exists independent of individuals and societies. Secondly, that this reality can be uncovered and explored by human knowledge and that, in doing so, the truth is being discerned. Thirdly, that people obtain this knowledge as individuals, independent of societal influences and, fourthly, that the key way to obtain this knowledge is through the use of reason. The result of these assumptions is that any other form of "truth" is viewed as false, which results in the creation of the type of dichotomies discussed previously. In contrast, an ability to uncover the "objective" truth will result in the knower having power and control both over this objective reality and also over themselves; a normative reality which once again emphasises the Cartesian dualism between reason and emotions.

In contrast to this Cartesianism, critical epistemology (which itself encompasses many variants) views knowledge as constructed within, and permeated by, its particular individual and social context (see, for example, Teubner, 1989). It arises out of, and cannot be disentangled from, the values and cultural contexts within which individuals and societies operate. Cartesian dualism's claims to neutrality and objectivity are, therefore, false. In fact, it is perpetuating social inequalities by ignoring them and refusing to acknowledge their existence. Williams (1993) argues that, firstly, the facts which reason shapes into knowledge are not independent, but rather arise out of cultural contexts and individual experiences. Secondly, the interpretation of facts requires value judgements and choices to decide between alternative readings. Such value judgements may well have moral and political implications. Thirdly, reason cannot be distanced from emotions and values because all three form integral parts of the interpretation of facts and problems. This vision of knowledge as a construct that is particular and sited challenges the idea of a universal reality and truth. Instead, it is accepted that there may be a large number of valid interpretations and understandings and even moralities. The knower does not have power and control over an objective reality, instead both the knower and the known influence and reconstruct each other.

What is key in terms of emotions and legal education is that this process of construction, be it by individuals or within society as a whole, does not have to (and arguably cannot) be achieved solely through the application of reason. Emotions and reason, cognition and affect, thoughts and feelings, all have a role to play within this on-going process of construction and re-construction. Thus the dichotomies can be erased, or at least lessened, and a richer, deeper process of knowing, being and creating takes place (Jaggar, 1989).

This critical epistemology represents a fundamental challenge to the focus on neutrality, rationality and a "scientific" quest for the objective truth which has characterised the doctrinal tradition and also permeates other approaches to legal education (for example, the use of empirical methods within socio-legal studies). However, it has been heavily criticised by many mainstream scholars. For example, Sherry (1996) argues that reason should be distinguished from personal beliefs. She suggests that failing to do this leads to a situation where epistemology fails to protect against morally or politically unsafe views with extreme and disturbing viewpoints and actions being granted a form of validity. For example, an anti-semitic or Holocaust denier's view of the world would be valid in their world, if not in the world of others. How, then, can such a belief be repudiated?

Williams acknowledges the power of similar arguments in her discussion of feminist legal epistemology. She suggests that feminists have suggested a variety of different ways to avoid being "left with no truth at all" (1993, p. 89). These include adopting a "standpoint" epistemology which privileges the view of oppressed groups (however defined) above those of others; taking some form of "pragmatic" approach to determining what best meets the required end (however defined) or trying to identify a "a standard for judgment that is in some sense culturally independent but still not transcendent" (Williams, 1993, p. 93). The key issue with all of these approaches lies in producing a clear and detailed guide and Williams herself, while calling for the latter solution, accepts that this is a work in progress. Therefore, while an array of alternatives by which to tackle the pitfalls of critical epistemology have been identified, there is arguably no coherent roadmap provided on how to avoid these.

Where the value in such a critical epistemology lies in terms of emotions and legal education is that it demonstrates that there is more than one approach. It is not the case that reason has to be prioritised and prized and emotions ignored or suppressed. This may seem alien to those steeped in existing legal traditions and trained to "think like a lawyer" but it provides an important counterbalance to many of the dominant narratives within legal education. As a legal academic or law student, it may be that there is not a pressing need to choose between the two epistemological traditions (and it may also be that we are relatively poorly equipped to do so). However, simply understanding that there are alternative narratives and approaches has a value in itself.

The continuing debate over critical epistemology should not detract from the contribution made to legal education by both critical legal scholars and feminist legal scholars. The critiques of the doctrinal tradition in legal education in Chapter 1 draw on the work of Goodrich (1996), Kennedy (1982) and Stanley (1988). The work of these authors flows from the critical legal studies movement which developed in the late twentieth century. Unger identifies two key characteristics of the movement. Firstly, its critique of "formalism and objectivism" and secondly its use of the law as an instrument to advance "leftist aims" (1983, pp. 564, 567). Unger describes "formalism" in a broad sense, contrasting its faith in legal justification with open-ended philosophical or ideological debates. He suggests that critical legal studies challenge the idea that legal doctrine can only be discerned through a neutral, apolitical analysis. He describes "objectivism" as the idea that legal materials create and maintain a coherent and defensible body of doctrine, rather than simply reflecting the outcome of practical pressures or power struggles. The characteristics he attributes to "formalism" and "objectivism" clearly reflect those that were identified in Chapter 1 as part of the doctrinal tradition and their rejection mirrors the general critical epistemology described previously.

The aims identified by Unger may be viewed as somewhat broad and this is reflected in criticism that critical legal studies is not a coherent movement, but instead a broad community of people who share similar political aims and a disquiet at doctrinal approaches to law. Certainly, in 1992, Goodrich suggested that the English form of the critical legal studies movement was theoretically fragmented and marginalised with little impact on analysis or curriculum. At that time, he viewed it as being at an early stage of its development. However, by 1999 his view was that the movement's lack of a clear identity had led to it becoming absorbed into the mainstream (although the presence of a thriving annual UK Critical Legal Conference perhaps suggests this is an over-generalisation).

In any event, although the critical legal studies movement has perhaps had relatively little overall impact in the UK, it has arguably had a disproportionately significant impact in its critique of the doctrinal tradition and through its critique of the suppression of emotion within legal education and law more generally. A key theme in the articles by Kennedy (1982), Stanley (1988) and Goodrich (1996) is the suppression of emotions which legal education requires and its perpetuation of a peculiarly homogeneous and restrictive legal culture and hierarchy. Despite this being a relatively small body of work, it has reached a larger audience than would perhaps be expected. However, Goodrich has also highlighted the limitations of the critique provided, suggesting (in 1999) that little had been done to attempt to practically reform the legal curriculum. This suggests that, while the critical legal studies movement was arguably important and significant in drawing academic attention to the practices of law schools, it did not itself have the impetus to fully develop or implement this critique. In part, at least, this can be attributed to the availability of a fuller feminist critique and pedagogy (Menkel-Meadow, 1988). This is not entirely separate from the critical legal studies movement and shares a common epistemology, but also arguably has a more complex and richer geneology, including a varied but longstanding engagement with work on emotions (Fischer, 2016).

Feminist legal studies

There are a significant number of strands of feminist thought, with Tong (1989) identifying seven key approaches (liberal, Marxist, radical, psychoanalytical, socialist, existentialist and postmodern), whilst emphasising the intersections between each of these. Beasley provides a similar list of approaches whilst also emphasizing the role of those feminists focusing on race/ethnicity. She argues that, without resorting to a neat definition, there are a number of recognisable characteristics linking each of these approaches; in particular that they involve:

> A critical response to traditional theorizing which thereby alters what may be discussed and how it may be discussed. That critique challenges assumptions of male supremacy/centrality.
>
> (1999, p. 117)

Specifically in relation to legal feminist thought, Naffine identifies three key chronological phases.[1] The first of these is a phase which focuses on "the male monopoly of law" (1990, p. 2). This involves a focus on women's battle to obtain equality within the present system against efforts to preserve male domination. The emphasis of this phase is on formal equality and the law itself is seen as essentially rational and fair but not yet possessing fully developed anti-discrimination legislation. There are clear parallels here with the positivist view of law and both the doctrinal and liberal traditions' portrayal of law as essentially neutral and autonomous. In relation to legal education, an example of Naffine's first phase can be found in the focus on increasing the number of women within the legal academy. This was arguably an important precursor to feminist legal studies becoming a larger part of the law school (Davies, 2013).

The second phase identified by Naffine consists of a deeper objection to the overall system which views it as embodying "a male culture, a male way of doing things" (1990, p. 3). In other words, claims of legal rationality and fairness are essentially a smokescreen which hide or attempt to obfuscate law's actual partiality to men and their view of the world. This male view of society involves an atomised, individual approach where each person only cares for, and seeks to protect, their own rights. It also insists on objectivity and the maintenance of distance between the "fact-finder" and "the subjects of the dispute" at the expense of a more healthy involvement and proximity (Naffine, 1990, p. 7; see also MacKinnon, 1983). In opposition to this "male" view, Gilligan suggested that there is a female "care ethic" which leads to differences in decision-making, reasoning and leadership styles (1993, p. 100). In relation to legal education, an example of Naffine's second phase can be found in Garner's suggestion that "caring, sensitive and devoted teachers" could provide a version of the Socratic approach in USA law schools that was "feminist friendly" (2000, p. 1643). This implies that the analytical, impersonal questioning most frequently associated with this approach represents a form of maleness, whereas a more empathetic and gentle approach embodies feminine virtues.

The third key phase in feminist legal thought identified by Naffine is one which concedes that law is male-dominated and full of biases but rejects the idea that this has arisen in an organised, consistent and conspiratorial fashion. Instead, the reality of law is that it has elements which are messy, contextualised, subjective and irrational, despite its claims to the contrary. In other words, although the law constructs a set of (masculine) legal ideals these are not attainable by either sex. Vital dimensions (usually associated with women) are missing as it reflects the "priorities of the dominant patriarchal social order" (which will usually themselves not be clear or consistent) (Naffine, 1990, p. 13). A key theme in this approach is the rejection of "grand theory" and a commitment to "the study of particular instances of law's oppression of women" (Naffine, 1990, p. 13). This approach, in particular the focus on individual instances of oppression, has links to the wider postmodern/poststructuralist feminist movement which became more prominent in the 1980s and 1990s. This movement rejects the idea of women as a homogenous or unified grouping and avoids championing any group identity (for example, female, gay, black). Instead it focuses on "destabilizing the manifold operations of power" which it describes in terms of "particularity and multiplicity" (Beasley, 1999, pp. 82–83; see also Frug, 1992).

One of the advantages of such a nuanced approach is that it does avoid generalizations about gender and other differences and enables commentators to take into account not only a person's sex but also their race, religious orientation and other identities they possess, acknowledging the importance of intersectionality. However, this rejection of universal principles and the embrace of fluidity also arguably means that it is difficult for such feminists to function as a cohesive movement for practical change or even to identify what should be changed and how. There are clear connections here with the debate over determining how and to what extent "truth" can be gauged using critical legal epistemology (Williams, 1993). Ramachandran (1998) raises similar concerns, suggesting that the challenge for feminism is how best to achieve the unity required of a political movement which wishes to effect change whilst avoiding perpetuating the forms of exclusion it is challenging, or, conversely, becoming too fragmented and dis-unified to act. Smart (2002) disputes this, suggesting that an overriding general theory itself does not provide a clear tactic for practical politics as by its nature it must operate at a level of abstraction which leaves it open to interpretation. However, this debate perhaps reflects Tong's comment (quoted previously) about each form of feminism only providing a partial and provisional answer – no single phase of feminist legal thought appears adequate on its own (and indeed, many other valuable but less prominent strains could also be identified, such as Marxist and socialist approaches).

In relation to legal education, Rhode critiques earlier feminist discussions by suggesting that they have generally proceeded on one of two levels: the first level involves focusing on "inadequacies that directly concern gender" such as the underrepresentation of women in academic positions and the devaluation of women's classroom participation (1993, p. 1549). This appears to reflect the first phase of feminist legal thought as discussed by Naffine (1990). The second level emphasises Gilligan's view of women as having a fundamentally different approach to legal and moral problems. This appears to reflect the second phase of feminist legal thought as discussed by Naffine (1990). Rhode argues that, while the second approach allows for a deeper analysis than the first, it does so in terms which can be over-simplistic and too essentialist. She argues that the similarities between men and women are more striking than the differences, but that the key is to acknowledge the diversity, contextual variations and multiple identities involved in mediating gender differences:

> For feminists concerned with legal education, the point is to ground critiques in normative principles, not essentialist premises. In short, we can affirm concerns that resonate with women's experiences, but on the basis of feminist commitments, not biological categories.
>
> (Rhode, 1993, p. 1554)

Drawing feminist work on legal education together, there is the sense of a valuable critique of mainstream legal practice and education which has, in turn, fed into law and emotions scholarship. It is arguable that there is still a lack of a cohesive vision of an alternative, feminist law school, let alone one focused on emotions. Indeed, even the suggestion of an alternative vision is possibly something which would be rejected by some feminists as too essentialist. However, some particularly relevant suggestions for the future of law schools have been made (particularly by USA commentators) which, largely implicitly, suggest the incorporation of emotions into this environment. These include the rejection of an adversarial model of legal education in favour of a more inclusive and collaborative model (Sturm, 1998), an increased focus on narrative and other forms of contextual analysis (Watkins, 2011: Farber and Sherry, 1993) and the encompassing of more varied forms of pedagogy and skills development (see, for example, Rhode, 1993).

Law and emotions scholarship

As discussed previously, feminist legal scholars' critiques of legal education and the key issues they have raised have fed into a body of work on law and emotions. In her 2006 taxonomy, Maroney argues that the distinguishing features of law and emotions scholarship are, firstly, its premise that emotions can and should be studied and are highly relevant to law and, secondly, its approach of taking a legal question and bringing to it a perspective grounded in the study or theory of emotions. She identifies six approaches to emotions within the literature: emotion-centered, emotional phenomenon, emotion-theory, legal doctrine, theory-of-law and legal actor (Maroney, 2006, p. 119).

The first of these, emotion-centred, looks at how a particular emotion is or should be reflected in law (for example, disgust or fear). Aligned with this, emotional phenomenon considers the mechanism by which that emotion is expressed and how this could be reflected in law (for example, the impact of affective forcasting – predicting how you will feel after a certain event – on decision-making). The third, emotion-theory, applies a certain theory, or theories, of emotions to consider how they are or should be reflected in law (an approach which will be taken in Chapter 3). The fourth, legal doctrine, analyses the relationship between emotions and a certain area of legal doctrine, exploring how they are, can be or ought to be incorporated into it (for example, by discussing the loss of control defence in relation to manslaughter which was referred to in Chapter 1). The fifth, theory-of-law, takes a particular theoretical approach to law and analyses the approach to emotions within it. This reflects the approach taken in this chapter by analysing the socio-legal view of emotion. The sixth, legal-actor approach, focuses on how emotions do and should influence and affect such actors in their interaction with the law. An example of this would be the studies of the emotional labour used within the legal profession that were referred to in Chapter 1.

Applying these categories to legal education, it appears that emotion-theory, theory-of-law and the legal actor approach all have a possible resonance. The first, emotion-theory, because the view of emotions subscribed to is likely to influence the perception of its relevance and usefulness. The second, theory-of-law, because it enables an exploration of different normative frameworks for the incorporation of emotions into legal education (such as comprehensive law and emotional intelligence). The last, legal actors, because it can encompass law students and legal academics.

Abrams (from a feminist legal studies viewpoint) identifies three different trends or currents in law and emotions scholarship – "recognition, reconnaissance and regulation" (2009, p. 302). The recognition current involves the acknowledgement that emotions play a part in legal transactions and decision-making. Abrams suggests that this view is still not universally accepted. This is demonstrated as recently as 2015 when Grossi undertook another, briefer, survey of law and emotions scholarship. Her starting point was to suggest that "emotions are not considered fit for the study of law" (2015, p. 55), thus suggesting that little has changed in the overall approach of law to emotions since Maroney's 2006 taxonomy. Abrams (2009) argues that there are two arguments behind this unwillingness to accept that emotions have a part to play in legal matters. Firstly, there is the argument that legal transactions are largely focused on areas where emotions are irrelevant. In other words, the law deals with rational actions, such as the entering into of a contract, where there are no extrinsic emotions. Secondly, there is the argument that legal decision-making derives its character and legitimacy from its objective, neutral nature. This legitimacy is therefore challenged if emotions are incorporated.

The preceding arguments resonate strongly with the doctrinal and liberal traditions of legal education and the way they frequently dichotomise emotions and reason using Cartesianism as their dominant epistemology (Williams, 1993). As recently as 2013, Solomon suggested that many legal authors simply dismiss emotion as "mere sentiment" which "confuse and distort the rational deliberations of justice" (2013, p. 292). Abrams and Keren are perhaps a little less scathing, but suggest that most legal scholars "remained committed to a core of detached, impersonal decision-making, though they acknowledged that it could be tinged at times with infusions of affect" (2010, p. 2008). Interestingly, Abrams cites the law's growing interest in, and acceptance of, the neurosciences as another example of its fascination with science, suggesting that it is seen as embodying a form of objectivity which is acceptable within law. In contrast, Abrams and Keren argue that law and emotions scholarship has been less well accepted because:

> It does not aim simply to correct legal subjects' decisionmaking in favor of rationality – the primary normative impetus in behavioral law and economics scholarship – but to modify legal doctrine to acknowledge and encompass affective response, or use law to channel, moderate, or foster the emotions.
> (Abrams and Keren, 2010, pp. 1999–2000)

However, despite reservations amongst the legal academy, Abrams (2009) does suggest that a number of legal scholars have moved on from such a recognition of emotions to create a current of reconnaissance. This involves drawing on research and findings on emotion from other disciplines, such as psychology or sociology to inform the law's engagement with a particular emotion. The third and final current is that of regulation. Abrams describes this as:

> A turn toward the task of normative prescription. In scholarship of this type, legal academics ask what particular insights about the emotions entail for the redirection of the law in particular areas.
> (Abrams, 2009, p. 304)

It moves away from considering the broad issues of whether emotions are or should be involved in a particular area and instead considers how, when and through which type of legal interventions. Abrams argues that this focus on regulation is crucial for determining how law and emotions interact (2009, p. 305). However, she acknowledges that there are objections to this. The first objection relates to the idea that the law becoming involved in emotions is actually a form of thought control, entering a domain which law should not be part of. Of course, this does assume that law and emotions can be separated. Bandes begins her groundbreaking book on *The Passions of Law* with the statement that "emotion pervades the law" (1999, p. 1). She argues that the law is imbued with emotions, often messy and unruly, and so ancient and deeply ingrained that they are "largely invisible" (Bandes, 1999, p. 2). Whether her work demonstrates emotions actually forming part of the law, or is another demonstration of the law's emotive subject matter, is perhaps arguable. However, the work of Bandes and others clearly illuminates the way in which emotions inter-connect with the law, despite it seeking to disregard or perhaps even conceal their existence. This illustration of the emotive subject matter of law is arguably itself sufficient to demonstrate that the law and legal actors should at least have a basic knowledge of emotions and their effects.

The second objection identified by Abrams reflects the concerns of Sanger (2001), which were referred to in Chapter 1 – that the emotions lose their authenticity when embodied in law. This appears to apply more to their embodiment through legislative provisions than fields such as legal education. However, it does emphasise the need to have, and communicate, a nuanced understanding of emotions, for example, avoiding assuming that all negative emotions are destructive and debilitating (Forgas, 2011).

Although the preceding taxonomies demonstrate a significant breadth and depth in law and emotions scholarship generally, there is relatively little literature specifically on emotions in legal education. Returning to Maroney's six categories, it appears that the only one to have been dealt with is that of legal actors, with the focus largely being on the emotional and psychological wellbeing of law students, in particular the negative effect that legal education can have on this (Bromberger, 2010). In terms of the currents of law and emotions scholarship identified by Abrams (2009), it appears that research in relation to legal education is still largely at the recognition stage. The only one full-length book to discuss this topic in-depth is "*Affect and Legal Education. Emotion in Learning and Teaching the Law*". The editors of this collection themselves suggest that the topic is "relatively invisible" in legal education literature (Maharg and Maughan, 2011, p. 1). They state that:

> If this book serves to illuminate how important affect is to a broad range of approaches to legal education, and to legal academics as well as law students, then it will have served its pioneering purpose.
>
> (Maharg and Maughan, 2011, p. 8)

The chapters contained in the collection are wide-ranging, beginning with a section on neuroscience then discussing legal educators and then learning. However, there is no one unifying theme and no attempt to construct any form of normative framework. Although insights are drawn on from neuroscience and psychology, there is surprisingly little from educational theory, suggesting that the reconnaissance current which Abrams refers to has still not been fully developed in this area.

Comprehensive and integrative law

Given the relatively early stage of scholarship on emotions in legal education, it is informative to briefly consider the ways in which feminist and critical approaches, together with wider insights from spiritual, philosophical and scientific disciplines, are currently being applied to the legal profession. Although in jurisdictions such as the UK the law degree is not primarily professional in nature, there remain close links between legal education and the legal profession and the latter may have a significant influence on the former.

Largely emanating from the USA, in recent years there has been the development of two movements which argue for a more holistic approach to legal practice, namely, comprehensive law (Daicoff, 2006) and integrative law (Wright, 2016). The distinction in, and relationship between, these two movements remains somewhat unclear, but both have in common their critique of existing modes of legal practice and their championing of models where the legal professional is positioned as a counsellor or problem-solver who heals conflicts or rifts within society (Scott,

2008). For example, the heuristic of therapeutic jurisprudence, which is embraced within comprehensive and integrative law, regards law as a "social force" which can therefore have therapeutic or anti-therapeutic behaviours and consequences in terms of its effect on psychological wellbeing including "the law's impact on emotional life" (Wexler, 2000, p. 125). All things being equal, a lawyer should therefore seek to maximise therapeutic effects on their client and minimise anti-therapeutic effects as a valid and important part of their role.

For this book, the relevance of these movements is in the way they acknowledge (and even embrace) the role of emotions within legal practice. In particular, notions such as emotional wellbeing and emotional intelligence are commonly included within them (see, for example, Daicoff, 2012). Whilst this could merely be seen as harnessing elements of emotions as a form of "soft skill", in fact, there is a recognition (at least in part) that emotions are more fundamental to legal practice. For example, Brookes argues for a relational framework for lawyering based on a new epistemology which incorporates the understanding that "Recognising and integrating the data from feelings and emotions is a critical process in effective legal practice" (2011, p. 336).

However, these movements do present a number of difficulties when seeking to translate their findings to the integration of emotions in legal education. Their practice orientation has meant a significant focus on practical approaches and case studies, arguably at the expense of a fully developed theoretical basis (Wexler, 2010; Slobogin, 1995). Indeed, a concept such as integrative law incorporates such a wide range of insights that it can be viewed as offering a veritable smorgasboard of theories within its remit. In addition, neither comprehensive law nor integrative law are currently mainstreamed within the jurisdictions in which they are advocated (despite some progress in the USA) (see, for example, Jones and Kawalek, 2018, in relation to the UK).

Therefore, in many ways, the comprehensive and integrative law movements share the opportunities, but also the challenges, of critical legal studies, feminist legal studies and law and emotions scholarship. On the one hand, they raise the potential for emotions to become an integral part of law (particularly legal education). On the other hand, they do not provide a fully developed or mainstreamed theoretical model to draw upon. This does raise the question of whether such a model is required for emotions to be acknowledged within legal education. It is arguable that this is unnecessary when such a broad range of evidence on the importance and value of emotions exists across disciplines and throughout the various aspects of personal, professional and educational existence. However, for law schools where the focus has traditionally been on the "scientific" and who are accustomed to the purported certainty of the doctrinal approach, it can be seen that such an established model would be attractive. It is possible that the only way to develop such a model is for emotions to become more mainstreamed within legal education, leading to greater understanding of their role within this context, but to do this may require a shift that goes beyond that occasioned to date by narrower forms of socio-legal studies if the insights of more sympathetic approaches are to be harnessed more fully.

Conclusion: constructing tentative foundations

A variety of different approaches to both the law and legal education have been explored within this chapter. When a broader definition of socio-legal studies is taken, it can be seen that it encompasses a wide range of scholarship on law and emotions, drawing from interdisciplinary work and critical jurisprudence. Although the idea that emotions do have a role to play in legal education has certainly not found unqualified acceptance throughout the legal academy, it has obtained sufficient recognition for some scholars to move on towards a more nuanced analysis of the role of emotions in specific areas (see, for example, Abrams, 2009 and Maroney, 2006). However, despite this, there is only a very sparse body of literature specifically on emotions and legal education. Work on critical legal studies, feminist legal theory and the comprehensive and integrative law movements does provide useful insights and a recognition of the potential role of emotions, but it has not yet begun to construct a full and cohesive normative theoretical framework for the role of emotions in legal education. Within socio-legal studies, there lies the potential, but for this to be developed a fuller understanding of what emotions are and their role needs to be developed, to demonstrate their centrality in law.

Note

1 There are also arguments that feminism is entering a fourth phase, focused on a dramatic shift in power within society (Donovan, 2012).

References

Abrams, K. (2009) "Barriers and Boundaries: Exploring Emotion in the Law of the Family", *Virginia Journal of Social Policy & the Law*, 16(2), 301–321.

Abrams, K. and Keren, H. (2010) "Who's Afraid of Law and the Emotions?", *Minnesota Law Review*, 94(6), 1997–2074.

Adler, M. and Simon, J. (2014) "Stepwise Progression: The Past, Present, and Possible Future of Empirical Research on Law in the United States and the United Kingdom", *Journal of Law and Society*, 41(3), 173–202.

Bandes, S. A. (1999) "Introduction", in Bandes, S. A. (ed), *The Passions of Law*, New York and London, New York University Press, 1–15.

Bartie, S. (2010) "The Lingering Core of Legal Scholarship", *Legal Studies*, 30(3), 345–369.

Beasley, C. (1999) *What is Feminism? An Introduction to Feminist Theory*, Sydney, Allen & Unwin.

Bromberger, N. (2010) "Enhancing Law Student Learning – the Nurturing Teacher", *Legal Education Review*, 20(1–2), 45–57.

Conaghan, J. (2013) *Law and Gender*, Oxford, Oxford University Press.

Cotterrell, R. B. M. (2006) *Law, Culture and Society: Legal Ideas in the Mirror of Social Theory*, Aldershot, Hampshire and Burlington, VT, Ashgate Publishing.

Cownie, F. (2004) *Legal Academics Culture and Identities*, Oxford and Portland, Oregon, Hart Publishing.

Daicoff, S. (2006) "Law as a Healing Profession: The "Comprehensive Law Movement" ", *Pepperdine Dispute Resolution Law Journal*, 6(1), 1–63.

Daicoff, S. S. (2012) "Expanding the Lawyer's Toolkit of Skills and Competencies: Synthesizing Leadership, Professionalism, Emotional Intelligence, Conflict Resolution, and Comprehensive Law", *Santa Clare Law Review*, 52(3), 795–874.

Davies, M. (2013) "Law's Truth and the Truth about Law: Interdisciplinary Refractions", in Monro, V. E. and Davies, M. (eds), *The Ashgate Research Companion to Feminist Legal Theory*, Aldershot, Ashgate Publishing.

Dickson-Swift, V., James, E. L., Kippen, S. and Liampattong, P. (2009) "Researching Sensitive Topics: Qualitative Research as Emotion Work", *Qualitative Research*, 9(1), 61–79.

Donovan, J. (2012) *Feminist Theory, Fourth Edition: The Intellectual Traditions*, New York and London, Continuum International.

Economic and Social Research Council (1993) *Review of Socio-Legal Studies*, London, ESRC.

Farber, D. A. and Sherry, S. (1993) "Telling Stories Out of School: An Essay on Legal Narratives", *Stanford Law Review*, 45(4), 807–855.

Feldman, R. (2009) "Law's Misguided Love Affair with Science", *Minnesota Journal of Law, Society and Technology*, 10(1), 95–116.

Fischer, C. (2016) "Feminist Philosophy, Pragmatism, and the "Turn to Affect": A Genealogical Critique", *Hypatia*, 31(4), 810–826.

Forgas, J. P. (2011) "Affect in Legal and Forensic Settings: The Cognitive Benefits of Not Being Too Happy", in Bornstein, B. H. and Wiener, R. L. (eds), *Emotion and the Law. Psychological Perspectives*, New York, Springer, 13–44.

Frug, M. J. (1992) *Postmodern Legal Feminism*, New York, Routledge.

Garner, D. D. (2000) "Socratic Misogyny? Analysing Feminist Criticisms of Socratic Teaching in Legal Education", *Brigham Young University Law Review*, 2000(4), 1597–1650.

Genn, H., Partington, M. and Wheeler, S. (2006) *Law in the Real World: Improving Our Understanding of How Law Works Final Report and Recommendations*, The Nuffield Inquiry on Empirical Legal Research.

Gilligan, C. (1993) *In a Different Voice Psychological Theory and Women's Development*, Cambridge, Massachusetts, Harvard University Press.

Goodrich, P. (1992) "Critical Legal Studies in England: Prospective Histories", *Oxford Journal of Legal Studies*, 12(2), 195–236.

Goodrich, P. (1996) "Of Blackstone's Tower: Metaphors of Distance and Histories of the English Law School", in Birks, P. (ed), *Pressing Problems in the Law Volume 2 What are Law Schools for?* Oxford, Oxford University Press.

Goodrich, P. (1999) "The Critic's Love of the Law: Intimate Observations of an Insular Jurisdiction", *Law and Critique*, 10(3), 343–360.

Grossi, R. (2015) "Understanding Law and Emotion", *Emotion Review*, 7(1), 55–60.

Guth, J. and Ashford, C. (2014) "The Legal Education and Training Review: Regulating socio-legal and Liberal Legal Education", *The Law Teacher*, 48(1), 5–19.

Harris, D. R. (1983) "The Development of Socio-Legal Studies in the United Kingdom", *Legal Studies*, 3(3), 315–333.

Holmes, O. W. (1897) "The Path of the Law", *Harvard Law Review*, 10, www.constitution.org/lrev/owh/path_law.htm (accessed 1 July 2018).

Howson, A. (2013) *The Body in Society: An Introduction*, 2nd edn, Cambridge and Malden, MA, Polity Press.

Hutchinson, T. and Duncan, N. (2012) "Defining and Describing What We Do: Doctrinal Legal Research", *Deakin Law Review*, 17(1), 83–119.

Jaggar, A. M. (1989) "Love and Knowledge: Emotion in Feminist Epistemology", *Inquiry*, 32(2), 151–176.

Jones, E. and Kawalek, A. (2018) "Dissolving the Stiff Upper Lip: Opportunities and Challenges for the Mainstreaming of Therapeutic Jurisprudence in the United Kingdom", *International Journal of Law and Psychiatry* [early access].

Kennedy, D. (1982) "Legal Education and the Reproduction of Hierarchy", *Journal of Legal Education*, 42(4), 591–615.

MacKinnon, C. A. (1983) "Feminism, Marxism, Method and the State: Towards Feminist Jurisprudence", *Signs*, 8(4), 635–658.

Maharg, P. and Maughan, C. (2011) "Introduction", in Maharg, P. and Maughan, C. (eds), *Affect and Legal Education. Emotion in Learning and Teaching the Law*, Aldershot, Ashgate Publishing, 1–10.

Maroney, T. A. (2006) "Law and Emotion: A Proposed Taxonomy of an Emerging Field", *Law and Human Behaviour*, 13(2), 119–142.

McCrudden, C. (2006) "Legal Research and the Social Sciences", *Law Quarterly Review*, 122, 632–650.

Menkel-Meadow, C. (1988) "Feminist Legal Theory, Critical Legal Studies, and Legal Education or "The Fem-Crits Go to Law School"", *Journal of Legal Education*, 38, 61–85.

Murphy, B. and McGee, J. (2015) "Phronetic Legal Inquiry. An Effective Design for Law and Society Research?", *Griffith Law Review*, 24(2), 1–26.

Naffine, N. (1990) *Law and the Sexes Explorations in Feminist Jurisprudence*, London, Allen & Unwin.

Ramachandran, B. (1998) "Re-Reading Difference: Feminist Critiques of the Law School Classroom and the Problem with Speaking from Experience", *Columbia Law Review*, 98(7), 1757–1794.

Rhode, D. L. (1993) "Missing Questions: Feminist Perspectives on Legal Education", *Stanford Law Review*, 45(6), 1547–1566.

Sanders, A. (2015) "Poor Thinking, Poor Outcome? The Future of the Law Degree after the Legal Education and Training Review and the Case for Socio-Legalism", in Sommerlad, H., Harris-Short, S., Vaughan, S. and Young, R. (eds), *The Futures of Legal Education and the Legal Profession*, Oxford and Portland, Hart Publishing.

Sanger, C. (2001) "The Role and Reality of Emotions in Law", *William & Mary Journal of Women and the Law*, 8(1), 107–113.

Scott, C. (2008) "Doctors as Advocates, Lawyers as Healers", *Hamline Journal of Public Law and Policy*, 29(2), 331–399.

Sherry, S. (1996) "The Sleep of Reason", *Georgetown Law Journal*, 84, 453–484.

Siems, M. M. and Mac Sithigh, D. (2012) "Mapping Legal Research", *Cambridge Law Journal*, 71(3), 651–676.

Slobogin, C. (1995) "Therapeutic Jurisprudence: Five Dilemmas to Ponder", *Psychology, Public Policy and Law*, 1(1), 193–219.

Smart, C. (2002) *Feminism and the Power of Law*, London, Routledge.

Solomon, R. C. (2013) "Sympathy and Vengeance: The Role of The Emotions in Justice", in Van Goozen, S. H. M., Van de Poll, I. E. and Sergeant, S. A. (eds), *Emotions: Essays on Emotion Theory*, New York and London, Psychology Press.

Stanley, C. (1988) "Training for the Hierarchy? Reflections on the British Experience of Legal Education", *The Law Teacher*, 22(2), 78–86.

Sturm, S. P. (1998) "From Gladiators to Problem-Solvers: Connecting Conversations about Women, the Academy and the Legal Profession", *Duke Journal of Gender Law and Policy*, 4, 119–147.

Teubner, G. "How the Law Thinks: Toward a Constructivist Epistemology of Law", *Law & Society Review*, 23(5), 727–758.

Tong, R. (1989) *Feminist Thought. A Comprehensive Introduction*, Boulder, CO, Westview Press.

Twining, W. (2014) "LETR: The Role of Academics in Legal Education and Training: 10 Theses", *The Law Teacher*, 48, 94–103.

Unger, R. M. (1983) "The Critical Legal Studies Movement", *Harvard Law Review*, 96(3), 561–675.

van Gestel, R. and Micklitz, H. (2011) *Revitalizing Doctrinal Legal Research in Europe: What about Methodology?* European University Institute Working Papers Law 2011/05.

Vick, D. W. (2004) "Interdisciplinarity and the Discipline of Law", *Journal of Law and Society*, 31(2), 163–193.

Watkins, D. (2011) "The Role of Narratives in Legal Education", *Liverpool Law Review*, 32(2), 113–133.

Webb, J. (2006) "The "Ambitious Modesty" of Harold Arthur's Humane Professionalism", *Osgoode Hall Law Journal*, 44(1), 119–155.

Wexler, D. B. (2000) "Therapeutic Jurisprudence: An Overview", *Thomas M. Cooley Law Review*, 17(1), 125–134.

Wexler, D. B. (2010) *From Theory to Practice and Back Again in Therapeutic Jurisprudence: Now Comes the Hard Part*, Arizona Legal Studies, Discussion Paper No. 10–12.

Williams, S. H. (1993) "Feminist Legal Epistemology", *Berkeley Women's Law Journal*, 8, 63–105.

Wright, J. K. (2016) *Lawyers as Changemakers: The Global Integrative Law Movement*, Chicago, ABA Publishing.

3 Emotions as a transformative force

Introduction: what is an emotion?

Chapters 1 and 2 of this book have both touched upon the role and purpose of emotions. The notion that reason and emotions are intertwined, that cognition and emotions cannot be separated, and that to do so is damaging to both, is fundamental to the premise of this book. To have a truly transformative effect on legal education, emotions must be more than evolutionary throwbacks, brute instinctive reactions or dangerous impulses that undermine rationality and mislead cognition. Instead, emotions must (and do) have an important role to play in our thought processes, decision-making, judgements and reactions. This chapter traces how philosophical and scientific thought has developed from largely embracing forms of Cartesian dualism (that term again!) to the position where there is now a wide range of findings and new theories which challenge traditional conceptions of emotions, those widely held beliefs that form the basis of their disregard and suppression within the law school.

Given the continual evolution of research into, and discussion on, emotions, it would take far more than an introduction to a chapter, a chapter, or even a book, to try and fully answer the question of what an emotion actually is. There are a broad range of definitions which are not always easy or possible to reconcile (see the list given in Kleinginna and Kleinginna, 1981, as an example of this). However, as a starting point, the following definition positions emotions within the welter of experiences and processes occurring within each individual (and which they bring with them into legal education):

> Emotion is a subjectively experienced feeling that is related to affect and mood.
> (Kohn and Keller, 2015, p. 547)

This quotation is a relatively uncontentious starting point for exploring the role of emotions, but may itself need some explanation. The notion of "affect" refers to the broader array of apparently non-cognitive functions which are present within individuals, often focused on "moods, attitudes, preferences" (Shuman and Scherer, 2014, p. 18). It is the underlying flow of underlying feelings of pleasantness or unpleasantness (valence) and calm or agitation (arousal) (Feldman Barrett, 2017, p. 72). When there is a high level of valance, this results in the higher intensity episodes that are experienced as emotions (Bornstein and Wiener, 2010, p. 1).[1] The questions to be explored in the remainder of this chapter are around why these emotions arise and what purpose (if any) they serve.

The lure of Cartesian dualism

This book has already introduced the notion of Cartesian dualism as one which separates reason and emotions and deifies the former at the expense of the latter. However, this form of division in fact has older roots, with the differences in approach to emotions taken by the philosophers of Ancient Greece. The pre-Socratic philosophers were interested in the nature of the soul and the process of thinking, with varied theories suggesting that thoughts were held within the air, in fire or in varying parts of the human anatomy (including the brain) (Crivellato and Ribatti, 2007). However, it can be argued that the philosophical study of emotions began with Plato (Knuuttila, 2004). He viewed the human soul as divided in three – reason (*logos*, located in the head), spirits (*thymos*, located in the chest) and appetites (*epithymétikon*, located near the liver) (Plato, 1974; Crivellato and Ribatti, 2007). Although various commentators have interpreted each of these spheres somewhat differently, they are commonly viewed as equating to cognition, emotions and motivation (Scherer, 2011, p. 332; for a different interpretation see Solomon, 2000, p. 4).

From this notion of the tripartite soul, a number of general conceptions about emotions have developed which can be traced through later philosophical discussion on emotions, notably the work of Descartes, and which still persist today. Indeed, the Introduction to this book has already explored the Cartesian view that emotions are bodily sensations which travel to, and excite, the mind, which in turn must control and regulate them. These conceptions form a philosophical basis for the notion that each element of consciousness is separate and discrete and that there is a hierarchy, with cognition (including reason and rationality) in the highest position, exercising control and wisdom over the lesser, more base aspects such as emotions (Scherer, 1995; although Coplan (2010) suggests that Plato viewed emotions as impervious to reason). This is the received wisdom on the rightful place of emotions that still pervades the law as a whole (Bailey and Knight, 2017) and manifests itself within key paradigms in legal education (in particular, the doctrinal and liberal traditions). As a result, as demonstrated in Chapters 1 and 2, the imperative in law schools has most commonly been to eradicate the influence of emotions to ensure that the "science" of law is as rigorous and unsullied as possible.

Indeed, in society generally, it is these Platonic and Cartesian visions of cognition (represented by reason and rationality) and emotion as separate and largely antithetical, which have received the most support up until the latter decades of the twentieth century (Scherer, 2011; Hey and Leathwood, 2009). This is, of course, a fairly sweeping generalization when applied to centuries of history and philosophy. For example, Bantock (1986, p. 125) refers to the "peculiarly creative tension" of both cognition and emotion in Renaissance education and also refers to the late eighteenth-century Romanticism's emphasis on feelings and emotions. Even within the Enlightenment period, philosophers such as David Hume and Adam Smith defended the importance of what they described as "the moral sentiments" (Smith, 2006; Hume, 2003). However, it was not until the latter part of the nineteenth century that the work of Charles Darwin (1809–1882) on emotions contributed to a resurgence in scientific and philosophical interest that has led to broader changes in the way emotions are conceptualised and understood (Oatley et al., 2006).

Darwin's focus was on the expression of emotions, for example, through facial expressions, blushing and crying. He argued that these largely resulted from either habituation (learning to use these expressions following repeated exposure) or were inherited and innate (evolving from the habits of ancestors):

> Actions which were at first voluntary, soon become habitual, and at last hereditary, and may then be performed even in opposition to the will. Although they often reveal the state of the mind, this result was not at first either intended or expected.
>
> (Darwin, 1890, p. 377)

Gendron and Feldman Barrett (2009, p. 316) summarise Darwin's theory as viewing emotions as mental states which cause stereotypic bodily expressions. His focus was on the expression of emotions, rather than the cause and generation of the mental state itself. Therefore, he does not specify a particular cause of emotions. However, Gendron and Feldman Barrett attribute to Darwin's work the development of what is now commonly termed as basic emotions theory. This theory has been further developed by individuals such as Tomkins and McCartur who identified a number of what they classified as "primary affects" and argued that "each of the primary affects is controlled by an innate "program" which has been inherited" (1964, pp. 121, 119). These affects (or emotions) are generated by facial expressions and, later, through the memory of those innate reactions.

A key current proponent of basic emotions theory is Ekman, who identifies a set of fundamental emotions which he argues are common to all cultures (and even across primate species), including anger, fear, sadness and enjoyment:

> There are separate discrete emotions, which have evolved to prepare us to deal with fundamental life tasks.
>
> (Ekman, 1992a, p. 170)

Ekman (1999, p. 46) identifies a number of meanings for the term "basic" within this approach. Firstly, there is the way in which individual emotions are characterised as each being individual and different. Secondly, there is the notion that emotions have evolved as a result of "their adaptive value in dealing with *fundamental life tasks*" [author's italics]. In other words, the emotion experienced in relation to a particular event (such as a threat of immediate danger) will be the one that has developed in the ancestral past, species-wide, as the best solution towards attaining the relevant goal within that situation. For example, a sense of fear will be generated if an individual holding a gun comes into view, causing the spectator to flee the danger. Ekman distinguishes these basic emotions from other "affective phenomena", viewing them as a special class compared to other emotional states or moods, on a number of grounds. This includes their rapid onset, short duration and the universal signals and physiology involved (Ekman, 1999, p. 56).

This approach still has a significant level of support within the contemporary scientific community and is the origin of the numerous online quizzes that invite you to test your emotional intelligence or emotional quotient by identifying an emotion from an image of a person's facial expression. Overall, basic emotions theory characterises different emotions as a series of largely physiological responses, each with their own neural programming, which largely occur as a result of the evolutionary process and the need for individuals to adapt to their environment (Ekman, 1999; 1992a; 1992b). This appears, at first glance at least, to lend support to the notion of a form of Cartesian dualism between reason (as a part of cognition) and emotions and thus the traditional approach of the law and legal education. If emotions are largely evolutionary throwbacks, the supremacy of reason and rationality is assured and becomes justifiably enshrined within the law and law schools.

Shortly after Darwin's theory was developed, a second influential theory, which deals with the physiology of emotions and can therefore be viewed as a form of basic emotions theory, was presented by William James (1842–1910). He argued that, contrary to the notion that a mental perception generated a mental reaction which generated a bodily expression, in fact:

> My thesis on the contrary is that *the bodily changes follow directly the* PERCEPTION *of the exciting fact, and that our feeling of the same changes as they occur* IS *the emotion.* [author's italics and emphasis]
>
> (James, 1884, pp. 189–190)

In other words, rather than a person's perception generating an emotion which led to bodily changes (such as blushing or recoiling with fear), it was that individual's bodily changes which in fact generated the felt emotion. This theory became known as the James-Lange theory after similar ideas were developed in parallel by Carl Lange (1834–1900) with its view of emotions as a function of sensory and motor areas rather than a specific system devoted to emotional functions (LeDoux and Phelps, 2000, p. 157). However, Gendron and Feldman Barrett (2009, p. 324) caution against wholly equating the work of James with that of Lange arguing that Lange followed Darwin's more fixed basic emotions approach whilst James allowed for more variability within emotional responses. A different theory was also developed by Walter Cannon (1871–1945) and Philip Bard (1998–1977), known as the Cannon-Bard theory, which viewed a person's bodily reaction and felt emotion as occurring simultaneously (Cannon, 1927). Another influential theory (arguably more in-keeping with the appraisal theories discussed ahead) is the "two factor theory". This identifies emotions as generated via a sequence of a physical state of arousal being "labelled" with an appropriate emotion through a person's cognitive function, drawing on external cues (Schachter and Singer, 1962, pp. 382–383). For example, when walking down a dark passageway at night if a figure with a gun appears your body will draw on your knowledge of dark passageways and guns to interpret your physical reaction as the emotion of fear (Schachter and Singer, 1962, p. 380).

Although most neuroscientists would now dispute the James-Lange hypothesis that the bodily change generates the emotion, they do accept that bodily experiences interact with or moderate the emotional sensation experienced (Dalgleish, 2004). Hence emotions are, at least in part, bodily functions. The embodied character of emotions once again brings them up against the prejudices of Cartesian dualism with the mind (representing cognition, reason and rationality) being seen as elevated above the more base, embodied nature of emotions (Conoghan, 2013). There is a lack of acknowledgement of the bodily and embodiment within law schools and an emphasis on the textual and oral (Philippopoulos-Mihalopoulos, 2012; Mertz, 2007). Therefore, the physiological aspects of emotions once again perpetuate their suppression and disregard within legal education.

In terms of understanding the mechanisms generating emotions within the brain, traditional theories also perpetuated the notion of cognition and emotions as separate by positing a hierarchical biological structure. In broad terms, a commonly held view developed viewing the brain as consisting of three discrete levels: the first, primitive level of the brain was seen as dealing with the basic functions required for survival; the middle, more recently evolved level (known as the limbic system) was perceived as generating emotions; and the top and most recently evolved level, the cortex, was hailed as the seat of cognition, reason and rationality (MacLean, 1949). This mirrors the form of master and slave metaphor referred to in the Introduction to this book (Solomon, 2000, p. 3) and once again positions emotions as inferior and potentially irrelevant.

Nevertheless, despite these characterisations of emotions within basic emotions theory, it is interesting to note that contemporary versions have begun to acknowledge "the important role of cultural and social learning processes in every aspect of emotion" and view emotions as in some ways moderated through each individual's experience, despite their evolutionary nature (Ekman, 1992b, p. 550). For example, Panksepp (2000, p. 143) argues that although many aspects of emotions are genetically engrained across species, there is also the existence of "Higher Sentiments" which may be unique to individual humans and combine innate and cognitive factors. He provides a taxonomy of emotions with various levels and indicates that the more subtle emotional responses (such as jealousy or shame) are those which arise when basic emotions are combined with cognitive functions (Panksepp, 2011, p. 1800). Effectively, the basic emotions become ingredients of subtler social emotions which are mediated by each individual's cognitive processes, thus suggesting emotional responses are not simply physiologically programmed.

This brief discussion indicates that, even within basic emotions theory, there is some acknowledgement at least of the importance and value of emotions. Indeed, Schulkin et al. characterise both Darwin and James as part of an "adaptationalist view" which sees emotions not as purely negative and passive states, but as "responses and behaviours" which "were selected by evolutionary forces as part of successful adaptation" (2003, p. 16). This characterisation also appears to apply to other contributors such as Tomkins and McCartur (1964), Ekman (1999, 1992a, 1992b) and Panksepp (2011, 2000). As such, this view does ascribe some use and value to emotions (and increasingly acknowledges the influence of external forces such as cultural and social and possibly even cognitive factors). However, by focusing on the perceived separateness of emotions from cognition and their seemingly physiological functions, such scientists appear to have implicitly retained the tradition of Cartesian dualism and can be broadly classified as "feeling", "sensation" or "non-cognitive" theorists (Coplan, 2010, p. 137).

There is a clear synchronicity between basic emotions theory and the development of legal education's traditional paradigms. The Platonic and Cartesian tradition, which perceives emotions largely as bodily responses, is mirrored in legal education by the doctrinal tradition's "fears that ungovernable emotion would inflame the vaunted reason of the law" (Abrams and Keren, 2010, p. 2028). In the same way that basic emotions theory has gradually acknowledged some cultural, social role or even cognitive role for emotions, some within the liberal tradition of law schools have arguably touched upon the role of emotions (see, for example, Webb, 2006). However, overall, both the doctrinal and liberal paradigms share common ground with basic emotions theory in refusing to accept that emotions have a significant role within cognition, reason and rationality. By moving on to consider the changing view on the role of emotions within mainstream philosophical and scientific thought, this chapter will demonstrate that these traditional conceptions and synchronicities no longer provide a sufficient or appropriate premise upon which to base legal education's understanding of, and approach to, emotions.

Emotion and reason intertwined

In the same way that socio-legal studies has presented the dominant challenge to the doctrinal approach in law, a newer approach to emotions within the scientific community, known as appraisal theories, has challenged the traditional Cartesian dualism which dominated the previous conceptualisations of emotions (Moors et al., 2013; Oatley et al., 2006). Unlike Plato's view of emotions as untameable by reason, this approach views emotions themselves as forms of judgement. The key figure associated with this view of the emotions is the ancient Greek philosopher Aristotle, who referred to both the psychological experiences and physiological changes of an emotion and viewed them as caused by a person's assessment of an object (Aristotle, 1985; see also Kristjánsson, 2012, p. 1).

Appraisal theory is commonly held in opposition to basic emotions theory (Gendron and Feldman Barrett, 2009). However, one of the originators of modern theories of appraisal in emotions, Magda Arnold (1903–2002), did not appear to see the two approaches as polarised. Instead, she argued that existing approaches had focused on the sequence "emotion-expression-action" whereas the explanation for emotions lay in the preceding sequence of "perception-appraisal-emotion"

(Arnold, 1960, p. 182; see also Feldman Barrett, 2017). In particular she argued that:

> Normal emotion carries with it the reference to an object or situation that is known in some way.
>
> (Arnold, 1960, p. 170)

In other words, it is an individual's perception and appraisal of an object or situation which initiates the emotion and the accompanying physiological changes. This will only arise if the object is perceived as affecting the individual by being either good or bad, present or absent or easy or difficult to obtain (or avoid). This appraisal will be immediate, automatic, intuitive and non-intellectual but may later be intensified or modified by a purposeful, reflective appraisal (Arnold, 1960, p. 143). Arnold suggested that the emotions experienced as a result of this appraisal would also leave a residue which would develop a quicker, easier repetition in future, leading to the formation of emotional attitudes and habits. She also made a distinction between emotions, which indicated an attitude to an object, and a feeling, which referred to one aspect of its object; for example, you may feel the emotion of love towards your husband or wife, but whether this was a pleasant sensation would be dependent on feeling.

One of the key proponents of an appraisal theory of emotion is Lazarus (1991). He terms the two appraisal mechanisms as "primary" and "secondary". The function of the "primary" appraisal is to recognise that the individual has something at stake, for example, if the situation is likely to cause harm to or, conversely, assist with the achievement of a personal goal. In other words, it has an impact on that person's wellbeing (Lazarus and Smith, 1988, p. 284). The "secondary" appraisal focuses on how the individual can cope with the situation, or use it to their advantage. It considers the coping resources and options that a person has. If it appears that this is an encounter that can be handled and may work out positively, that is likely to result in a positive emotional response, whereas uncertainty or concerns about the outcome will result in negative emotions (Lazarus and Smith, 1988).

Moors suggests that there are a variety of "flavours" of appraisal theories which have different theories on the underlying mechanisms and whether the emotion is viewed as constructed from, or as an automatic response to, an appraisal (2014, p. 304). However, she argues that the two common assumptions between all appraisal theories are firstly, that emotions are triggered by a stimulus and contain a variety of common components; and secondly, that a form of appraisal regulates the relationship between the stimulus and the components (Moors, 2014; Moors et al., 2013). In terms of the relationship between cognition and emotions, Ellsworth suggests that:

> Appraisal theorists believe that thought and emotion are largely inseparable, that emotions arise from the organism's perceptions – its appraisals – of environmental changes that are relevant for its well being.
>
> (Ellsworth, 2013, p. 125)

Therefore, appraisal theorists commonly view emotions as non-cognitive, although this is not a universal view; for example, Lazarus (1991) views emotions as cognitive in nature (as will be discussed later). Although appraisal theorists may characterise emotions as non-cognitive, they also view them as inextricably linked to cognitive processes (Ellsworth, 2013; Moors et al., 2013; Oatley et al., 2006). This close inter-relationship between emotions and cognition is arguably the most significant shift to arise from changes in philosophical and scientific perceptions of emotions. It challenges the pervasive notion of cognition and emotions as separate, dualistic, or even opposing, and positions emotions as important, if not key, to individuals' thoughts by demonstrating how cognition and emotions are intertwined. A striking illustration of the importance of emotions working alongside reason comes from Damasio (2006), whose somatic-marker hypothesis argues that it is physical changes in the body which generate emotions. He describes an individual (Elliot) who suffered a brain injury which retained his intellectual functions wholly intact but left him appearing to lack what Damasio termed as "secondary", or complex, emotions (2006, p. 137). Damasio gives a telling description of trying to arrange a subsequent appointment with Elliot at the end of one session. What should have been a simple identification of an appropriate date turned into a half an hour deliberation as Elliot weighed up the advantages and disadvantages of each, equally valid, date in turn, but appeared unable to reach a decision. He had no form of emotional response or instinct to guide his choice and was therefore unable to choose.

In relation to decision-making generally, Pfister and Böhm (2008) argue that emotions in fact have four key functions. They provide information which indicates the potential effect of the decision on wellbeing, they facilitate faster decision-making (in contrast to the unfortunate Elliot), they sort the relevance of different factors by directing attention to the most salient of these and they generate commitment to the eventual decision that is reached. More recently, Lerner et al. (2015), reviewing thirty five years of literature, have identified eight different themes currently being explored around the ways in which emotions interact with decision-making. They suggest that the overwhelming evidence demonstrates that "emotions powerfully, predictably, and pervasively influence decision making" (Lerner et al., 2015, p. 5). The importance of emotions in other key mental processes has also been increasingly explored; for example, it is well-established that emotions affect the way individuals process information. Positive emotions are associated with an ability to view the bigger picture, whilst negative emotions tend to generate a focus on specific details (Gasper, 2004). Similarly, emotions play a significant role in how people interpret and respond to information and the formation and retrieval of memories (for a useful summary of some key studies see McConnell and Eva, 2012). Overall, the current literature stemming from appraisal theories, and wider discussion of emotions, provide a vast array of evidence and examples of the necessity for emotions to interact with, and influence, cognition (Storbeck and Clore, 2007; Schwarz, 2000).

This body of literature has been also been supported, and influenced, by accompanying shifts in understanding of the brain mechanisms involved in emotions. The notion of a form of hierarchical system, with emotional workings being contained within the limbic system (and controlled by the cortex) has been questioned. For example, it is argued that it has proved impossible to devise criteria to select which structures and pathways form a part of it (LeDoux and Phelps, 2000). Instead, Panksepp (2000, p. 141) argues that there are now three approaches to the brain mechanisms of emotions – a "generalized emotions theory" which sees them as constructed from a variety of raw parts via learning mechanisms; a "central affective programs" approach which sees emotions as global brain states that emerge from central brain processes; and a variety of hybrids which focus on the different components which contribute from both the brain and body. Panksepp himself supports the idea of central affective programmes, which he attributes to MacLean (1949). He cites LeDoux and Phelps (2000) as an example of the "generalized emotions theory" and Damasio (2006) as an example of a researcher who embodies a hybrid approach with his hypothesis that the body itself provides the biological "landscape" which translates into emotions (2006, p. 173).

Regardless of which of the previous three approaches to brain mechanisms are taken, it is significant to note that none of these simply place emotions as forming an inferior, subjugated function lying beneath cognition; instead a more sophisticated and nuanced understanding of emotions is being developed. As a result, the notion of cognition and emotions as intertwined is no longer outlandish or groundbreaking, instead it is an accepted part of contemporary science and philosophy (Damasio, 2006; Nussbaum, 2001). Once again, there is a synchronicity here with the development of socio-legal studies as there is a clear shift in approaches to emotions, just as there has been a shift in approaches to law and legal research. However, within legal education, the acknowledgement of emotions still arguably lies at the boundaries of acceptance, even within socio-legal scholarship. Therefore, a potential divide is emerging as emotions scholarship moves forward rapidly, but legal education remains largely tethered to traditional, and often outdated, concepts of emotions.

Having said that, there is evidence that the idea of cognition and emotions being intertwined or integrated is gradually beginning to be reflected in the legal sphere by the forms of law and emotions scholarship discussed in Chapter 2. For example, Bandes and Blumenthal (2012, p. 164) refer to emotions as "dynamic processes that are integral to decision-making", contrasting this with the "folk knowledge" which views emotions as impulsive and irrational. A range of studies within law are beginning to explore how emotions interact with cognition throughout the legal sphere in areas as diverse as the judiciary (Anleu et al., 2015) and constitutional design (Sajó, 2010). Overall, the vision that drives these draws on contemporary scientific and philosophical insights and is summarised well by Bandes and Blumenthal when they describe emotions thus:

> They influence the way we screen, categorize, and interpret information; influence our evaluations of the intentions or credibility of others; and help us decide what is important or valuable. Perhaps most important, they drive

> us to care about the outcome of our decision making and motivate us to take action, or refrain from taking action, on the situations we evaluate.
>
> (Bandes and Blumenthal, 2012, pp. 163–164)

It is clear that emotions have the potential to have an extremely significant impact on law. If cognition, reason and rationality are intertwined with emotions, this implies that reason will be impoverished and impaired if emotions are suppressed or disregarded (Harris and Schultz, 1993). For legal education, this provides both a challenge and an opportunity. It challenges the existing limits of the doctrinal and liberal traditions and also places an imperative on the socio-legal approach to fully embrace law and emotions scholarship and begin the process of incorporating this into the law school in earnest.

Constructing realities

The preceding discussion summarises some of the key evidence demonstrating that emotions have a role and worth as an integral part of cognition, reason and rationality, including thought processes, decision-making and many other aspects of consciousness. Although appraisal theories have arguably been key in challenging Platonic and Cartesian views of emotions, alongside the evolving understanding of brain mechanisms, the conceptualisation of emotions as intertwined with cognition also permeates a wide range of other current theories of emotions. For example Pessoa (2013), drawing on network theory, has characterised traditional notions of the relationship between cognition and emotions as antagonistic and segregated. Instead, he argues that:

> Parcelling the brain into cognitive and affective regions is inherently problematic, and ultimately untenable for at least three reasons: first, brain regions viewed as 'affective' are also involved in cognition; second, brain regions viewed as 'cognitive' are also involved in emotion; and critically, third, cognition and emotion are integrated in the brain.
>
> (Pessoa, 2008, p. 148)

Another significant approach to emotions, which emphasises their relationship with cognition, focuses on the ways in which emotions are constructed, either by individuals or within society. This approach therefore shares an epistemological base with the critical and feminist approaches to legal education discussed in Chapter 2, viewing knowledge as partial and situated in a particular societal and cultural context. Whilst these approaches are focused on the way in which knowledge and learning is created and constructed within the law school, constructivism in theories of emotions focuses on the ways in which an emotional experience is constructed. There are two aspects to this; firstly, the role of the individual and their thought processes and bodily reactions (Feldman Barrett, 2017) and, secondly, the role of external social and cultural influences in the construction of emotions (Boiger and Mesquita, 2012). Depending on the theorist, each of these aspects may be highlighted to a greater or lesser extent. One of the leading proponents of constructivism within theories of emotion is Feldman Barrett, who argues that:

> Emotions are not reactions to the world. You are not a passive receiver of sensory input but an active constructor of your emotions. From sensory input and past experience, your brain constructs meaning and prescribes action.
>
> (Feldman Barrett, 2017, p. 31)

In other words, emotions are once again demonstrated to have a significant value rather than being classified as irrational physiological urges, but this time the meaning, experience (and the neurological processes involved) are viewed as personal to each individual because of their differing understanding and experience of, and interactions with, the world. Whilst Feldman Barrett's work explores the neurological processes involved in the individual's construction of emotions in depth, she also acknowledges the importance of social and cultural influences in creating the experience. The idea that emotion is socially constructed was developed by Averill who argues that:

> An emotion is a transitory social role (a socially constituted syndrome) that includes an individual's appraisal of the situation and that is interpreted as a passion rather than an action.
>
> (Averill, 2005, p. 254)

Boiger and Mesquita (2012) give a range of examples to illustrate this concept, focusing on the ways in which social interactions and relationships influence emotional responses. For example, the way in which emotions are constructed and evolve during a marital row depends on the reactions of each spouse, with defensiveness on the part of one increasing anger on the part of the other, or an apology from one eliciting a very different response. Similarly, the ways in which caregivers will respond to an infant's indications of their affective states will influence the way in which the infant's emotional responses develop. They emphasise the fluid and dynamic nature of emotions in such situations and also indicate the importance of cultural context within the interpretation and understanding of different emotions.

According to such constructivist theories, emotions are therefore (at least in part) a function of cognition. This is because enacting a social role involves its active cognitive interpretation by an individual, involving a highly personal, evaluative appraisal (Averill, 2005). Averill views the object which is being appraised as something which does not exist outside the meaning imposed on it by the individual. In other words, it constitutes "a meaning imposed on the environment – a cognitive construct, so to speak" (2005, p. 252). For Averill, even the sense of being overwhelmed or consumed by an emotion can be explained by the individual's interpretation of their own behaviour. The idea of an emotion as a social role also leads him to dispute basic emotions theory, suggesting that there are an "indefinite" number of emotions which can be constructed (Averill, 2005; see also Boiger and Mesquita, 2012).

The constructivist theory of emotions once again presents a clear challenge to the Cartesian dualism and the focus on a particular form of reason and rationality which is prevalent in both law and legal education. It adds a different dimension in its emphasis on social and cultural influences and their role in the emotional experience. This is important in terms of the lived experience of the law school, because it demonstrates that the emotions experienced within it will be, if not generated, at the very least influenced, by the broader culture of that particular institution as well as the norms and culture of legal education and the law more generally. For many stakeholders within the law school, this often equates to narrow and rigid forms of "thinking like a lawyer" (James, 2008) (a point which is further discussed in Chapter 6).

Different concepts of cognition

The general approach of appraisal theories views the initial appraisal leading to an emotion as requiring subsequent logical and rational reflection. It does not require emotions to form a part of cognition, simply to interact with it (Arnold, 1960, p. 143). However, some theories of appraisal, alongside constructivist theories of emotions, move further towards the notion that emotions themselves are part of cognition. This views emotions as not just intertwined with, but actually a part of, cognition. For example, Nussbaum argues that:

> Emotions are not just the fuel that powers the psychological mechanism of a reasoning creature, they are parts, highly complex and messy parts, of this creature's reasoning itself.
>
> (Nussbaum, 2001, p. 3)

In other words, emotions become characterised as cognitive, evaluative judgements which appraise an object as invested with value or importance. A key distinction here lies in the nature of the appraisal. Whereas for Arnold this is automatic and intuitive (at least at first), for Nussbaum and others they embody a propositional attitude. In other words, for an emotion to be present, it must be generated by an attitude directed at a proposition. The many variants of this form of approach are generally termed as cognitive because of the role of evaluative judgement they ascribe to emotion. The traditional debate between cognitive and non-cognitive theories is perhaps best encapsulated in the fierce debate between Lazarus (1984) and Zajonc (1984).[2] Zajonc argues that:

> Many emotional phenomena can be explained and have been explained without invoking cognitive processes of any kind.
>
> (Zajonc, 1984, p. 118)

He views affect as independent from cognition and as having primacy in the generation of emotions. In other words, emotions arise independently of cognition and precede its input (Zajonc, 1980). He argues that the minimum information process required for an emotion is "pure sensory input" and therefore a cognitive input is not required as a pre-condition (Zajonc, 1984, p. 122). In contrast, Lazarus's appraisal theory requires cognition to be a pre-condition because to experience an emotion (as opposed to a sensory preference), an individual must appraise an object or situation and then comprehend "that their well-being is implicated in a transaction, for better or worse" (1984, p. 124).

The debate between proponents of basic emotions theory and those who have developed a cognitive theory of emotions has been described as one of "nature-versus-nurture" (Saarni, 2000, p. 311) with the biological, evolutionary nature of basic emotions challenged by the notion of emotions as evaluative judgements. The debate can also have significant implications; for example, if emotions do not require a cognitive element, there is the potential for people to be manipulated without knowing that they are being manipulated – because they experience an emotion quickly, automatically and before cognition. If you subject them to something they have an affective reaction to, but so fast that they do not consciously recognise it, this can be viewed as a form of subliminal priming or conditioning (Murphy and Zajonc, 1993). However, to distinguish between theories of emotion as being either cognitive or non-cognitive in the way in which Zajonc (1984), Lazarus (1984) and others attempt to do implies a clear definition of these terms. Coplan suggests that in fact there has been "confusion" over the definition of the term cognition itself (2010, p. 138; see also Kappas, 2006).

Both Coplan (2010) and, earlier, Deigh (1994) focus on defending a non-cognitive theory of emotions by arguably attributing to such a theory some of the characteristics commonly associated with cognitive theories. For example, one key component of the cognitive vision of emotions has traditionally been viewed as intentionality, "the property of being directed at or toward something" (Deigh, 1994, p. 826). However, Deigh argues that this can be incorporated into non-cognitive accounts, because although it is a common property it is not essential to the generation of emotions. He argues that the difference arises in the link cognitivists make between intentionality and propositional thoughts by employing a narrow concept of cognition. Debes (2009, p. 2) also cautions against equating the term "cognitive" with "intentional", arguing that non-cognitive theories (such as the previously discussed James-Lange theory) cannot all be said to overlook or discard the role of intentionality. More generally, Coplan argues that it is not necessary to employ cognitive theories to invest emotions with value:

> If it is possible for bodily feelings and patterns of bodily change to register information and communicate something about the world and our relationship to it, then emotion can be meaningful and significant without needing to be cognitive.
>
> (Coplan, 2010, p. 141)

A different approach has been taken by other commentators who, rather than focusing on the distinction between cognitive and non-cognitive and the primacy of either, acknowledge emotions as including a wide range of different elements. For example, Johnson-Laird and Oatley approach this by viewing emotions as "communications" with physiological, social and cognitive elements and dividing them into three categories – "basic", "object-orientated" or "complex" (2000, p. 461; see also Kappas, 2006). Alternatively, Prinz (2004, p. 1) argues against such divisions and suggests that all emotions are fundamentally similar. However, he moves away from basic emotions theory by stating that all emotions are culturally informed and involve an affective appraisal:

Perhaps the recent summary given by Scherer and Moors best captures the contemporary view of the role and function of emotions when they seek to identify the common ground between different theories of emotions. They state that:

> Theorists generally agree that emotion should be viewed as an interface between an organism and its environment, constantly mediating between changing events and social contexts on the one hand and the individual's responses and experience on the other. . . . There is also substantial agreement that emotion episodes comprise different components such as appraisal of the situation, action preparation, physiological responses, expressive behavior, and subjective feelings.
>
> (2019, p. 14.3).

If the cognitive theories of emotion are accepted, then this has an even more significant potential impact on both law and legal education than the notion that emotions and cognition are intertwined or integrated. Indeed, it could be argued that it supports Bandes' (1999) argument that emotions are, in fact, a part of law. If the focus of the doctrinal and liberal traditions are on the cognitive processes of reason and rationality, then if emotions are also a cognitive function they must form a part of that focus. It also provides further authentication for the growth in law and emotions scholarship. However, to focus on this specific point is arguably too essentialist when some theorists are challenging the need to categorise emotions as either cognitive or non-cognitive. In essence, regardless of whether emotions are defined as cognitive or non-cognitive, or whether some form of hybrid approach is taken, the emphasis is, once again, on emotions as having a role in cognition, reason and rationality which goes beyond that which has traditionally been ascribed to it by both law and legal education.

Emotional intelligence as a new perspective?

This chapter's discussion of debates around emotions and cognition would not be complete without reference to the concept of emotional intelligence. Intelligence is the term often used as a measure of abilities commonly associated with cognitive functions, including "the ability to reason, plan, solve problems, think abstractly, comprehend complex ideas, learn quickly and learn from experience"

(Gottfredson, 1997, p. 13). Traditionally, it has been defined as general intelligence or "g" – a general, unitary faculty of intelligence (Spearman, 1904). This view is still supported by the majority of scientists today and suggests that intelligence is largely hereditary and static (after childhood) with a biological basis (Gottfredson, 1997; Howe, 1997). It has also formed the basis for the IQ tests popularised by the US military in World War I and now commonly found in educational and work environments (Mackintosh, 1988).

However, a range of different models of intelligence have been suggested, including Sternberg's triarchic theory (Sternberg et al., 2000) and Gardner's multiple intelligences (1983). When considering cognition and emotions, the most pertinent theory is that of emotional intelligence. Originated by Salovey and Mayer (1990), this theory has become heavily popularised in recent years through the publications of Daniel Goleman (1998; 1996). There are a number of different models of emotional intelligence, but Mayer et al.'s definition captures its fundamental premise:

> We define EI as the capacity to reason about emotions, and of emotions to enhance thinking. It includes the abilities to accurately perceive emotions, to access and generate emotions so as to assist thought, to understand emotions and emotional knowledge, and to reflectively regulate emotions so as to promote emotional and intellectual growth.
>
> (Mayer et al., 2004, p. 197)

The Salovey and Mayer model strives to focus on abilities and to avoid identifying expressions of emotional intelligence as a part of its remit (Mayer et al., 2008). However, Goleman's model has been developed into a far broader set of emotional competencies, which appear to encompass a range of both abilities and personality traits, for example, conscientiousness and empathy (Boyatzis et al., 2000). Other models, such as that of Bar-On (2006), are also fairly broad-ranging in their scope.

The concept of emotional intelligence has come under sustained attack from mainstream science (see, for example, Waterhouse, 2006a, 2006b; Murphy, 2006). Arguably one of the weaknesses in all models of emotional intelligence is their lack of engagement with theories of emotions as a whole to support their position. In relation to Salovey and Mayer's model, the reference to reasoning "of emotion" in the preceding quotation almost appears to imply a cognitive approach. Their reference to emotions conveying knowledge about an individual's relationship with the world could reflect some form of appraisal theory with a reference to "the functional role of emotions as communication signals" (Mayer et al., 2008, p. 506). In addition, they have referred elsewhere to the role of basic emotions (Mayer et al., 2000, p. 107). Averill (2004) has attempted to analyse their approach and suggests that it is effectively an updated version of the James-Lange theory (1884), with reference to Damasio (2006) as well.

Goleman's representation of emotions is also ambiguous, to say the least. He views the emotional and rational as "semi-independent faculties" with "distinct, but interconnected circuitry" which need to operate in "tight harmony" to achieve the well-balanced person (1996, p. 9). He does appear to subscribe to Ekman's theory of basic emotions and refers to their evolutionary importance, but overall there is a lack of clarity around how the notion of emotional intelligence fits with scientific and philosophical conceptualisations of emotions. Therefore, the notion of emotional intelligence has only limited weight when seeking to demonstrate the importance and value of emotions in those terms.

However, despite this lack of conceptual clarity, emotional intelligence has become a phrase that is commonly used throughout society and, increasingly, within legal education and practice (Jones, 2018). It is therefore possible that the popularity of the idea of emotional intelligence could contribute to a broader societal and legal shift towards re-evaluating the place of emotions, despite its theoretical shortcomings. It is arguable that it is best to view the phrase itself as a form of shorthand, which encompasses a range of valuable emotional competencies, rather than contributing directly to the question of what emotions are, but this should not diminish its importance in raising the profile of emotions on a large scale.

Conclusion: situating emotions within legal education

The discussion in this chapter over the philosophical and scientific definitions of emotions, their neurological basis, their social or cultural significance and the meaning of cognition has revolved around the relationship between emotions and cognition. The significance of this for legal education in particular lies in the largely unchallenged way that concepts of reason and rationality have been framed as solely cognitive functions which have no connection or relevance to emotions (Maharg and Maughan, 2011; James, 2008; Harris and Schultz, 1993).

The discussion of the scientific community's changing perceptions of emotion has demonstrated three broad approaches (although each contains numerous facets and nuances). Firstly, there is basic emotions theory, which views emotions as largely pre-determined by evolution and habit (Ekman, 1992a; Tomkins and McCartur, 1964). This could be broadly termed as a dualist approach, which views emotions as independent of cognitive abilities. Such conceptualisations often stem from interpretations of Cartesian dualism which, as previously discussed, have led to a view of emotions as irrational and in need of control and subjugation by cognition (Hey and Leathwood, 2009; Schutz et al., 2006; Descartes, 1989; Plato, 1974). Nevertheless, as seen in the preceding discussion, this approach still does assign a value and use to emotions and increasingly acknowledges the possibility of cognitive and other elements influencing them (Panksepp, 2000; Ekman, 1992b). Perhaps as a result of this shift, a wholly "dualist" approach appears to be becoming increasingly rare in the scientific world.

A parallel has been highlighted between such a "dualist" approach and the doctrinal and liberal traditions of undergraduate legal education in England and Wales. Such an approach has led to both the law and legal education focusing on reason and rationality as functions of cognition, and largely disregarding or suppressing emotions. While philosophical and scientific perceptions of emotions have gradually moved on from this, the evidence in Chapters 1 and 2 suggests it is still the dominant paradigm within legal education.

The approach directly opposed to that of the "dualists" is one which could be termed "emotions as reason". This characterises emotions as having a cognitive, evaluative function which makes them an integral part of the reasoning process itself – whether this be as a judgement (Nussbaum, 2001) through an individual's constructed experience (Feldman Barrett, 2017) or via the construction of social and cultural imperatives (Averill, 2005). In terms of parallels with the law overall, this is more akin to the radical approach of authors such as Bandes (1999). The emphasis on the construction of emotions also mirrors the critical epistemology espoused by feminist legal scholars and critical legal scholars (see, for example, Naffine, 1990 and Kennedy, 1982), an epistemological approach which acknowledges the need for emotions to be a part of legal education, although it has not yet provided a coherent theoretical framework for achieving this.

The third approach to emotions can perhaps be termed as "emotions and reason". This can be found in a wide variety of forms, from the mixture of cognition and physiology in the accounts of Damasio (2006) and Johnson-Laird and Oatley (2000), to various defences of emotions as a non-cognitive force which nevertheless have an important role to play in the lives of individuals (see, for example, Coplan, 2010; Prinz, 2004; Deigh, 1994). Perhaps its strongest and fullest exposition is found in the development of a range of appraisal theories (Moors, 2014; Moors et al., 2013; Lazarus, 1991; Arnold, 1960) with their conceptualisation of emotions as immediate and intuitive judgements combined with a cognitive evaluation. This "emotions and reason" approach is arguably the one which offers the most practical potential for its transfer to legal education. It is an approach which requires law schools to acknowledge the presence and importance of emotions, without requiring a radical epistemological shift to occur which (as will be discussed in subsequent chapters) would be very difficult in the current climate of both higher education generally and legal education specifically.

To argue that law and legal education should only focus on narrow, non-emotional, cognitive forms of reason and rationality is to rely on mostly discredited quasi-scientific theories stemming largely from a tradition of Cartesian dualism. To argue that emotions are a fully cognitive function is to introduce a radical suggestion which may be rejected by many as not fully substantiated or tested. However, to state that cognition and emotions are intertwined, with both contributing to reason and rationality, is to offer a valid compromise which reflects developments in philosophical and scientific thought on emotions without requiring a shift which would arguably be akin to a doctrinalist becoming a critical legal scholar. It also enables acknowledgement of the truism that the subject matter of both the law and legal education is itself emotive. The growth of socio-legal studies and its challenge to the doctrinal tradition demonstrate that there is an opportunity for a pluralistic approach to be taken across law schools. By seeking to broaden concepts of reason and rationality, rather than displace them, an "emotions and reason" approach mirrors the direction taken by socio-legal studies and offers a way to acknowledge and utilise emotions within legal education. This can be done in a manner which harnesses, rather than opposes, what Schlag has termed "the enchantment of reason" (1998) and the quest for the scientific which was highlighted in Chapter 1 (Feldman, 2009a, 2009b). Whilst it will still provide a significant challenge to the established norms of the law school, it offers the potential for drawing together the increasing breadth of contemporary legal education with the strong evidence-base which research into emotions now provides. The following chapter will begin to contextualize this approach within higher education more generally, to see how acknowledging emotions in this fashion fits within the wider educational and political environments and discourses which (at least in part) shape the development of law schools.

Notes

1 This is a common definition of affect, encompassing emotional states. However, Feldman Barrett's definition separates affect from emotion (2017, p. 72).

2 This is one extract from the debate between the two which ranges over a number of years.

References

Abrams, K. and Keren, H. (2010) "Who's Afraid of Law and the Emotions?", *Minnesota Law Review*, 94(6), 1997–2074.

Anleu, S. R., Blix, S. B. and Mack, K. (2015) "Researching Emotion in Courts and the Judiciary: A Tale of Two Projects", *Emotion Review*, 7(2), 145–150.

Aristotle (1985) *Nicomachean Ethics*, Indianapolis, Hackett Publishing Company.

Arnold, M. B. (1960) *Emotion and Personality. Volume 1 Psychological Aspects*, London, Cassell & Company.

Averill, J. R. (2004) "A Tale of Two Snarks: Emotional Intelligence and Emotional Creativity", *Psychological Inquiry*, 15(3), 228–233.

Averill, J. R. (1980) "A Constructivist View of Emotions", in Plutchik, R. and Kellerman, H. (eds) (1980) *Theories of Emotion*, New York: Academic Press reproduced in Price, C. (ed.) (2005) *Emotion*, Milton Keynes, The Open University, 306–312, 318–322 and 326–329.

Bailey, M. L. and Knight, K. J. (2017) "Writing Histories of Law and Emotion", *The Journal of Legal History*, 38(2), 117–129.

Bandes, S. A. (1999) "Introduction", in Bandes, S. A. (ed), *The Passions of Law*, New York and London, New York University Press, 1–15.

Bandes, S. A. and Blumenthal, J. A. (2012) "Emotion and the Law", *Annual Review of Law and Social Science*, 8(1), 161–181.

Bantock, G. H. (1986) "Educating the Emotions: An Historical Perspective", *British Journal of Educational Studies*, 34(2), 122–141.

Bar-On, R. (2006) "The Bar-On Model of Emotional-social Intelligence", *Psicothema*, 18(1), 13–25.

Boiger, M. and Mesquita, B. (2012) "The Construction of Emotion in Interactions, Relationships, and Cultures", *Emotion Review*, 4(3), 221–229.

Bornstein, B. H. and Wiener, R. L. (2010) "Emotion and the Law: A Field Whose Time Has Come", in Bornstein, B. H. and Wiener, R. L. (eds), *Nebraska Symposium on Motivation. Emotion and the Law. Psychological Perspectives*, New York, Dordrecht, Heidelberg, London, Springer, 1–12.

Boyatzis, R. E., Goleman, D. and Rhee, K., (2000) "Clustering Competence in Emotional Intelligence: Insights from the Emotional Competence Inventory (ECI)", *Handbook of Emotional Intelligence*, 99(6), 343–362.

Cannon, W. B. (1927) "The James-Lange Theory of Emotions: A Critical Examination and an Alternative Theory", *The American Journal of Psychology*, 39(1/4), 106–124.

Conoghan, J. (2013) *Law and Gender*, Oxford, Oxford University Press.

Coplan, A. (2010) "Feeling without Thinking: Lessons from the Ancients on Emotions and Virtue-Acquisition", *Metaphilosophy*, 41(1–2), 132–151.

Crivellato, E. and Ribatti, D. (2007) "Soul, Mind, Brain: Greek Philosophy and the Birth of Neuroscience", *Brain Research Bulletin*, 71, 327–336.

Dalgleish, T. (2004) "The Emotional Brain", *Nature Reviews Neuroscience*, 5(7), 582–589.

Damasio, A. (2006) *"Descartes" Error*, London, Vintage.

Darwin, C. (Edited by Darwin, F.) (1890) *The Expression of the Emotions in Man and Animals*, 2nd edn, London, John Murray.

Debes, R. (2009) "Neither Here nor There: The Cognitive Nature of Emotion", *Philosophical Studies*, 146(1), 1–27.

Deigh, J. (1994) "Cognitivism in the Study of Emotions", *Ethics*, 104, 824–854.

Descartes, R. (Translator Voss, S. H.) (1989) *The Passions of the Soul*, Indianapolis, Hackett Publishing.

Ekman, P. (1992a) "An Argument for Basic Emotions", *Cognition and Emotion*, 6(3/4), 169–200.

Ekman, P. (1992b) "Are There Basic Emotions?", *Psychological Review*, 99(3), 550–553.

Ekman, P. (1999) "Basic Emotions", in Dalgleish, T. and Power, M. (eds), *Handbook of Cognition and Emotion*, New York, John Wiley & Co.

Ellsworth, P. C. (2013) "Appraisal Theory: Old and New Questions", *Emotion Review*, 5(2), 125–131.

Feldman Barrett, L. (2017) *How Emotions are Made: The Secret Life of the Brain*, London, Macmillan.

Feldman, R. (2009a) *The Role of Science in Law*, Oxford, Oxford University Press.

Feldman, R. (2009b) "Law's Misguided Love Affair with Science", *Minnesota Journal of Law, Society and Technology*, 10(1), 95–116.

Gardner, H. (1983) *Frames of Mind. The Theory of Multiple Intelligences*, London, Heineman.

Gasper, K. (2004) "Do You See What I See? Affect and Visual Information Processing", *Cognition and Emotion*, 18(3), 405–421.

Gendron, M. and Feldman Barrett, L. (2009) "Reconstructing the Past: A Century of Ideas About Emotion in Psychology", *Emotion Review*, 1(4), 316–339.

Goleman, D. (1996) *Emotional Intelligence*, London, Bloomsbury.

Goleman, D. (1998) *Working with Emotional Intelligence*, London, Bloomsbury.

Gottfredson, L. S. (1997) "Mainstream Science on Intelligence: An Editorial with 52 Signatories, History, and Bibliography", 24(1), *Intelligence*, 13–23.

Harris, A. P. and Schultz, M. M. (1993) ""A(nother) Critique of Pure Reason": Toward Civic Virtue in Legal Education", *Stanford Law Review*, 45(6), 1773–1805.

Hey, V. and Leathwood, C. (2009) "Passionate Attachments: Higher Education, Policy, Knowledge, Emotion and Social Justice", *Higher Education Policy*, 22(1), 101–118.

Howe, M. J. A. (1997) *IQ in Question. The Truth about Intelligence*, London, Sage Publications.

Hume, D. (2003) *A Treatise of Human Nature*, New York, Dover Publications.

James, C. (2008) "'Lawyers' Wellbeing and Professional Legal Education", *The Law Teacher*, 42(1), 85–97.

James, W. (1884) "What is an Emotion?", *Mind*, 9, 188–205.

Johnson-Laird, P. N. and Oatley, K. (2000) "Cognitive and Social Construction in Emotions Brain", in Lewis, M. and Haviland-Jones, J. M. (eds), *Handbook of Emotions*, 2nd edn, New York and London, The Guilford Press.

Jones, E. (2018) "Making Practice More Affective: Emotional Intelligence as a Fundamental Meta-Competency", *European Journal of Current Legal Issues*, 24(1).

Kappas, A. (2006) "Appraisals are Direct, Immediate, Intuitive, and Unwitting . . . and Some are Reflective. . . ." *Cognition and Emotion*, 20(7), 952–975.

Kennedy, D. (1982) "Legal Education and the Reproduction of Hierarchy", *Journal of Legal Education*, 32(4), 591–615.

Kleinginna, P. R. and Kleinginna, A. M. (1981) "A Categorized List of Emotion Definitions, with Suggestions for a Consensual Definition", *Motivation and Emotion*, 5(4), 345–379.

Knuuttila, S. (2004) *Emotions in Ancient and Medieval Philosophy*, Oxford, Oxford University Press.

Kohn, R. and Keller, M. B. (2015) "Emotions", in Tasman, A., Kay, J., Lieberman, J. A., First, M. B. and Riba, M. (2015) *Psychiatry Volumes 1 & 2*, 4th edn, Chichester, West Sussex, John Wiley & Sons, 547–568.

Kristjánsson, K. (2012) *Aristotle, Emotions, and Education*, Aldershot and Burlingham, Ashgate Publishing.

Lange, C. G. (1885) "The Mechanism of the Emotions", in Rand, B. (ed), (1912) *The Classical Psychologists*, Boston, Houghton Mifflin.

Lazarus, R. S. (1984) "On the Primacy of Cognition", *American Psychologist*, 39(2), 124–129.

Lazarus, R. S. (1991) "Progress on a Cognitive-Motivational-Relational Theory of Emotion", *American Psychologist*, 46(8), 819–834.

Lazarus, R. S. and Smith, C. A. (1988) "Knowledge and Appraisal in the Cognition-Emotion Relationship", *Cognition and Emotion*, 2(4), 281–300.

LeDoux, J. E. and Phelps, E. A. (2000) "Emotional Networks in the Brain", in Lewis, M. and Haviland-Jones, J. M. (eds), *Handbook of Emotions*, 2nd edn, New York and London, The Guilford Press.

Lerner, J. S., Li, Y., Valdesolo, P. and Kassam, K. S. (2015) "Emotion and Decision Making", *Annual Review of Psychology*, 66, 1–45.

Mackintosh, N. J. (1988) *IQ and Human Intelligence*, Oxford, Oxford University Press.

MacLean, P. D. (1949) "Psychosomatic Disease and the "Visceral Brain" Recent Developments Bearing on the Papez Theory of Emotion", *Psychomatic Medicine*, 11, 338–353.

Maharg, P. and Maughan, C. (2011) "Introduction", in Maharg, P. and Maughan, C. (eds), *Affect and Legal Education. Emotion in Learning and Teaching the Law*, Aldershot, Ashgate Publishing, 1–10.

Mayer, J. D., Salovey, P. and Caruso, D. R. (2000) "Emotional Intelligence as Zeitgeist, as Personality, and as a Standard Intelligence", in Bar-On, R. and Parker, J. D. A. (eds), *Handbook of emotion Intelligence*, New York, Jossey-Bass, 92–117.

Mayer, J. D., Salovey, P. and Caruso, D. R. (2004) "Emotional Intelligence: Theory, Findings and Implications", *Psychological Inquiry*, 15(3), 197–215.

Mayer, J. D., Salovey, P. and Caruso, D. R. (2008) "Emotional Intelligence. New Ability or Eclectic Traits", *American Psychologist*, 63(6), 503–517.

McConnell, M. M. and Eva, K. W. (2012) "The Role of Emotion in the Learning and Transfer of Clinical Skills and Knowledge", *Academic Medicine*, 87(10), 1316–1322.

Mertz, E. (2007) *The Language of Law School. Learning to "Think like a Lawyer"*, Oxford, Oxford University Press.

Moors, A. (2014) "Flavours of Appraisal Theories of Emotion", *Emotion Review*, 6(4), 303–307.

Moors, A., Ellsworth, P. C., Scherer, K. R. and Frijda, N. H. (2013) "Appraisal Theories of Emotion: State of the Art and Future Development", *Emotion Review*, 5(1), 119–124.

Murphy, K. A. (ed) (2006) *A Critique of Emotional Intelligence. What Are the Problems and How Can They Be Fixed?* London, Lawrence Erlbaum Associates.

Murphy, S. T. and Zajonc, R. B. (1993) "Affect, Cognition, and Awareness: Affective Priming with Optimal and Suboptimal Stimulus Exposures", *Journal of Personality and Social Psychology*, 64(5), 723–739.

Naffine, N. (1990) *Law and the Sexes Explorations in Feminist Jurisprudence*, London, Allen & Unwin.

Nussbaum, M. (2001) *Upheavals of Thought: The Intelligence of Emotions*, Cambridge, Cambridge University Press.

Oatley, K., Keltner, D. and Jenkins, J. M. (2006) *Understanding Emotions*, 2nd edn, London: Blackwell Publishing.

Panksepp, J. (2000) "Emotions as Natural Kinds within the Mammalian Brain", in Lewis, M. and Haviland-Jones, J. M. (eds), *Handbook of Emotions*, 2nd edn, New York and London, The Guilford Press.

Panksepp, J. (2011) "The Basic Emotional Circuits of Mammalian Brains: Do Animals Have Affective Lives?", *Neuroscience and Biobehavioral Reviews*, 35, 1791–1804.

Pessoa, L. (2008) "On the Relationship Between Emotion and Cognition", *Nature Reviews Neuroscience*, 9(2), 148–158.

Pessoa, L. (2013) *The Cognitive-Emotional Brain: From Interactions to Integration*, Cambridge, Massachusetts and London, England, The MIT Press.

Pfister, H. M. and Böhm, G. (2008) "The Multiplicity of Emotions: A Framework of Emotional Functions in Decision Making", *Judgment and Decision Making*, 3(1), 5–17.

Philippopoulos-Mihalopoulos, A. (2012) "Mapping the Lawscape: Spatial Law and the Body", in Bankowski, Z., Del Mar, M. and Maharg, P. (eds), *Beyond Text in Legal Education*, Edinburgh, Edinburgh University Press.

Plato (1974) *Republic*, Indianapolis, Hackett Publishing Company.

Prinz, J. (2004) "Which Emotions are Basic", in Evans, D. and Cruse, P. (eds), *Emotion, Evolution and Rationality*, Oxford, Oxford University Press, 1–19.

Saarni, C. (2000) "The Social Context of Emotional Development", in Lewis, M. and Haviland-Jones, J. M. (eds), *Handbook of Emotions*, 2nd edn, New York and London, The Guilford Press, 306–322.

Sajó, A. (2011) "Emotions in Constitutional Design", *International Journal of Constitutional Law*, 8(3), 354–384.

Salovey, P and Mayer, J. D. (1990) "Emotional Intelligence", *Imagination, Cognition and Personality*, 9(3), 185–211.

Schachter, S. and Singer, L. R. S. J. (1962) "Cognitive, Social, and Physiological Determinants of Emotional State", *Psychological Review*, 69(5), 379–339.

Scherer, K. R. (1995) "Plato's Legacy: Relationships Between Cognition, Emotion and Motivation", *Geneva Studies in Emotion and Communication*, 9(1), 1–7.

Scherer, K. R. (2011) "On the Rationality of Emotions: Or, When Are Emotions Rational?", *Social Science Information*, 50(3–4), 330–350.

Scherer, K. R. and Moors, A. (2019) "The Emotion Process: Event Appraisal and Component Differentiation", *Annual Review of Psychology*, 70, 14.1–14.27.

Schlag, P. (1998) *The Enchantment of Reason*, Durham, Duke University Press.

Schulkin, J., Thompson, B. L. and Rosen, J. B. (2003) "Demythologizing the Emotions: Adaptation, Cognition, and Visceral Representations of Emotion in the Nervous System", *Brain and Cognition*, 52(1), 15–33.

Schutz, P., Hong, J. Y., Cross, D. I. and Osbon, J. N. (2006) "Reflections on Investigating Emotion in Educational Activity Settings", *Educational Psychology Review*, 18(4), 343–360.

Schwarz, U. (2000) "Emotion, Cognition, and Decision Making", *Cognition and Emotion*, 14(4), 433–440.

Shuman, V. and Scherer, K. R. (2014) "Concepts and Structures of Emotions", in Pekrun, R. and Linnenbrink-Garcia, L. (eds), *International Handbook of Emotions in Education*, New York and London, Routledge, 13–35.

Smith, A. (2006) *The Theory of Moral Sentiments*, New York, Dover Publications.

Solomon, R. C. (2000) "The Philosophy of Emotions", in Lewis, M. and Haviland-Jones, J. M. (eds), *Handbook of Emotions*, 2nd edn, New York and London, The Guilford Press.

Spearman, C. (1904) ""General Intelligence", Objectively Determined and Measured", *American Journal of Psychology*, 15, 201–293.

Sternberg, R. J., Forsythe, G. B., Hedlund, J., Horvath, J. A., Wagner, R. K., Williams, W. D., Snook, S. A. and Grigorenko, E. L. (2000) *Practical Intelligence in Everyday Life*, Cambridge, Cambridge University Press.

Storbeck, J. and Clore, G. L. (2007) "On the Interdependence of Cognition and Emotion", *Cognition and Emotion*, 21(6), 1212–1237.

Tomkins, S. S. and McCartur, R. (1964) "What and Where Are the Primary Affects? Some Evidence for a Theory", *Perceptual and Motor Skills*, 18(1), 119–158.

Waterhouse, L. (2006a) "Multiple Intelligences, the Mozart Effect and Emotional Intelligence: A Critical Review", *Educational Psychologist*, 41(4), 207–225.

Waterhouse, L. (2006b) "Inadequate Evidence for Multiple Intelligences, the Mozart Effect and Emotional Intelligence Theories", *Educational Psychologist*, 41(4), 247–255.

Webb, J. (2006) "The "Ambitious Modesty" of Harold Arthur's Humane Professionalism", *Osgoode Hall Law Journal*, 44(1), 119–155.

Zajonc, R. B. (1980) "Feeling and Thinking. Preferences Need No Inferences", *American Psychologist*, 35(2), 151–175.

Zajonc, R. B. (1984) "On the Primacy of Affect", *American Psychologist*, 39(2), 117–123.

4 Situating emotions within the politics and policies of academia

Introduction: a shifting backdrop

Shifts in the conceptualisation of emotions and the growing perception of them as intertwined with, if not part of, cognition, demonstrate significant developments in their understanding within philosophical and scientific thought. There are some parallels (drawn in Chapter 3) between the differing approaches to emotion (termed there as "dualist", "emotions as reason" and "emotions and reason") and the paradigms to be found within legal education. Perhaps the most notable of these is between the Cartesian dualism of basic emotions theory and the traditional doctrinal and liberal traditions in law schools, which largely expect emotions to be disregarded or suppressed (Jones, 2018a; Maroney, 2006). However, there is also an increasing discrepancy between the scientific and the legal. On the one hand, the newer appraisal and cognitive theories of emotions have received mainstream acceptance within the scientific community (Feldman Barrett, 2017; Damasio, 2006). On the other hand, within legal education even the newer paradigm of socio-legal studies, which can now claim to be fully integrated (or absorbed, depending on your viewpoint) into law schools (Siems and Mac Sithigh, 2012; Cownie, 2004), still largely ascribes to a basic emotions theory which separates emotions and reason and ignores their interaction. Broader socio-legal and critical legal approaches (namely, critical and feminist legal studies and law and emotions scholarship) have made some headway in acknowledging the value of emotions and their inter-relationship with law, showing their potential for future inclusion and use within legal education (Abrams and Keren, 2010; Bromberger, 2010; Sturm, 1998). However, the impact of these upon contemporary legal education is partial and they have not yet been either mainstreamed or normalised in the same way that research methods from the social sciences have been.

It would be easy to assume that the wider politics and policies of higher education have contributed to this lack of recognition, militating against the acknowledgement of emotions within law schools, but the reality is more nuanced and complex than that. In fact, broader developments in higher education in recent years have led to a significant interest in employability and skills development. In turn, this has led to increased calls for emotional abilities to be acknowledged and utilised as a set of so-called soft skills (see, for example, Juergens, 2005, and Silver, 1999, in relation to USA legal education).[1] These skills often draw upon on the competency-based model of emotional intelligence proposed by Goleman (1998; 1996) and discussed in Chapter 3. They are increasingly seen as important in terms of graduate employability (Pertegel-Felices et al., 2014; Dacre Pool and Qualter, 2013).[2]

The growing focus on employability, skills and soft skills throughout higher education is inextricably linked to the neo-liberal marketisation of universities in recent years in countries such as the UK, Australia and the USA. Therefore, the suggestion that the use of emotions should be characterised in higher education as a form of soft skill leads to them becoming part of a complex neo-liberal ideology which is often seen as conflicting with traditional notions of the role of the university (Thornton, 2014; Lynch, 2006; Collier, 2005). This has significant implications as the way in which the neo-liberal university is characterised not only colours the structural and environmental backdrop against which emotions are being integrated, it also influences, and even generates, emotions itself and attempts to determine the ends for which emotions are utilised. Therefore, the politics and policies of academia can have a fundamental impact on the role of emotions within law schools.

Higher education's new role

The changes within the politics and policies of higher education can best be understood by exploring the shifting answer to the question "what is a university (or, indeed, a law school) for?" In 1966, the answer of the Chair of the recent UK Parliamentary Committee on Higher Education's report on higher education (hereafter the "Robbins Report") was that higher education's purpose is as follows:

> To attempt to understand the world, to contemplate and to analyse its values – these are activities which, even if they were never associated with practical advantage, would still lend meaning and dignity to life on this planet.
>
> (Robbins, 1966, p. 5)

This captures the image of the university as an ivory tower; a place that is "unashamedly elite" and separate from the concerns of everyday life (Smith and Webster, 1997, p. 3). Indeed, Lynch argues that universities have traditionally "traded on their Enlightenment inheritance that they are the guardians and creators of knowledge produced for the greater good of humanity in its entirety" (2006, p. 3). It captures a view of the role of the university which is reminiscent of Newman (1994) and the liberal view of legal education espoused by, amongst others, Bradney (2003) with the sense of law schools' value not being about preparation for the legal profession but instead lying in the way they foster individual (and societal) knowledge and understanding. Within this view there is little need for wider, vocationally orientated skills: instead the focus is on intellectual, more particularly cognitive, development (Whitson, 1998; Bradney, 1987).

It should be noted that, even at the time of the Robbins Report, there were challenges to any notion of higher education as solely a good in itself. The Report itself identifies one of the four aims of higher education as "instruction in skills suitable to play a part in the general division of labour" (the Robbins Report,

1963). More broadly, commentators have challenged the notion of the post-war era as a "golden age" in higher education (Tight, 2010, p. 106), with suggestions that the perception of universities as favoured elite institutions has never been wholly accurate (Fanghanel, 2012, p. 4). The post-war economic boom, an increase in the public's respect for academics (following their contribution to the war effort) and the generation of greater funding through increased numbers of students all did contribute to a sense of privilege in the post-war period (Tight, 2010, p. 107). However, any such "golden age" for universities generally was limited and partial in scope, revolving around a "few favoured institutions" for a "brief moment" in time (Ramsden, 2003, p. 5). This makes it important to recognize that, within higher education generally, and universities specifically, there has always been a certain amount of diversity in purpose and aims, including the potential for a range of different viewpoints on skills. Nevertheless, it is clear that the traditional core aspiration, if not the reality, was for the liberal ideal of the university as a public good, benefiting society generally, rather than focusing on the development of vocational skills.

With regard to law schools, particularly in the UK, the longstanding tensions between vocational and liberal aims have been touched upon in Chapter 1, meaning the question of their purpose and aims has never been definitively resolved. However, the conventional view is that "the modern English law school is in most important respects a post Second World War creation" with university law schools seeking greater recognition from the wider academy in this period (Twining, 1994, p. 26). In 1971, the Committee on Legal Education in their report on legal education (hereafter the "Ormrod Report") was confident enough to conclude that:

> The struggle to establish the study of Law, and particularly of English law, as an academic discipline in the universities has succeeded.
>
> (Ormrod Report, 1971, para. 44(1))

This suggests that a liberal form of legal education, in accordance with the Robbins Report's view of higher education as a public good, was well-established during this era. Indeed, Twining (1994) argues that the Ormrod Report facilitated this move towards assimilating law schools into the wider university by declining to impose significant restrictions or requirements for professional formation onto the undergraduate law degree in England and Wales. However, he also points out that this move towards integration with the wider academy left the law schools vulnerable to the same wider pressures which began to unfold upon higher education as a whole from the 1970s onwards. These pressures, as discussed ahead, include a huge increase in student numbers and growing demands for a focus on skills, soft skills and employability which can offer both opportunities and challenges for the acknowledgment and utilization of emotions within legal education.

In terms of student numbers, Telling (2018, p. 4) suggests that a wider post-war vision of social mobility and meritocracy, heralded in the Robbins Report itself, drove the increasing growth in student numbers.[3] The Robbins Report identified that in 1870 only around 1% of the population was in full-time education at the age of 19. By 1938 this had only risen to around 2%. In 1962 the figure was 7%, nearly all of them in higher education (Robbins Report, 1963, para. 43). In contrast, in 2017 it was reported that 49% of people in the UK would have entered into higher education by the age of thirty (Adams, 2017). At the time of the Robbins Report (1963), there were thirty-one universities across the UK with the power to award degrees. In 2016/17, there were 162 publically funded higher education institutions within the UK (Universities UK, 2017).

The growth of legal education in the post-war era largely mirrored the growth in higher education generally, with Wilson reporting a total of twenty-three university law schools offering full degrees in 1965, including seventeen in England, one in Wales, one in Northern Ireland and four in Scotland (Wilson, 1966). The total number of undergraduate students studying law full time in England, Wales and Northern Ireland had risen from 1,515 in 1938 to 4,204 in 1965 (Wilson, 1966). A further survey in 1975 indicated that a full law degree was now available in thirty universities and nineteen polytechnics and other institutions maintained by local authorities. The total number of undergraduate students studying full time had increased to 7,072 (Wilson and Marsh, 1975). In 2016/17 over 18,000 students in the UK graduated from an undergraduate law degree (Higher Education Statistics Agency, 2017).

These changes in numbers in higher education generally, and law schools in particular, demonstrate that higher education has shifted from an elite few to a mass process which, Smith and Webster argue, has now become the norm: attending university now “merely marks a stage in life” (1997, p. 2). The larger number and broader range of students now involved in higher education, combined with the advance of neo-liberalism, has been the catalyst for an increasing focus on the importance of skills generally, not just those related specifically to intellectual development (Chamorro-Premuzic et al., 2010; Barrie, 2006; Bennett et al., 1999). Thus it has raised the profile of those vocationally oriented or employability skills which are often characterised as including elements of emotional competency. The graduate attributes frameworks generated by higher education providers will typically include not only specific subject components but also “study skills, digital literacices and other 21st century skills” (Advance HE, 2018). Such skills may well include an emotional component, for example, the ability to collaborate or work with others is typically included. To collaborate effectively involves reading the emotions of others and managing your own emotions in your response. There is also an increasing narrative around the notion of resilience, which involves being able to emotionally deal with and adapt to change and uncertainty.

The advance of neo-liberalism

The election of Margaret Thatcher’s UK Conservative Government in 1979 and Ronald Reagan as president of the USA in 1981 heralded the introduction of a neo-liberal ideology which, as the dominant political and governmental ideology in many Western societies, now defines how higher education is characterised (Bessant et al., 2015; Holborow, 2012; Lynch, 2006). The origins of neo-liberalism in the UK stem from the New Right form of Conservatism which became dominant within the party in the late 1970s and formed the mainstay of Thatcherism (Eccleshall, 1994). This attributed many social and economic problems to what Jay terms "ungovernability" (1994, p. 146). In other words, the idea that overblown expectations from the electorate, unchecked expansion in the public sector and the ability of groups such as trade unions to put pressure on the government had created issues such as inflation, rising taxes and increasing public expenditure. The solution to this was perceived to lie in "rolling back the state". This involved decentralising and liberalising the economy through policies such as "free trade, open markets, privatisation, deregulation and a decrease in the welfare role played by state" (Bessant et al., 2015, p. 419; see also Mudge, 2008). In other words, maximising the operation of the free market and minimising government regulation (Thornton, 2001a). Its hallmark is "a vision of society as a marketplace" (Joshee, 2008, p. 56). This is in contrast to the Keynesian welfare or "interventionalist" state which used government intervention to redistribute wealth and generate employment (Sommerlad et al., 2015, p. 4).

In terms of higher education, this focus on the dominance of the market means that universities are both expected to meet the demands of students as consumers and provide graduates with a high level of skills to enable them to graduate into the workplace and contribute as much as possible to the productivity of their employers (Bessant et al., 2015; Ball, 2009; National Committee of Inquiry into Higher Education, 1997). As Telling describes it, the notions of meritocracy which drove the post-war expansion in higher education have been replaced by free market concepts where higher education has become characterised as a private good, with universities acting as "competing businesses" (2018, p. 5).

Paradoxically, at the same time as state functions are being reduced in many areas, neo-liberalism also involves the strengthening of government authority against external pressures from the electorate and public sector (Jay, 1994). Thus neo-liberalism is commonly associated with New Public Management theory. This involves heavily centralised control of the public sector and the introduction of private sector discourses focused on improving efficiency (Bessant et al., 2015; Lane, 2000). One manifestation of this is arguably the increased controls exercised over universities, which includes a series of government policies aimed at requiring skills and employability to form a key aspect of higher education (see, for example, Department for Business, Innovation and Skills, 2014; Browne, 2010). This level of control has also become internalised within universities, with increased focus on accountability, audit and metrics at all levels (Olssen, 2016).

The impact of neo-liberalism is not limited to specific reforms in higher education or the public sector. Instead, it has now become hegemonic in contemporary society (Fine and Saad-Filho, 2017). Blalock suggests that it has moved beyond a form of policy and become "a set of principles and modes of governance so ingrained as to constitute the common sense of the age" (2014, p. 83). She argues that these principles have become so embedded that they are no longer seen as contentious and its assumptions become largely unchallenged. This echoes Thornton's suggestion that "the market as the leitmotif of neo-liberalism has permeated every nook and cranny of society" (2012, p. 265). As a result, it is arguable that, if using emotions as a form of soft skill can be demonstrated to fit within this ideology, it will be easier to increase their role within legal education. However, at the same time, this leads to questions over how neo-liberalism has impacted on higher education and whether its ideological tenets should be embraced in this way.

Shore and Davidson (2014) emphasise that despite some common themes, neo-liberalism is not homogenous and uniform and therefore its impact will vary in accordance with local circumstances and policies. In addition, it is impossible to treat universities, even within one country, as a single homogenous mass which will be affected in a standardised and uniform manner. Nevertheless, neo-liberalism has had a significant impact on universities overall. Collier (2004) argues that there are four themes that have emerged in the present-day university: the corporatisation of the university; a focus on useful knowledge (as opposed to knowledge for its own sake); a new form of managerialism; and new measures of performance and accountability. Each of these can be linked back to facets of neo-liberalism (although Collier does not explicitly seek to do this). Equally, each of these arguably has an impact on the inclusion and treatment of skills in higher education generally and legal education specifically, particularly the use of emotions as a form of soft skill.

In relation to corporatisation, Collier uses the term to depict "a heightened *interconnection* between the objectives, goals and practices of the business and academic worlds" [author's italics] (2004, p. 510). One illustration of this is the shift away from state funding of universities towards a system of tuition fees which arguably repositions students as the consumers of higher education (Bessant et al., 2015; Giroux, 2012; Holborow, 2012). This movement has been criticised by a number of commentators, including Bessant et al. (2015) who argue that it leads students to view higher education as a private financial investment aimed at maximising their future earning potential, rather than as a public good. Universities are forced to compete for the business of students and the less popular subjects may become surplus to requirements, whilst institutions increasingly seek to emphasise their credentials in terms of skills development and employability to remain competitive (Bartram, 2016). McCulloch (arguing that "co-producer" would be a more appropriate term) does summarise some positive aspects of the term consumer in this context, for example, in encouraging students' voice to be heard (2009, p. 173). However, he acknowledges the difficulties this characterisation also causes, for example, by placing less emphasis on the active role of students within the learning process.

The role and content of learning are also relevant to Collier's next theme, the focus on useful knowledge. He argues that academics are now in a position where knowledge has to be viewed as "a resource to help create wealth and competitive advantage" (2005, p. 479). Thornton (2001b) agrees with this, arguing that the university has become a form of knowledge industry, subject to the demands of the market. This can be linked to increases in public funding since the massification of the system (although the focus has increasingly shifted onto the generation of income through other means, including research funding and consultancy work). This, Barrie (2006) argues, has led for demands for universities to show that they are providing value for money by satisfying the demand for useful outputs. In other words, more esoteric knowledge is likely to be disregarded and devalued and knowledge that has the potential to generate an economic contribution to society is prized. This is often in the form of applied knowledge, the "know how" over the "know what" (Thornton, 2012, p. 237). As "profit-making economic entities" universities must generate knowledge to be transferred to the economy and "foster commercialization" (Holborow, 2012, p. 97).

Such a focus is a fundamental shift from the previous liberal conception of universities as a public good whose status relies on their objective inquiry (Lynch, 2006). Instead of universities providing a form of neutral space for discourse (Barnett, 2005) they instead represent private interests competing within a marketplace. Once again, this appears to link to the idea of a broader skillset as increasingly important, with skills providing the "know how" previously referred to by Thornton. In addition, an increasing emphasis on a new form of managerialism and the introduction of new measures of performance and accountability (Collier's third and fourth themes) has led to a significant emphasis on institutions and individual academics generating tangible and measurable outcomes in all aspects of higher education, including in terms of skills and employability (Olssen, 2016; McCowan, 2015). This neo-liberal agenda, and the need to develop an increasingly large and diverse cohort into effective learners, has led to a widespread acceptance within higher education that a wider, more vocationally orientated set of skills are a key part of the university's remit (Tymon, 2013,; Holmes, 2013). This, in part at least, is necessary to meet the demands of employers who are increasingly recognising the value of soft skills within the workplace and demanding such competencies from their employees (Stewart, 2016; Schutte and Loi, 2014). For example, law firms are demonstrating an increasing awareness of the need for forms of emotional literacy amongst lawyers to ensure that they can offer high levels of personalised client care (Jones, 2018b).

Drummond et al. (1998) identify three different approaches to incorporating skills which may be taken by universities. Firstly, embedding skills throughout the curriculum; secondly, developing freestanding skills courses; and thirdly, using work placements or other work-based learning. Star and Hammer suggest that the focus on skills has been played out in different ways, according to the perspective of individual academics. They argue that some view a more diverse cohort as lacking required skills for university study, thus creating "problems . . . requiring remedial intervention from support staff". Conversely, other members of the academy have chosen to take a "student-centred approach" which adjusts their teaching to the needs of the cohort (Star and Hammer, 2008, p. 239). Regardless of which approach is taken, it can be seen that developing relevant skills within the student body is a key part of the process. In addition to the preceding approaches, there are also examples of centralised, university-wide initiatives to embed skills into the undergraduate degree to enhance employability (see, for example, Fallows and Steven, 2000). Baker and Henson (2010) argue that the advantage of such interdisciplinary initiatives is that they ensure an equal provision across faculties, with appropriate leaders implementing it. In other words, it effectively circumvents any resistance amongst academic staff or particular faculties. However, this is something that could be seen as dangerous for those such as Cownie and Bradney (2005) who view academics as key in resisting neo-liberal incursions into universities. It may also underestimate the levels of resistance present within higher education.

In terms of the effectiveness of implementing the skills agenda, in 1998, Drummond et al. suggested that there is "little evidence of effective practice on any large scale" (1998, p. 23). They pointed to a range of different obstacles to implementation at institutional and departmental levels as well as in relation to individual academics. These ranged from institutional intransigence to lack of resources and knowledge of best practice to individual academics' desire to focus on research. Despite the increasing inclusion of skills provision within universities since this time, there still appear to be a number of barriers remaining. For example, Cranmer (2006) points to the difficulties in matching the skills required in employment to the skills focused on at universities. Boden and Nedeva discuss the divergence between universities who focus on a relatively narrow range of skills to "directly prepare students for jobs" and those (such as Oxford and Cambridge) where "broad-based knowledge and cultural capital are still the currencies that students accumulate" (2010, p. 48). At a more individual level, Baker and Henson refer to the belief of "many" academics that the degree should only cover "issues of direct academic significance" (2010, p. 63). Hewitt (2008) also points to difficulties in assessing skills where traditional methods may not be appropriate, but more innovative methods may be seen as more subjective and thus less acceptable. Therefore, it is likely the effectiveness of implementation varies significantly depending on where and who is involved, which skills are selected and which methods are used to impart these.

In fact, the response of universities to the neo-liberalization of higher education overall is contested amongst academics. Some view the universities as having responded somewhat too vigorously and transformed themselves into corporate entities (Giroux, 2012; McArthur, 2011). These commentators tend to view this as a negative transformation, arguing that it contravenes the fundamental tenets of higher education which are closely associated with the liberal vision of it as a public good. Instead, students are impoverished by the focus on them solely as consumers, being provided with a form of higher education that is increasingly vocational and shaped by the demands of employers. The public interest has therefore given way to "powerful consumer-oriented corporate networks" (Lynch, 2006, p. 3). However, other commentators view academics as being in a position to offer either covert or overt resistance to the shifts in public policy and climate, for example, by providing a sustained critique, explicitly identifying manifestations of neo-liberal policy to avoid its insidious pressures, forming international networks to collectively resist such policy, using information and communication technology to embed critical analyses into teaching and developing alternative pedagogies to promote powerful counter-narratives (Levidow, 2002; Williams, 2001). The extent to which this has occurred is difficult to ascertain; however, later writings clearly identify that neo-liberalism remains the dominant discourse of policy and politics within higher education, despite its practical implementation and acceptance being more mixed (Bessant et al., 2015 and Giroux, 2012).

The neo-liberal law school

When considering the impact of neo-liberalism on legal education specifically, it is necessary to once again return to the debate about the purpose of a law degree. If a law degree is viewed as largely vocational, preparing students for forms of legal practice, it is likely that the neo-liberal focus on employability and skills, including soft skills, will be seen as sympathetic to the ends of undergraduate legal education. Law can be seen as upholding and promoting neo-liberal ideology because of its strong connection to the state (Bowrey, 2013) and its application of knowledge and vocational links appear to fit well with neo-liberal principles. However, if it is seen as part of a liberal education which views knowledge as a good in itself and, for many proponents, promotes a form of good citizenship or develops the individual as a critical thinker, the demands of neo-liberalism can be seen as antithetical to the purpose of the law school (Mytton, 2005; Collier, 2004). Essentially, in a liberal form of legal education the university is being viewed as a public good, whereas a vocationally orientated system fits with the notion of it as transformed into a private enterprise. Hence Cownie argues that:

> A state which understands education as merely a commodity, primarily serving the needs of the economy by providing suitably skilled workers, clearly has a vocational focus and is likely to have little sympathy with the idea of a legal education which is primarily designed to produce independently-minded critical thinkers.
>
> (Cownie, 2010, p. 13)

Collier concludes that there are increasing indications that law schools are becoming "an industry preoccupied with economic rationalism, efficiency and the generation of income" (2004, p. 534). Thornton argues that legal academics are now sought after as new knowledge workers who must serve the state and produce other new knowledge workers (lawyers) to facilitate the market economy. As a result, she suggests that socio-legal topics have become dispensable as "technocratic, skills-based" courses are required. She depicts this as heralding a return to the doctrinal tradition and raises the danger of returning to the "trade school" mentality of the past (Thornton, 2001b, p. 10). However, an analysis of the last Research Excellent Framework in the UK suggests that, in research terms at least, socio-legal studies have not been squeezed out (Research Excellence Framework, 2015). This seems to add weight to Cownie and Bradney's argument (2005) that the picture painted by Thornton is too stark.

Mirroring the wider university, there are some signs that this perceived threat to the liberal foundations of the law school is being successfully counterbalanced (or at least moderated) by legal academics. Collier and Bradney in particular are cautiously optimistic over the impact of such changes in the university law school to date. Bradney (2011; 2003) suggests that the legal academy has proved able to effectively resist attempts at commercialisation. He argues that law schools can manage the processes involved in a way which leaves sufficient opportunities to pursue their own agendas, although this does assume the required will and vision is in place to do so. Collier also argues that a system of university management formerly based on "patronage, elitism and unaccountability" has become more egalitarian and pluralistic in nature (2004, p. 534). He agrees that such neo-liberalism sits uneasily with the ideal of a liberal law school, but at the same time, he sounds a note of caution in viewing these changes as damaging to the legal academy or law students:

> Any general claim that law schools are, as a result of these changes, more oppressive and difficult environments in which to work than in the past, or that these university – business links are themselves somehow new, must thus be treated with a considerable degree of caution.
>
> (Collier, 2014, p. 216)

The preceding quotation demonstrates that, while there is clearly room for continued unease and uncertainty about the influence of neo-liberalism on legal education, to date its impact on law schools appears to have been less significant or ingrained than first imagined (or feared). Nevertheless, it is the dominant paradigm in higher education overall and therefore forms the backdrop for any changes which take place within law schools. This means its influence must be taken account of when considering the role of skills in legal education and whether emotions can and should be incorporated as a form of soft skill.

In terms of the role of skills within legal education, Boon (1998, p. 158) argues that its origins can be found in the 1930s legal realist movement in the USA and the development of forms of clinical legal education. However, the acknowledgement of skills in the UK has been complicated by the uneasy relationship between the law schools and the legal professions and the distinction between the academic and vocational stages of training (Boon, 1998, p. 159). The Ormrod Report in 1971 suggested that the purpose of the undergraduate law degree (the academic stage) should be to impart legal principles and key legal subjects and also develop the "intellectual processes" required for "thinking like a lawyer": in other words, the ability to reason "logically and analytically". Although this therefore suggests the incorporation of some academic skills, it is clear that the development of more vocational skills is intended to be at the professional stage of training (Ormrod Report, 1971, para. 102, 101, 125). This focus on developing academic skills was emphasised further in 1996 by The Lord Chancellor's Advisory Committee on Legal Education and Conduct ("ACLEC") whose illustrative statement of outcomes for the undergraduate law degree included reference to "general transferable intellectual skills" (ACLEC, 1996, p. 66).

The following year, Harris and Jones, in their survey of UK law schools, indicated that there was "widespread agreement" that "lawyering skills" such as "library research, legal reasoning, case analysis" should be included in the undergraduate law degree (1997, p. 49). This appears to mirror the ACLEC statement in its focus on academic skills. However, they suggested there was "much less of a consensus" over the extent to which vocational skills should be incorporated (Harris and Jones, 1997, p. 49). Their findings from responses to surveys by seventy-six law schools were that 56.6% (43) did incorporate such vocational skills; 79% (30) of these were new university (former polytechnic, post-1992) law schools. Of the law schools which included such skills, 30% (13) provided stand-alone skills units, 14% (6) embedded them into the overall curriculum, 51% (22) used both methods and two primarily used case studies and mooting (Harris and Jones, 1997). Their conclusion was that there was "substantial diversity" in whether or not such skills were incorporated and, if so, how this was implemented (Harris and Jones, 1997, p. 97).

A subsequent survey of law schools in 2004 (Harris and Beinart, 2005, pp. 309–310) found that out of fifty-eight law schools who responded, 26% (15) had a compulsory module (or part of a module) relating to "lawyers' professional responsibilities". Another 8% (5) offered this on an optional basis. A total of 55% (35) offered mooting on either a compulsory or voluntary basis and 40% (23) offered courtroom skills. Overall, 80% of respondents (46) offered some form of "practical skills" module (or part thereof). The post-1992 university law schools were found to be more likely to offer these types of skills-focused activities and modules, and only 3% (1) did not cover other "practical skills" (for example, interviewing), whereas 14% (4) of old university law schools did not cover these. Harris and Beinart (2005) conclude that this range of practices may represent a lack of coherency over the purpose of the undergraduate law degree.[4] It could equally demonstrate a range of purposes in different university settings. However, it is clear that overall in the eight year period between these two settings, skills, in particular vocational skills, were becoming more prominent within law schools (particularly, it seems, within post-1992 universities). This is reflective of the increasing neo-liberalization of the law schools within this period.

The Quality Assurance Agency's (QAA) current benchmarking statement for law in the UK states that a law graduate should be "a well skilled graduate with considerable transferable generic and subject-specific knowledge, skills and attributes" (2015, p. 4). The list of twelve "skills and qualities of mind" that a law graduate should possess does appear to focus heavily on legal and academic skills, such as critical analysis and evaluation. However, the reference to "self-management" and "engagement with their own personal and professional development, and academic integrity" do both suggest a place for wider skills (although the definition of self-management focuses largely on the idea of reflective learning) (QAA, 2015, p. 7).

The general contention over which skills should be included within a law degree is reflected in academic debate of the matter. At one end of the spectrum, Bradney argues that it is appropriate for legal academics to research, at a theoretical level, any conceptual or other issues that arise in relation to professional legal skills to increase knowledge about legal practice. However, he also states that "law schools cannot be involved in training people in such skills. Training as an end is inimical to the pursuit and acquisition of knowledge" (Bradney, 1987, p. 130). In contrast, Bridges (1993), writing in relation to higher education generally, suggests that integrating skills into liberal forms of education is essential if education is to fulfil its aim of providing students with a positive freedom. He argues that the aspirations which are now framed as skills are those which enable students to transfer their knowledge and understanding to the social, political and economic worlds, thus empowering them in these spheres. In the context of legal education, Ragavan develops this argument, suggesting that "the ability to apply particular skills in specific contexts will contribute to student success in the diverse environment they will encounter, especially in a globalised market" and arguing that this is an appropriate part of a liberal legal education (2012, pp. 16, 20). Bell has also made a similar argument, suggesting that the language of "transferable skills" is necessary to communicate to employers and others the intellectual achievements of students receiving a liberal form of education (2000, p. 178).

The preceding discussion of skills within legal education suggests that there is a widespread acceptance of the need for law students to develop academic and intellectual skills which can be applied to law. Although there appear to be differences between universities, it is likely that most (if not all) institutions implement these as part of their strategies for developing effective learners. However, the acceptance of the need for skills which are vocational in nature is more qualified and their use and implementation is more variable and diverse. The most likely approach for many in the legal academy, and within law schools as a whole, will be to find a form of middle way. As Rigg argues:

> The real difficulty lies in charting a course between the liberal ideal and the vocational reality which upholds the integrity of the subject matter and forecloses any potential "dumbing down" criticism.
>
> (2013, p. 410)

The way this is accomplished is likely to vary very significantly between different universities. However, the previous discussion on the neo-liberalisation of higher education as a whole and its focus on economic worth and market forces suggests that the balance is likely to gradually shift towards the acknowledgement and incorporation of more vocational skills – prizing those which are seen as directly relevant to graduate employability, rather than those which display good citizenship and critical thinking. The question then arises as to how well emotions fit within this type of skillset and whether this can (and should) impact their acknowledgement and use within law schools.

Soft skills and emotional competencies

So far this chapter has assumed that readers will share a form of common understanding over the term "skills". The growing skills agenda throughout universities means that the terms "skills" and "soft skills" are widely used in literature on higher education generally and legal education in particular. It is somewhat surprising, therefore, that these words are rarely clearly defined. Barrie, in the Australian context, refers to the fact that a "bewildering array of terms" has developed to describe different graduate qualities with many being used interchangeably, such as "skills" and "attitudes" (2006, p. 217). Bennett et al. had previously raised similar concerns in the UK context, suggesting a conflation between "skills" and "attributes" and a failure to distinguish between different types of skills, such as "core" and "transferable" (1999, p. 74). This lack of definitional clarity is particularly apparent when it comes to the notion of "soft skills". Chamorro-Premuzic et al. define soft skills as "a range of competencies that are independent of, albeit often developed by, formal curricula and rarely assessed explicitly" (2010, p. 221). They contrast this with subject and content-specific skills that are formally assessed. They acknowledge that the characterisation of such skills varies widely between disciplines, suggesting that this makes an assessment of their usefulness harder to make. They also suggest that some characterisations include forms of personality traits which influence academic performance whilst remaining stable, for example, openness to new ideas and conscientiousness (Charmorro-Premuzic and Furnham, 2006). Andrews and Higson provide a similar definition of soft skills, referring to "generic skills and competencies required of graduates in the workplace" (2008, p. 419). This reference to the "workplace" implies a vocational quality to these skills, which perhaps stems from the authors' focus on the business degree in four countries. However, it is mirrored implicitly in Chamorro-Premuzic et al.'s discussion of the role soft skills could have in helping graduates to achieve "not only academic but also occupational goals" upon graduation (2010, p. 222).

Taken as a whole, the preceding discussion suggests that there are no clear definitional boundaries in relation to soft skills and, while various categorisations exist, there is no single, agreed conceptualisation. However, they tend to be categorised as those skills which are harder to quantify or assess and which relate more to graduate employability than academic performance. These include references to management of the self and personal development (Bennett et al., 1999). Perhaps what is most significant for the purpose of this chapter is the way that common definitions of soft skills appear to encompass emotional competencies, often framed as emotional intelligence (Andrews and Higson, 2008; Rowe et al., 2008). This characterisation is somewhat ironic when emotional intelligence's scientific origins focused on its challenge to the traditional concept of "g", suggesting it in fact represents a fundamental shift in how intelligence, and therefore cognition, should be perceived (Mayer et al., 2004). Nevertheless, there is increasing evidence that neo-liberalism has sought to co-opt emotions, particularly emotional competence, as a form of soft skill for economic and ideological ends. For example, D'Aoust argues that neo-liberalism includes "highly emotional components, ranging from consumption desire to workforce management" (2014, p. 269), but she suggests that these are being used to create attachments to neo-liberal ideology, and hence dissipate resistance to it. Kiersey suggests that not only are emotions used to generate attachment and commitment to neo-liberal goals, but their wider value has also been acknowledged as part of the "human capital" required for economic productivity (2014, p. 358). The creation of workers who have affective capabilities such as empathy is now viewed as providing greater economic productivity and thus meeting a key goal of neo-liberal ideology. In terms of individuals, this means an emphasis on self-regulation and self-improvement in a way which implies a recognition of, and role for, emotions. However, it is emotions being used for the neo-liberal ends of equipping citizens to become self-reliant and entrepreneurial and thus able to "participate responsibly and effectively as citizens" (Lupton, 1999, p. 297; see also Clegg and David, 2006).

At first glance, Lynch appears to take a different view of the relationship between neo-liberalism, soft skills and emotions, suggesting that neo-liberalism continues the liberal tradition of the rational, autonomous subject and prizes self-regulation and governance, replicating the tradition of Cartesian dualism:

> It is disregarding of the role that emotions play in our relationships and our learning, and correlatively indifferent to the central role of care and love relations in defining who we are.
>
> (Lynch, 2006, p. 5)

Burke also echoes this in stating that the neo-liberal concept of the person is one which refuses to acknowledge "our relational existence in and with the world" (2015, p. 389). Although seemingly contradictory, it is arguable that the views of D'Aoust (2014) and Kiersey (2014) are in fact compatible with those of Lynch (2006) and Burke (2015). In neo-liberal ideology emotions are being used to regulate a person's behaviour and strengthen their ideological ties. They are not being used or valued as a way to develop and nurture relationships, or in a manner which challenges the Cartesian dualism that relegates emotions to irrational impulses which can be manipulated for economic means. In terms of skills, this means that acknowledging and ultilising emotions can be viewed in neo-liberal terms as creating useful soft skills for increasing employability and productivity. However, this is likely to be within a narrow conceptualisation which views relational aspects as irrelevant or worthless, unless they can be demonstrated to have economic value. Within higher education, such soft skills become part of the shift towards study as a private good which will equip students as skilled workers or "human capital" to generate economic prosperity (Levidow, 2002, p. 229).

Overall, neo-liberal ideology places skills at the core of higher education (Bessant et al., 2015; Lynch, 2010) in a way which allows for a greater awareness and appreciation of so-called soft skills, including emotional competencies. However, this growing acknowledgement also raises a number of problematic questions about the ideological underpinnings of any attempts to include emotions within legal education and over whether their categorisation as a soft skill diminishes their importance within cognition, reason and rationality. The value and significance now placed on a wider range of skills within higher education appears to significantly increase the potential for the acknowledgement and utilisation of emotions as a form of soft skill, but in doing so it appears that emotions will become part of a neo-liberal ideology which is contested by many academics and which characterises university education as a private good focused on economic ends. Within this characterisation, emotions fundamentally remain viewed as a series of irrational impulses, but they are acknowledged and, to some extent, valued because of their perceived ability to be manipulated for economic and ideological ends.

Emotional competence for legal competence

In terms of the role of emotions within legal education specifically, there have been a handful of articles which argue for their importance as a form of soft skill, particularly in relation to clinical legal education (see, for example, Juergens, 2005). In the USA and Australia, this argument is usually based around the theories of multiple intelligences and emotional intelligence, applying them to legal education.[5] As early as 1999, Silver in the USA context suggested that "by the time one graduates from law school the skills that have been validated rarely include emotional, empathetic intelligence" (1999, p. 1174). She argued that students need to prepare for the emotional effects practising law can have on themselves and their clients, and that emotional intelligence can equip them with the tools to identify and manage these effects. Since then, a number of other USA commentators have developed similar arguments (for example, Montgomery, 2008). Cain describes a weekly class on emotional intelligence he ran as part of a University of Denver College of Law internship (work experience) programme. Two of the key goals of this class were encouraging students to apply emotional intelligence to their internship and, subsequently, their legal practice, as well as considering its application at an institutional level. He concludes that it was a "successful and rewarding" experience, although the small numbers involved (eleven attendees with only four responding to an evaluative survey) make it difficult to draw any wider conclusions (Cain, 2003, p. 17).

James (2008a), discussing emotional intelligence in an Australian context, notes that the postgraduate, fundamentally vocational nature of legal studies in the USA has meant that the focus of commentators has been largely on how to provide students with assistance in preparing for the rigours of life in legal practice. He argues that clinical legal education is important in teaching students how to put the law, and their role as lawyers, into a real-life context and suggests that:

> The concept of emotional intelligence provides the best theory for the kind of personal development that clinical legal education seems to encourage in students.
>
> (James, 2008a, p. 94)

Ways to incorporate emotional intelligence could include reflection on feelings and emotion in small groups, keeping a reflective journal, incorporating emotionally intelligent techniques into negotiation and interview training, providing appropriate mentoring and using mindfulness training (James, 2005). James's research into graduates of the University of Newcastle Law School (in Australia) who were practising as lawyers demonstrated a "very relevant" correlation between high levels of emotional intelligence and greater job satisfaction at work (James, 2008b, p. 132). Although work on the incorporation of emotional intelligence is less developed in the UK, there are also indications that it is becoming an area of increasing interest (Jones, 2018b). However, as discussed in Chapter 3, the term "emotional intelligence" is itself highly contested in scientific circles and its use may well further muddy the already murky waters of the soft skills agenda. There is perhaps an irony that the law school, with its emphasis on cognition, reason and rationality, has chosen to largely focus on this concept when the broader philosophical and scientific work on emotions is still commonly ignored. Indeed, the literature on applying concepts such as emotional intelligence to legal education demonstrates both the potential for emotions to be used as a form of soft skill, but also the dangers of it becoming very narrow and vocational in its focus. There is little (if any) acknowledgement of the type of inter-relationship with cognition that was discussed in Chapter 3. Failing to acknowledge the broader role of emotions can lead to such soft skills being dismissed as "a waste of time" or "too touchy feely" (student comments reported in Cain, 2003, pp. 11–12). To avoid this, the inter-relationship between emotion and cognition, particularly reason and rationality, needs to be emphasised, taking the "emotions and reason" approach suggested in Chapter 3.

Definitions within legal education

The Legal Education and Training Review (LETR) provides an illustration of the potential dangers of failing to provide a clear scientific basis and definitional certainty when exploring the role of soft skills within the legal sphere. Discussing the requirements for legal practice, it provides a list of "knowledge, skills and attributes" that are currently prescribed by various professional legal bodies (Chapter 2, Annex 1). It also provides tables demonstrating the ranking of importance by various legal professions of "knowledge items" and "skills and attributes" (Tables 2.4 and 2.5). However, it does not explain the distinction between the two. An analysis of these tables suggests that the "knowledge items" refer to understanding of particular legal topics, whereas the "skills and attributes" encompass a wide array of suggestions. These range from the ability to apply understanding of a legal topic (for example, problem-solving and explaining legal issues) to broad personality traits (for example, honesty, integrity and common sense) to non-legal abilities (for example, speaking a different language). The common thread that defines this as a "skill" is not explained. Perhaps it can therefore be assumed that any item not constituting "knowledge" is, by its otherness, assumed to be a skill.

What is particularly notable is that the Report refers specifically to the importance of the affective dimension, describing it as "critical to professional practice" (2013, para. 4.83). This is a groundbreaking and potentially transformative acknowledgement which suggests an important role for emotions. However, its failure to include any definition of affect and its use of broad and often contentious terms such as "empathy", "resilience" and the ubiquitous "emotional intelligence" has arguably enabled stakeholders within the profession to continue to largely ignore this dimension. The lack of a clear framework for its implementation has led to the Report's championing of the affective being largely disregarded (Jones, 2018c).

Conclusion: touching the void

The discussion of skills in this chapter has demonstrated that these have become an increasingly key part of the remit of higher education. For universities this has meant an acceptance of the need to develop not only more traditional academic skills, but also those which relate more to employability (Holborow, 2012; Barrie, 2006; Levidow, 2002). In a sense, the law school has always been somewhat torn between the academic and the vocational and therefore is better placed than some disciplines to respond to this challenge. However, the limited evidence available suggests that implementation of the skills agenda has been somewhat uneven to date (Harris and Beinart, 2005; Harris and Jones, 1997).

Underlying this focus on skills is a neo-liberal ideology which is challenging for many within higher education, not least those within the legal academy (Collier, 2014; Thornton, 2014). The idea of education as a commodity within a knowledge economy, the corporatisation of internal university practices and procedures and the consumerization of students have all been highly contentious. However, within the law school, views on the impact of this neo-liberalization vary considerably. There are suggestions of increasing vocationalism and the erosion of the socio-legal curriculum (Thornton, 2001b), but at the same time there are indications of resistance and of burgeoning interest in areas of applied socio-legal work (Cownie and Bradney, 2005).

To argue that emotions should be incorporated into the offering of law schools as a form of soft skill or competency is appealing because it correlates neatly with the neo-liberal ideology that is now so pervasive within the higher education sector, and its growing acknowledgement of emotions as potentially useful tools within the knowledge economy (D'Aoust, 2014; Kiersey, 2014). However, at the same time, it is problematic for precisely that reason. Within the law school, there are still schisms between those who argue for a vocational form of legal education and those who view it as a liberal degree. For those law schools and members of the legal academy who view vocationalism as key, the idea of utilising emotions as a soft skill could be promoted and developed, using concepts such as emotional intelligence. However, characterising the use of emotions within law solely as a soft skill is not a complete or wholly satisfactory solution. To label and categorise emotions in this way does not fully acknowledge their value and inter-relationship with cognition, reason and rationality. It could also alienate those members of the legal academy who are seeking to resist neo-liberal ideology and those who wish to avoid vocationalism becoming an increasing part of legal education. Perhaps most significantly, the use of emotions as part of the wider skills agenda is not ideologically neutral and could be viewed as supporting, or even promoting, a neo-liberal form of higher education that is contested by many.

The remaining three chapters of this book will each discuss a different way in which emotions play a (largely unacknowledged) role within legal education at present. Each of these have the potential to be acknowledged and developed, giving emotions a further foothold with the law degree as much more than simply a form of soft skill and potential tool for further neo-liberalisation.

Notes

1 The definition of "soft skills" is discussed within the chapter. The use of this term should not be taken to indicate agreement with its implications. The notion of skills associated with emotions being in some way non-essential or separate from so-called "hard skills" is highly problematic.

2 The term "competency" is often used interchangeably with the term "skill" within the literature on soft skills in higher education. Boyatzis describes a competency as "a capability or ability" (2011, p. 12). This chapter will refer to the term "skill" as one encompassing "competencies".

3 In the USA context, Stevens (2001, p. 205) also refers to the number of war veterans seeking places.

4 As recently as 2013, the Legal Education and Training Review in England and Wales (LETR) noted that the question of which skills should be dealt with in the undergraduate law degree was contentious. Student and trainee respondents indicated they wanted more skills and employability-focused activities at this level, whereas academic and Bar respondents raised concerns (LETR, 2013).

5 There is also some acknowledgement of the potential of therapeutic jurisprudence in this area (Baker, 2006), as a heuristic which focuses on wellbeing and therefore seems to impliedly incorporate emotions.

References

Abrams, K. and Keren, H. (2010) "Who's Afraid of Law and the Emotions?", *Minnesota Law Review*, 94(6), 1997–2074.

Adams, R. (2017) *Almost Half of all Young People in England go on to Higher Education*, www.theguardian.com/education/2017/sep/28/almost-half-of-all-young-people-in-england-go-on-to-higher-education (accessed 26 September 2018).

Advance HE (2018) *Graduate attributes framework* https://www.heacademy.ac.uk/knowledge-hub/graduate-attributes-framework (accessed 30 January 2019).

Andrews, J. and Higson, H. (2008) "Graduate Employability, "Soft Skills" Versus "Hard" Business Knowledge: A European Study", *Higher Education in Europe*, 33(4), 411–422.

Baker, G. (2006) "Do You Hear the Knocking at the Door? A 'Therapeutic' Approach to Enriching Clinical Legal Education Comes Calling", *Whittier Law Review*, 28(1), 379–407.

Baker, G. and Henson, D. (2010) "Promoting Employability Skills Development in a Research-Intensive University", *Education + Training*, 52(1), 62–75.

Ball, M. (2009) "Learning, Labour and Employability", *Studies in the Education of Adults*, 41(1), 39–52.

Barnett, R. (2005) "Recapturing the Universal in the University", *Educational Philosophy and Theory*, 37(6), 785–797.

Barrie, S. C. (2006) "Understanding What We Mean by the Generic Attributes of Graduates", *High Education*, 51(2), 215–241.

Bartram, B. (2016) "Economic Motives to Attend University: A Cross-country Study", *Research in Post-Compulsory Education*, 21(4), 394–408.

Bell, J. (2000) "Key Skills in the Law Curriculum and Self-assessment", *The Law Teacher*, 34(2), 175–192.

Bennett, N., Dunne, E. and Carre, C. (1999) "Patterns of Core and Generic Skill Provision in Higher Education", *Higher Education*, 37(1), 71–93.

Bessant, S. E. F., Robinson, Z. P. and Ormerod, R. M. (2015) "Neoliberalism, New Public Management and The Sustainable Development Agenda of Higher Education: History, Contradictions and Synergies", *Environmental Education Research*, 21(3), 417–432.

Blalock, C. (2014) "Neoliberalism and the Crisis of Liberal Theory", *Law and Contemporary Problems*, 77, 71–103.

Boden, R. and Nedeva, M. (2010) "Employing Discourse: Universities and Graduate 'Employability' ", *Journal of Education Policy*, 25(1), 37–54.

Boon, A. (1998) "History is Past Politics: A Critique of the Legal Skills Movement in England and Wales", *Journal of Law and Society*, 25(1), 151–169.

Bowrey, K. (2013) "Audit Culture: Why Law Journals Are Ranked and What Impact This Has on the Discipline of Law Today", *Legal Education Review*, 23(1), 291–312.

Bradney, A. (1987) "The Place for Teaching Professional Legal Skills in UK University Law Schools", *Journal of Professional Legal Education*, 5(2), 125–133.

Bradney, A. (2003) *Conversations Choices and Chances the Liberal Law School in the Twenty-First Century*, Oxford and Portland, Oregon, Hart Publishing.

Bradney, A. (2011) "English University Law Schools, the Age of Austerity and Human Flourishing", *International Journal of the Legal Profession*, 18(1–2), 59–71.

Bridges, D. (1993) "Transferable Skills: A Philosophical Perspective", *Studies in Higher Education*, 18(1), 43–51.

Bromberger, N. (2010) "Enhancing Law Student Learning – the Nurturing Teacher", *Legal Education Review*, 20(1–2), 45–57.

Brooks, S. L. (2006) "Practicing (and Teaching) Therapeutic Jurisprudence: Importing Social Work Principles and Techniques into Clinical Legal Education", *St Thomas Law Journal*, 17(3), 513–530.

Browne, J. (2010) *Securing a Sustainable Future for Higher Education. An Independent Review of Higher Education Funding and Student Finance*, www.gov.uk/government/uploads/system/uploads/attachment_data/file/422565/bis-10-1208-securing-sustainable-higher-education-browne-report.pdf (accessed 29 September 2018).

Burke, P. J. (2015) "Re/imagining Higher Education Pedagogies: Gender, Emotion and Difference", *Teaching in Higher Education*, 20(4), 388–401.

Cain, P. J. (2003) "A First Step Toward Introducing Emotional Intelligence Into the Law School Curriculum: The "Emotional Intelligence and the Clinical Student" Class", *Legal Education Review*, 14(1), 1–17.

Chamorro-Premuzic, T. and Furnham, A. (2006) "Intellectual Competence and the Intelligent Personality: A Third Way in Differential Psychology", *Review of General Psychology*, 10(3), 251–267.

Chamorro-Premuzic, T., Arteche, A., Bremner, A. J., Greven, C. and Furnham, A. (2010) "Soft Skills in Higher Education: Importance and Improvement Ratings as a Function of Individual Differences and Academic Performance", *Educational Psychology: An International Journal of Experimental Educational Psychology*, 30(2), 221–241.

Clegg, S. and David, M. (2006) "Passion, Pedagogies and the Project of the Personal in Higher Education", *Twenty-First Century Society*, 1(2), 149–165.

Collier, R. (2004) ""We're All Socio-Legal Now?" Legal Education, Scholarship and the "Global Knowledge Economy" – Reflections on the UK Experience", *Sydney Law Review*, 26(4), 503–536.

Collier, R. (2005) "The Liberal Law School, the Restructured University and the Paradox of Socio-Legal Studies", *Modern Law Review*, 68(3), 475–494.

Collier, R. (2014) ""Love Law, Love Life" Neoliberalism, Wellbeing and Gender in the Legal Profession – the Case of Law School", *Legal Ethics*, 17(2), 202–230.

Committee on Higher Education (1963) *Higher Education Report*, Cmnd. 2154.

Committee on Legal Education (1971) *Report of the Committee on Legal Education*, Cmnd. 4595.

Cownie, F. (2004) *Legal Academics Culture and Identities*, Oxford and Portland, Oregon, Hart Publishing.

Cownie, F. (2010) "Contextualising Stakeholders in the Law School", in Cownie, F. (ed), *Stakeholders in the Law School*, Oxford and Portland, Oregon, Hart Publishing Limited.

Cownie, F. and Bradney, T. (2005) "Gothic Horror? A Response to Margaret Thornton", *Social & Legal Studies*, 14(2), 277–285.

Cranmer, S. (2006) "Enhancing Graduate Employability: Best Intentions and Mixed Outcomes", *Studies in Higher Education*, 31(2), 169–184.

Dacre Pool, L. and Qualter, P. (2013) "Emotional Self-efficacy, Graduate Employability, and Career Satisfaction: Testing the Associations", *Australian Journal of Psychology*, 65(4), 214–223.

Damasio, A. (2006) *"Descartes" Error*, London, Vintage.

D'Aoust, A.-M. (2014) "Ties that Bind? Engaging Emotions, Governmentality and Neoliberalism: Introduction to the Special Issue", *Global Society*, 28(3), 267–276.

Department for Business, Innovation and Skills (2014) *Research Paper. Improving the Student Learning Experience – A National Assessment*, www.gov.uk/government/uploads/system/uploads/attachment_data/file/311288/bis-14-700-improving-the-student-learning-experience.pdf (accessed 29 September 2018).

Drummond, I., Nixon, I. and Wiltshire, J. (1998) "Personal Transferable Skills in Higher Education: The Problems of Implementing Good Practice", *Quality Assurance in Education*, 6(1), 19–27.

Eccleshall, R. (1994) "Conservatism", in Eccleshall, R., Geoghegan, V., Jay, R., Kenny, M., Mackenzie, I. and Wilford, R. (eds), *Political ideologies an introduction*, 2nd edn, London and New York, Routledge, 60–90.

Fallows, S. and Steven, C. (2000) "Building Employability Skills Into the Higher Education Curriculum: A University-wide Initiative", *Education + Training*, 42(2), 75–83.

Fanghanel, J. (2012) *Being an Academic*, Abingdon and New York, Routledge.

Feldman Barrett, L. (2017) *How Emotions are Made: The Secret Life of the Brain*, London, Macmillan.

Fine, B. and Saad-Filho, A. (2017) "Thirteen Things You Need to Know About Neoliberalism", *Critical Sociology*, 43(4–5), 685–706.

Giroux, H. A. (2012) "Neoliberalism, Youth and the Leasing of Higher Education", in Hill, D. and Kumar, R. (eds), *Global Neoliberalism and Education and Its Consequences*, New York and London, Routledge.

Goleman, D. (1996) *Emotional Intelligence*, London, Bloomsbury.

Goleman, D. (1998) *Working with Emotional Intelligence*, London, Bloomsbury.

Harris, P. and Beinart, S. (2005) "A Survey of Law Schools in the United Kingdom, 2005", *The Law Teacher*, 39(3), 299–366.

Harris, P. and Jones, M. (1997) "A Survey of Law Schools in the United Kingdom, 1996", *The Law Teacher*, 31(1), 38–126.

Hewitt, A. (2008) "Producing Skilled Legal Graduates. Avoiding the Madness in a Situational Learning Methodology", *Griffith Law Review*, 17(1), 87–120.

Higher Education Statistics Agency (2017) *Higher Education Student Statistics: UK, 2016/17 – Qualifications achieved*, www.hesa.ac.uk/news/11-01-2018/sfr247-higher-education-student-statistics/qualifications (accessed 26 September 2018).

Holborow (2012) "Neoliberalism, Human Capital and the Skills Agenda in Higher Education – the Irish Case", *Journal for Critical Education Policy Studies*, 10(1), 93–111.

Holmes, L. (2013) "Competing Perspectives on Graduate Employability: Possession, Position or Process?", *Studies in Higher Education*, 38(4), 538–554.

James, C. (2005) "Seeing Things as We Are. Emotional Intelligence and Clinical Legal Education", *International Journal of Clinical Legal Education*, 9, 123–149.

James, C. (2008a) ""Lawyers" Wellbeing and Professional Legal Education", *The Law Teacher*, 42(1), 85–97.

James, C. (2008b) "Lawyer Dissatisfaction, Emotional Wellbeing and Clinical Legal Education", *Legal Education Review*, 18(1–2), 123–137.

Jay, R. (1994) "Democracy", in Eccleshall, R., Geoghegan, V., Jay, R., Kenny, M., Mackenzie, I. and Wilford, R. (eds), *Political ideologies an introduction*, 2nd edn, London and New York, Routledge, 118–152.

Jones, E. (2018a) "Transforming Legal Education Through Emotions", *Legal Studies*, 38(3), 450–479.

Jones, E. (2018b) "Making Practice More Affective: Emotional Intelligence as a Legal Meta-competency", *European Journal of Current Legal Issues*, 24(1).

Jones, E. (2018c) "Affective or Defective? Exploring the LETR's Characterisation of Affect and Its Translation Into Practice", *The Law Teacher* (forthcoming).

Joshee, R. (2008) "Neoliberalism versus Social Justice: A View from Canada", in Hopson, R. K, Yeakey, C. C. and Boakary, F. M. (eds), *Power, Voice and the Public Good: Schooling and Education in Global Societies*, Bingley, Emerald Group Publishing Limited.

Juergens, A. (2005) "Practising What We Teach: The Importance of Emotion and Community Connection in Law Work and Law Teaching", *Clinical Law Review*, 11(2), 413–424.

Kiersey, N. J. (2014) ""Retail Therapy in the Dragon's Den": Neoliberalism and Affective Labour in the Popular Culture of Ireland's Financial Crisis", *Global Society*, 28(3), 356–374.

Lane, J. E. (2000) *New Public Management*, London and New York, Routledge.

Legal Education and Training Review (2013) *Setting Standards. The Future of Legal Services Education and Training Regulation in England and Wales*, http://letr.org.uk/the-report/index.html (accessed 29 September 2018).

Levidow, L. (2002) "Marketizing Higher Education: Neoliberal Strategies and Counter-Strategies", in Robins, K. and Webster, F. (eds), *The Virtual University? Knowledge, Markets and Management*, Oxford, Oxford University Press, 227–248.

Lupton, D. (1999) "Developing the "Whole Me": Citizenship, Neo-liberalism and the Contemporary Health and Physical Education Curriculum", *Critical Public Health*, 9(4), 287–300.

Lynch, K. (2006) "Neoliberalism and Marketisation: The Implications for Higher Education", *European Education Research Journal*, 5(1), 1–12.

Lynch, K. (2010) "Carelessness: A Hidden Doxa in Higher Education", *Arts & Humanities in Higher Education*, 9(1), 54–67.

Maroney, T. A. (2006) "Law and Emotion: A Proposed Taxonomy of an Emerging Field", *Law and Human Behaviour*, 13(2), 119–142.

Mayer, J. D., Salovey, P. and Caruso, D. R. (2004) "Emotional Intelligence: Theory, Findings and Implications", *Psychological Inquiry*, 15(3), 197–215.

McArthur, J. (2011) "Reconsidering the Social and Economic Purposes of Higher Education", *Higher Education Research & Development*, 30(6), 737–749.

McCowan, T. (2015) "Should Universities Promote Employability?", *Theory and Research in Education*, 13(3), 267–285.

McCulloch, A. (2009) "The Student as Co-producer: Learning from Public Administration about the Student – University Relationship", *Studies in Higher Education*, 34(2), 171–183.

Montgomery, J. E. (2008) "Incorporating Emotional Intelligence Concepts into Legal Education: Strengthening the Professionalism of Law Students", *University of Toledo Law Review*, 39(2), 323–352.

Mudge, S. L. (2008) "What is Neo-liberalism?", *Socio-Economic Review*, 6(4), 706–731.

Mytton, E. (2005) "Legal Education: The Integrated Law School", *Web Journal of Current Legal Issues*, 4.

National Committee of Inquiry into Higher Education (1997) *Higher Education in the Learning Society*, http://www.educationengland.org.uk/documents/dearing1997/dearing1997.html (accessed 29 September 2018).

Olssen, M. (2016) "Neoliberal Competition in Higher Education Today: Research, Accountability and Impact", *British Journal of Sociology of Education*, 37(1), 129–148.

Pertegel-Felices, M. L., Castejon-Costa, J. L. and Jimeno-Morenilla, A. (2014) "Differences Between the Personal, Social and Emotional Profiles of Teaching and Computer Engineering Professionals and Students", *Studies in Higher Education*, 39(7), 1185–1201.

Quality Assurance Agency (2015) *Subject Benchmark Statement Law*, www.qaa.ac.uk/docs/qaa/subject-benchmark-statements/sbs-law-15.pdf?sfvrsn=ff99f781_8 (accessed 29 September 2018).

Ragavan, S. K. (2012) "Acquiring Skills for a Globalised World Through a Peer Mentoring Scheme: A UK Law School Experience", *The Law Teacher*, 46(1), 15–37.

Ramsden, P. (2003) *Learning to Teach in Higher Education*, Abingdon and New York, Routledge Falmer.

Research Excellence Framework (2015) *Overview Report by Main Panel C and Sub-Panels 16–26*, www.ref.ac.uk/media/ref/content/expanel/member/Main%20Panel%20C%20overview%20report.pdf (accessed 29 September 2018).

Rigg, D. (2013) "Embedding Employability in Assessment: Searching for the Balance Between Academic Learning and Skills Development in Law: A Case Study", *The Law Teacher*, 47(3), 404–420.

Robbins, L. C. (1966) *The University in the Modern World and Other Papers on Higher Education*, London, Melbourne and Toronto, Macmillan.

Rowe, A., Gardenscwartz, L. and Cherbosque, A. (2008) *Emotional Intelligence for Managing Results in a Diverse World. The Hard Truth about Soft Skills in the Workplace*, Mountain View, Davies-Black Publishing.

Schutte, N. S. and Loi, N. M. (2014) "Connections Between Emotional Intelligence and Workplace Flourishing", *Personality and Individual Differences*, 66, 134–139.

Shore, C. and Davidson, M. (2014) "Beyond Collusion and Resistance. Academic-management Relations Within the Neoliberal University", *Teaching and Learning*, 7(1), 12–28.

Siems, M. M. and Mac Sithigh, D. (2012) "Mapping Legal Research", *Cambridge Law Journal*, 71(3), 651–676.

Silver, M. A. (1999) "Emotional Intelligence and Legal Education", *Psychology, Public Policy and Law*, 5(4), 1173–1203.

Smith, A. and Webster, F. (1997) "Changing Ideas of the University", in Smith, A. and Webster, F. (eds), *The Postmodern University? Contested Visions of Higher Education in Society*, Buckingham and Philadelphia, Society for Research into Higher Education and the Open University Press.

Sommerlad, H., Harris-Short, S., Vaughan, S. and Young, R. (2015) "The Futures of Legal Education and the Legal Profession", in Sommerlad, H., Harris-Short, S., Vaughan, S. and Young, R. (eds), *The Futures of Legal Education and the Legal Profession*, Oxford and Portland, Hart Publishing.

Star, C. and Hammer, S. (2008) "Teaching Generic Skills: Eroding the Higher Purpose of Universities, Or an Opportunity for Renewal?", *Oxford Review of Education*, 34(2), 237–251.

Stevens, R. B. (2001) *Law School: Legal Education in America from the 1850s to the 1980s*, Chapel Hill and London, University of North Carolina Press.

Stewart, C., Wall, A. and Marciniec, S. (2016) "Mixed Signals: Do College Graduates Have the Soft Skills That Employers Want?", *Competition Forum*, 14, 276–281.

Sturm, S. P. (1998) "From Gladiators to Problem-Solvers: Connecting Conversations about Women, the Academy and the Legal Profession", *Duke Journal of Gender Law and Policy*, 4, 119–147.

Telling, K. (2018) "Selling the Liberal Arts Degree in England: Unique Students, Generic Skills and Mass Higher Education", *Sociology*, 1–17.

The Lord Chancellor's Advisory Committee on Legal Education and Conduct (1996) *First Report on Legal Education and Training*, London.

Thornton, M. (2001a) "The Demise of Diversity in Legal Education: Globalisation and the New Knowledge Economy", *International Journal of the Legal Profession*, 8(1), 37–56.

Thornton, M. (2001b) "Among the Ruins: Law in the Neo-Liberal Academy", *Windsor Yearbook of Access to Justice*, 20, 3–24.

Thornton, M. (2012) "The New Knowledge Economy and The Transformation of the Law Discipline", *International Journal of the Legal Profession*, 19(2–3), 265–281.

Thornton, M. (2014) "Legal Education in the Corporate University", *The Annual Review of Law and Social Science*, 10, 19–35.

Tight, M. (2010) "The Golden Age of Academe: Myth or Memory?", *British Journal of Educational Studies*, 58(1), 105–116.

Twining, W. (1994) *Blackstone's Tower. The English Law School*, London, Stevens & Sons/Sweet & Maxwell.

Tymon, A. (2013) "The Student Perspective on Employability", *Studies in Higher Education*, 38(6), 841–856.

Universities UK (2017) *Higher Education in Numbers*, www.universitiesuk.ac.uk/facts-and-stats/Pages/higher-education-data.aspx (accessed 26 September 2018).

Whitson, K. (1998) "Key Skills and Curriculum Reform", *Studies in Higher Education*, 23(3), 307–319.

Williams, J. J. (2001) "Franchising the University", in Giroux, H. A. and Myrsiades, K. (eds), *Beyond the Corporate University*, London, Rowman and Littlefield, 15–28.

Wilson, J. F. (1966) "Survey of Legal Education in the United Kingdom", *Journal of the Society of Public Teachers of Law (N. S.)*, 9, 1–144.

Wilson, J. F. and Marsh, F. B. (1975) "A Second Survey of Legal Education in the United Kingdom", *Journal of the Society of Public Teachers of Law (N. S.)*, 13, 239–331.

5 Embracing emotions within learning

Introduction: from rhetoric to reality

The preceding chapter demonstrates that emotions, in the form of soft skills, have now garnered some level of interest, possibly even acceptance, within higher education. In this sense, the growing skills agenda holds out potential, but its neo-liberal roots may prove damaging if emotions become viewed as little more than economically expedient. Therefore, it is necessary to move past ideological rhetoric and look at the role of emotions within the lived experience of the law school. At the core of this chapter is the idea that emotions play a fundamental part within learning that goes far beyond any acknowledgement of particular emotional competencies and, instead, imbues the entire learning experience, impacting on each individual in myriad tangible (and intangible) ways (Tyng et al., 2017). To fail to acknowledge this within legal education is, therefore, to deny a fundamental part of the learning process.

Experiences, emotions and engagement

To some extent, the starting point for this examination of the role of emotions within learning is once again neo-liberal in nature. Student learning (rather than education) is now identified as the ultimate goal of teaching (Ramsden, 2003; Armitage et al., 2007). This is, at least in part, as a result of the increasing focus on skills development, although it forms part of much broader changes in understanding of the nature of teaching, demonstrated by the evolving emphasis on different theories of learning discussed ahead. In the USA context, Barr and Tagg describe these changes as creating a paradigm shift from institutions which exist to "provide instruction" to institutions which exist to "produce learning" (1995, p. 14). The characterisation of this learning has also shifted. The absorption of information through a transmissional, didactic form of teaching has been (in theory, at least) largely supplanted by concepts such as "deep" and "active" learning which seek to engage students in the process rather than positioning them as passive recipients (Burridge, 2002, pp. 27–29). As an active participant, each student experiences (albeit largely unknowingly) an individual and intricate interaction of values, goals, motivation, expectations and engagement, which is imbued with, and profoundly influenced by, emotions (Tyng et al., 207; Linnenbrink-Garcia et al., 2016; Ahmed et al., 2010).

When considering the learning process and experience, there is a significant body of work, often focusing on compulsory schooling, which emphasises the importance of emotions (see, for example, Durlak et al., 2011; Zins et al., 2007). An illustration of the importance of emotions is given by Pekrun and Linnenbrink-Garcia (2014) who begin their edited collection on emotions and education by stating that:

> The classroom is an emotional place. The countless hours students spend attending class, completing projects, taking exams, and building social relationships translate into progress towards crucial life goals – holding a degree in education has never been of more personal, social, or financial significance than it is today. Accordingly, it is no wonder that educational settings abound with emotions. In these settings, emotions such as enjoyment of learning, curiosity, interest, hope, pride, anger, anxiety, shame, confusion, frustration, or boredom are frequent, pervasive, manifold, and often intense.
>
> (Pekrun and Linnenbrink-Garcia, 2014, p. 1)

Examples given in this collection include a discussion of the importance of regulating (managing) emotions in the learning environment, the role of emotional intelligence in education, the influence of emotions in perceptions of achievement, the relevance of specific emotions such as enjoyment, shame, pride, anxiety and boredom and the potentially transformative effects of social and emotional learning. More generally, the literature on emotions and learning has explored the individual student experience of learning (Ahmed et al., 2010) but also considered the impact of the broader emotional climate within the classroom, including the effect of peer-to-peer and student-teacher interactions (Grams and Jurowetzki, 2015), some elements of which will be returned to in Chapter 7. Shuman and Scherer (2014) suggest that the differing definitions of emotions used by a variety of educational commentators has led to a diverse range of projects, leading to "unique bodies of knowledge" (2014, p. 13). However, as theories of emotions increasingly acknowledge the way emotions intertwine with (or even form part of) cognition, it seems likely that these bodies will increasingly coalesce. Already, at the core of all these bodies is the well-evidenced proposition that emotions form an integral part of learning and the learning process. This is the case regardless of level of study, discipline, type of learning environment and teaching technique, although the shape of the role which emotions play may be influenced by each of these.

This proposition is a challenge to the conventional norms of education. Pons et al.'s research found that in 200,000 psychological and educational publications including "cognition" or "emotion" in the title (or equivalents) less than 4% referred to both. Those that did were generally relating them both to a third issue (such as gender) with "few" addressing the relationship between the two (Pons et al., 2011, p. 78). As an explanation for this, they refer to the long tradition of dualism that exists between cognition and emotions and suggest this has been perpetuated in education science. This explanation is supported by Immordino-Yang and Damasio's argument that educators within schools tend to view higher-level cognitive skills as "rational, disembodied systems" which are separate from emotion, rather than viewing them as grounded in a long history of emotional functions" (2011, p. 116).

In addition, the potential consequences of a greater acknowledgement of emotions have been critiqued. Ecclestone has been particularly vocal in criticising what she perceives as a focus on self-esteem and emotional intelligence which elevates "emotion and personal experience as valid educational goals" within education (Ecclestone, 2004, p. 117; see also Furedi, 2002). She argues that a focus on self-esteem has led to a focus on "emotional vulnerability" rather than agency (Ecclestone, 2004, p. 118). For example, failure in a formal assessment is now likely to be labelled as an "emotionally damaging" event. This, in turn, leads students and educators to believe they cannot succeed without support and encourages them to lower their aspirations where such challenges are involved, as well as focusing attention on individual feelings rather than the inequalities contained in the education system which provides such assessment (Ecclestone, 2004, p. 118). Overall, Ecclestone views this focus on therapeutic interventions as disempowering students who are easily labelled (by themselves and others) as having low self-esteem and being vulnerable. This leads to so-called therapeutic interventions which shift the focus away from personal autonomy and challenge (2004, pp. 111–113). Furedi sums this up by suggesting that "therapeutic culture invites people to view themselves as objects rather than subjects of their own destiny" (2002, p. 24).

Ecclestone's argument does appear to be based on the assumption that all social and emotional learning is focused on self-esteem. In fact, within the literature on social and emotional learning in compulsory schooling a far greater emphasis appears to be placed on the regulation and management of emotions (see, for example, Weare and Gray, 2003). In addition, there is a significant amount of discussion on the concept of self-regulation – the way students direct their own learning through belief in their ability to achieve a required result (Op 'T Eynde, 2007). This focuses on a student's belief in relation to a specific task, not their sense of self-worth generally. Therefore, as Bromberger argues, there is no necessary connection between the two concepts as an individual may have self-esteem generally, but have lower self-efficacy when carrying out a specific piece of work (2010, p. 49).

In her later work, Ecclestone does acknowledge the intertwined nature of emotions and reason as concepts, and the need to acknowledge this within education, stating that:

> It is therefore important to make explicit here that 'emotion' and 'reason' are just two of many conceptual formulations which show the impossibility of separating the pursuit of rational autonomy from the emotions (and sometimes passions) that inspire or maintain autonomy and that are often invested in presenting and defending it.
>
> (Ecclestone, 2011, p. 94)

Instead of challenging the notion that emotions form an inextricable part of learning, Ecclestone's core concern appears to be with the relative weighting afforded to reason and emotions and what this demonstrates about society's conception of the individual (Ecclestone, 2011, p. 95). Her argument is that the pendulum has swung too far in favour of emotions, leading to the prioritising of the therapeutic with an increasing disregard for subject-based knowledge and the wider cultural, political and social setting (2011, pp. 107–108). There are echoes here of wider concerns about neo-liberalism's characterisation, and use, of emotions (as discussed in Chapter 4) which ignores their relational value and places the onus on individual self-improvement in a way which can be problematic and shallow (Lynch, 2006). Ecclestone's work is thus important in generating an awareness of the need to ensure that the approach taken to emotions within legal education does not lead to unintended but disempowering consequences. Nevertheless, despite the need to be aware of this possibility and the potential incursions of neo-liberalism, what is key is that there is now a fundamental acceptance of the core proposition that learning requires a focus on the emotions as well as cognition (Pons et al., 2011; Immordino-Yang and Damasio, 2011).

Social and emotional learning programmes

An important way in which the inter-relation of cognition and emotions within learning can be demonstrated is through an examination of programmes focused on social and emotional aspects of learning. These are designed to ensure that:

> Children and adults acquire and effectively apply the knowledge, attitudes, and skills necessary to understand and manage emotions, set and achieve positive goals, feel and show empathy for others, establish and maintain positive relationships, and make responsible decisions.
>
> (Collaborative for Academic, Social and Emotional Learning, 2018)

Such programmes are predicated upon the necessity for social and emotional skills to be developed to equip students for adult life (Romasz et al., 2004). The literature on them also emphasises the links between their usage and children and young people's academic achievement (Elias, 2003). A number of meta-analyses support the effectiveness of social and emotional learning programmes in this regard. For example, Durlak et al.'s meta-analysis of 213 programmes within schools found that they "yielded significant positive effects" on the aspects of social and emotional behaviour and attitudes that were targeted, "enhanced" adjustments to behaviour and "improved academic performance on achievement tests and grades" with an average gain in academic achievement of 11% (Durlak et al., 2011, pp. 405, 417). They also concluded that such programmes were beneficial at all stages of compulsory schooling and could be facilitated by existing school staff, allowing them to be incorporated into the usual school routines. Durlak et al.'s meta-analysis identified two variables which "moderated positive student outcomes" (2011, p. 418). The first of these is the use of SAFE principles. This is the idea that social and emotional learning must be sequenced, active, focused and explicit. In other words, ordered with a logical development of skills, involving students' active participation in learning, focused with dedicated time allocated, and with particular emotional and social skills being explicitly identified and worked on (Bannerjee et al., 2014). The second variable is the manner in which the programme is implemented, requiring appropriate buy-in from staff. Problems with implementation were found to lead to a "negative impact" on outcomes (Durlak et al., 2011, p. 418).

Within the UK, one of the most commonly used programmes (although it is no longer government funded) is the Social and Emotional Aspects of Learning (SEAL) programme, which was introduced, initially as a pilot, in 2003. In their report for the UK government which led to the implementation of SEAL, Weare and Gray noted that "some emotions (such as sadness, anger) can block learning, while others (such as a sense of wellbeing, feeling safe and feeling valued) promote learning" (2003, p. 35). They also suggested that "it would appear from recent research emotional and social processes are fundamentally inseparable from cognitive processes" (Weare and Gray, 2003, p. 35). An evaluation of the programme in 2010 found that the results were somewhat mixed and emphasised the importance of adhering to the SAFE principles (Humphrey et al., 2010). A further evaluation in 2014 once again referred to the importance of these principles and also argued that it was necessary to integrate the programme throughout the curriculum and across the school (sometimes termed a whole school approach) for effective implementation:

> As revealed by our multi-informant design, a whole-school approach to SEAL that engages all staff and pupils was a key predictor of subjective ratings of school ethos, which in turn mediated associations with more positive social experiences for pupils, lower levels of persistent absence, and higher levels of attainment.
>
> (Bannerjee et al., 2014, p. 732)

This emphasis on engaging both staff and students and the integration of SEAL into "the fabric of the school" (Bannerjee et al., 2014, p. 732) highlights the importance of integrating social and emotional learning with the broader learning taking place. Within compulsory schooling, this involves incorporating such learning into the general curriculum, (Bannerjee et al., 2014; Durlak et al., 2011). Within higher education generally, and legal education specifically, this indicates the importance of emotions not simply being regarded as a pastoral issue, wholly removed from the academic content of courses.

Learning theories and experiences

If emotions do and should form a part of learning, it is necessary to explore the role of emotions within theories of learning. Armitage et al. define learning theories as "based on psychological understanding" and seeking to explain "what happens when learning takes place" (2007, p. 71). As such, they could be viewed as encompassing a broad range of constructs, including those of multiple intelligences and emotional intelligence (see Chapter 3). However, a common, if very wide, categorisation is to divide them into behaviourist, cognitive and constructivist theories (Ertmer and Timothy, 2013; Yilmaz, 2011; Fleming, 2011). In addition, there is a body of humanist learning theories which are traditionally associated with concepts such as emotional literacy through the work of authors such as Rogers (1983) and Steiner and Perry (1979). Whilst these are less commonly included in the literature on childhood theories of learning, they form part of the foundation of many adult learning theories (Armitage et al., 2007).

Behaviourist theories represent the more traditional forms of learning theory and involve "a mechanical, materialistic view of psychology, involving a close study of observable, objectively measurable behaviour" (Curzon, 2004, p. 35). In other words, they disregard any cognitive or emotional processes involved in learning and focus solely on measurable results. Interestingly, Curzon (2004) points out that early behaviourial theorists rejected notions of Cartesian dualism in the same way that many in the scientific community now have. However, the behaviourist reasoning for this rejection was the view of human nature as explainable in wholly mechanical terms – as a form of machine with no role for emotions. Another parallel with law and legal education is suggested by Bredo's (1997) comment that the early twentieth century turn to behaviourism stemmed from a desire to establish psychology as a legitimate science through a focus on measurable outcomes. This mirrors the development of the doctrinal tradition as a "scientific" approach to law to achieve validation for its academic study. A final parallel seems to be the positivistic nature of behavourism (Boghossian, 2006) which mirrors the doctrinal tradition's roots in a positivist approach to law (as discussed in Chapter 1).

Behaviourist theories can be divided into classical behaviourist theories and neo-behaviourist theories (Curzon, 2004). The classic theories can be traced back to individuals such as Ivan Pavlov (1849–1936), whose well-known experiment with a dog illustrated the significance of conditioning, and John Watson (1878–1958), whose experiments conditioned a young child to be afraid of a white rat (Fleming, 2011).[1] At the foundation of these experiments was the belief that all human behaviour is based on largely physiological responses to stimuli (suggesting interesting parallels with the basic emotions theory discussed in Chapter 3). As Watson explained:

> Psychology as the behaviorist views it is a purely objective experimental branch of natural science. Its theoretical goal is the prediction and control of behavior. Introspection forms no essential part of its methods, nor is the scientific value of its data dependent upon the readiness with which they lend themselves to interpretation in terms of consciousness.
>
> (Watson, 1913)

Neo-behaviourist theories can be characterised as viewing behaviour as largely "purposive" and "often directed by anticipations of consequences based on past experiences" (Curzon, 2004, p. 35). In other words, the behaviour will be directed towards a particular goal rather than being a solely physiologically determined reflex. One of the most well-known proponents of this was Burrhus Frederic Skinner (1904–1990), whose work focused on operant conditioning. An "operant" is a voluntary act which creates a consequence. The consequence will determine the probability of a change in the timing of a future response and therefore can be used to reinforce the response made by an individual (Bredo, 1997). As Skinner describes it:

> The consequences of behavior may "feed back" into the organism. When they do so, they may change the probability that the behavior which produced them will occur again.
>
> (Skinner, 2014, p. 59)

For Skinner, learning can be defined as a change in the response rate as a result of such reinforcement, making it easy to identify and observe (Bredo, 1997).

Within an educational setting, the behaviourist focus on conditioning means that the role of the teacher is key to learning taking place. The teacher must set behavioural objectives, break down the issue into components to be mastered step-by-step, produce the correct stimuli and determine the criteria for measuring the student's progress (Fleming, 2011). Boghossian (2006) emphasises that behaviourism (together with other theories of learning) is a construct to describe how people learn, without specifying the methods by which that learning will be delivered. However, he suggests that in higher education, behaviourism has become associated with a form of delivery dependent on lectures, the type of traditional transmissional mode which the contemporary focus on learning has shifted away from.

The description of behaviourist theories implies that emotions are to be disregarded, or viewed as irrelevant, when measuring an individual's learning. Skinner himself, when discussing feelings, referred to the work of James (1884) and suggested that:

> In short, the bodily conditions we feel are *collateral products* of our genetic and environmental histories. They have no explanatory force; they are simply additional facts to be taken into account.
>
> (Skinner, 1975, p. 43)

His focus was clearly on the environmental stimuli which he saw as generating all responses – cognitive and affective. Therefore, feelings were "one of the most fascinating attractions along the path of dalliance" (Skinner, 1975, p. 43). There has been some debate about the role of emotions within the reinforcement of responses (see, for example, Staats, 1988). However, overall behaviourism, overtly at least, appears to minimise or disregard the role of emotions within learning. In more general terms, there has been a wide range of critique of behavourist theories. Perhaps most concerning in terms of legal education is Bredo's argument (1997) that a behaviourist approach to learning is unable to develop an individual's analytical skills. The rigid, atomistic approach of dealing with each component in turn does not enable a learner to contextualise the learning and see the overall issue or problem that is being tackled. The focus on structured stimuli and reinforcement suggests a passive compliance with the teacher's goals which focuses on lower-order mental abilities. There is also the danger that forms of learning which are not necessarily measurable, such as abstract thinking, are disregarded (Armitage et al., 2007).

In 2006, Boghossian suggested that behaviourism had previously been the dominant construct in educational settings, but had now been supplanted by constructivism (Boghossian, 2006, p. 713). More recently, Illeris (2009) has suggested that behaviourism as a learning theory has few recent contributions and is only of very limited interest and application. While it is widely acknowledged as retaining a place in, for example, learning by rote (such as when law students memorise cases or legislation for an examination), it is no longer viewed as sufficient on its own as a learning theory (Pritchard, 2009). Therefore, it is necessary to consider the other learning theories which are now more dominant to examine their relationship with emotions.

What Bredo terms the "cognitive revolution" of the 1960s and 1970s involved a shift from the external observation and measurement of the behaviourists to a focus on internal, cognitive processes (1997, p. 23). This stemmed from a desire to understand the ways in which individuals understand and process information (Yilmaz, 2011). For a cognitivist "learning is equated with discrete changes between states of knowledge rather than with changes in the probability of response" (Ertmer and Timothy, 2013, p. 51). This knowledge is obtained through an individual's interaction with their environment. It is a dynamic process which involves an individual obtaining new information, using it to develop their existing knowledge, and then applying it to new situations, thus once again obtaining new information (Armitage et al., 2007). Cognitivism focuses on conceptualising this process by identifying the mental activity involved at each stage of it (Ertmer and Timothy, 2013). Bredo suggests that this focus shifted the perceived goal of learning from the behaviourists' aim of "rapidly getting the right answer" to an emphasis on acquiring "expert" rules which solve a problem more effectively than "novice" rules. This may involve obtaining the answer more quickly, but the aim is to use the correct practice in reaching it to make the experience replicable (Bredo, 1997, p. 29).

Although cognitive forms of learning theory encompass a wide variety of approaches, one of the most influential is that of Jean Piaget (1896–1980), who identified specific and sequential stages of intellectual development in childhood (Jarvis, 2003). For example, between the ages of twelve and nineteen is the final stage of development, in which a child becomes able to solve abstract, hypothetical problems in their mind (Aubrey and Riley, 2016). Another important cognitive theorist is Jerome Bruner (1915–2016) who explored the differing cognitive structures involved in individual disciplines of study, identifying general rules and concepts of which an understanding is required to enable individuals to process specific detail relating to the subject (Bredo, 1997).

Each cognitive learning theory has been subject to a range of critiques. However, Bredo identifies one overarching critique as a detachment from the individual's physicality. He argues that cognitivism focuses on the mental process "as a separate stage after sensory input and before motor response" and in doing so may involve "physical and emotional passivity" (Bredo, 1997, p. 30). This critique implies that cognitive learning theory disregards emotions and, therefore, ascribes to the form of Cartesian dualism described in Chapter 3, despite the increasing evidence that emotions are at least intertwined with cognition and may even form a part of cognition. The very fact that the theory has been critiqued for a lack of engagement with emotions suggests that there may be a growing awareness of this inter-relationship.

Cognitive learning theories have close links with constructivist learning theories. These once again return to the constructivist epistemology discussed in Chapter 3 (which was also the foundation for constructivist theories of emotion in Chapter 4). The interconnected nature of cognitive and constructivist theories is demonstrated by the differing approaches of a range of commentators. For example, Fleming (2011) categorises Piaget as a constructivist thinker, whereas Yilmaz (2011) suggests cognitive theories such as Piaget's were an inspiration to the constructivist movement. Pritchard (2009) suggests that, in fact, constructivism is one branch of the broader cognitive tradition. The key distinction which appears to be made by a number of commentators is that both behaviourist and cognitive learning theories take an "objectivistic" philosophical stance (Ertmer and Timothy, 2013, p. 54). In other words, the focus is on how an individual interacts (internally or externally) with their environment, with knowledge viewed as something that is available to be acquired. Therefore, there is a form of dualism between the knower and the known (Garrison, 1998). In contrast, constructivist learning theories are based on the epistemology of constructivism, and do not view knowledge as an independent entity which can be "mapped" onto the individual. Instead, they argue that "humans *create* meaning as opposed to *acquiring* it" (Ertmer and Timothy, 2013, p. 56). This means that, firstly, the focus must be on the learner and not the topic to be taught, and secondly, that there is no meaning outside that which is constructed by the learner. This is in direct opposition to the Platonic view of there being an objective reality and independent truths which human beings (through learning) are striving to uncover (Wangerin, 1988). Instead, it is the learner's experience, and their perception of these experiences, which have value in an educational setting (Boghossian, 2006).

Constructivist learning theories can themselves be subdivided in a range of ways. However, the key division appears to be between those which focus on individual cognitive processes (in a Piagetian fashion) and those which focus on social constructivism (O'Donnell et al., 2015). For example, Lev Vygotsky (1896–1934) viewed learning as a social activity, and one significantly influenced by the cultural context it takes place in (Powell and Kalina, 2009, p. 244). He argued (in relation to childhood development) that "the active part is here played by the organism which masters the means of cultural behaviour supplied by the environment" (Vygotsky, 1929). A common thread is that such constructivist theories are now commonly associated with student-based approaches to education. This generally involves characterising the teacher as a facilitator, rather than an authoritarian figure (Powell and Kalina, 2009), placing the learner in control, contextualising learning to make it meaningful and authentic, presenting information in a variety of different ways and supporting the use of problem-solving skills (Ertmer and Timothy, 2013). There is a focus on "scaffolding" – providing appropriate levels of support as the learner develops and (particularly in relation to social constructivism) on dialogue and collaboration (Pritchard, 2009, p. 25).

Some of the issues identified in critiques of constructivist learning theories include challenges to its underlying epistemological assumption that reality, and learning, is constructed (see the discussion in Boghossian, 2006) and the argument that constructivist reforms in education have become "the Trojan horse of Western imperialism", failing to unpack the cultural (and imperialistic) values and assumptions which lie behind their implementation (Bowers, 2005, p. 123). Kotzee (2010) argues that the link between constructivist epistemology and constructivist pedagogy is not fully theorised, leading to issues within formal learning settings. For example, he suggests that teachers may interpret a constructivist viewpoint as akin to a democracy whereby every learner's opinion is equally valid. The desire to avoid imposing opinions on others can lead to the teacher effectively being unwilling to teach anything. However, despite Kotzee's criticism of the use of constructivist learning theories, he acknowledges that "today, all learning theory in higher education seems tacitly to be cast in a constructivist mould" (Kotzee, 2010, p. 177). Phillips agrees, suggesting that "Across the broad fields of educational theory and research, constructivism has become something akin to a secular religion" (1995, p. 5).

The shift towards cognitivist and constructivist learning theories seems to offer much more scope for the acknowledgement and inclusion of emotions than the behaviourist paradigm. Despite this, to date, the role of emotions in these theories has rarely been explicitly acknowledged and explored. Jonassen (1991) argues that cognitive theories are still bound by the notion of Cartesian dualism and retain an implicit form of divide between emotions and reason, although more recently Ertmer and Timothy have suggested that cognitivist theories do acknowledge the influence of an individual's "thoughts, beliefs, attitudes and values" on learning (2013, p. 52).

Harking back to theories of emotions, there is evidence that emotions do play a significant, if still relatively un-theorised, part in theories of learning. The theories of emotions discussed in Chapter 3 demonstrate that emotions are intertwined with, if not part of, cognition. If this is the case then emotions cannot be excluded from any form of learning theory which focuses on the mental processes involved in the learning experience (as both cognitivist and constructivist theories do). A learning theory which fails to acknowledge the role of emotions is effectively implicitly requiring students to expend their time and resources in suppressing or disregarding them, rather than focusing on learning itself (Lund and Chemi, 2015, p. x). Instead, Garrison (1998) urges educators to acknowledge the body and its functions (including, in his view, emotions) as a core part of the curriculum. He argues for a form of pragmatic social constructivism which focuses on "embodied action" rather than "abstract Reason" and co-ordinates cognition and emotions together (Garrison, 1998, p. 44). Powell and Kalina (2009) also touch on the role of emotions in constructivist learning theories, stating that students learn through examples which they relate to either emotionally and cognitively and through meaningful experience which connects the two. Gates also supports this, suggesting that "The constructionist model views the emotional not in opposition to the rational, but rather in partnership with the rational. To think and act rationally, one must feel" (2000). A perfect illustration of the need for emotions to be acknowledged and utilised within legal education.

The preceding learning theories have largely been developed and discussed in relation to children of compulsory school age. Students taking a law degree will range in age. The majority of undergraduate law students in the UK overall are aged twenty or under, a trend which is increasing. However, there is still a significant proportion of students spanning a wide age range with just under 200,000 aged forty or over (Universities UK, 2014). Therefore, it is arguable that adult learning theories should be given equal, if not greater, weight when assessing the role of emotions within law schools. Key among adult learning theories is andragogy (Armitage et al., 2007), a theory developed by Knowles (1984). It emphasises the difference between child and adult learners and its key tenets include a perception of adults as self-directed learners, an emphasis on learning through experience, a need to accommodate the individual's readiness to learn and a focus on competency and performance-based orientation to learning (Knowles, 1984). In many ways, these characteristics appear to align with those generally associated with constructivist learning theories, in particular, the view of learners as active participants and the focus on their experience as being at the core of their learning (Knowles, 1984; Ecclestone, 2011). The emphasis on experiential learning is perhaps most commonly associated with Kolb's learning cycle (1984), which is a staple of teacher training and widely acknowledged (Armitage et al., 2007).

In terms of emotions, Knowles specifically states that learning is "an internal process controlled by the learners and engaging their whole being – including intellectual, emotional and physiological functions" (1984, pp. 55–56). This view of learning is derived from a humanist approach to education which differs from others in the significance it accords to the affective domain. In particular, it views emotions and feelings as forming key parts of the learning journey (McIntosh, 2010). For example, Rogers, a key proponent of humanist theories, defines the journey of learning as involving the "whole person", including both feelings and intuition as well as logic and intellect (1983, p. 20). Therefore, it can be seen that andragogy and the wider humanist tradition have a significant engagement with the emotions compared to the lack of detailed discussion within other learning theories. However, the extent to which humanist perspectives have permeated formal education is questionable. Gregory argues that they have become linked instead with self-improvement and that:

> The idea that formal (traditional) education might concern itself with the emotional and inner life of the person remains a curious and potentially risky idea to many.
>
> (Gregory, 2006, p. 115)

Cognitivist, constructivist and humanist learning theories all demonstrate a role for emotions within learning. It is humanist theories which have developed this farthest, but often outside formal learning environments, leaving difficulties in obtaining acceptance and translating their tenets into the higher education setting. The question, therefore, is how emotions can be incorporated within learning in higher education, particularly legal education. To explore this it is necessary to consider how emotions and learning interact within these environments.

Conceptualising emotions within higher education

Mirroring the body of literature on compulsory education, Leathwood and Hey argue that, traditionally, emotions have been disregarded or suppressed within higher education on the grounds that:

> The academy has traditionally been constructed as the paradigmatic site of pure rationality devoted to the dispassionate and objective search for truth – an emotion-free zone, reflecting the dominance of Cartesian dualism with its rational/emotional, mind/body, public/private, masculine/feminine split. Universities have epitomised the rational and valorised side of this dichotomy, with emotion rejected as subjective and irrational.
>
> (Leathwood and Hey, 2009, p. 429)

Nevertheless, there are echoes of the type of shift indicated earlier in this chapter, with several commentators noting that this dichotomy is being challenged by some educators within universities. Beard et al. (2007) argue that there has been little systematic analysis of theories of emotions within the pedagogy of higher education, but rather an implied acknowledgement of its role within learning as a result of the wider moves which promote engagement and active learning. Echoing the discussion of Ecclestone (2011), the key debate in higher education does appear to be shifting to how emotions should be theorised, not whether or not they should form a part of it. In particular, there are concerns that the neoliberalization of higher education and its emphasis on individuals and the market will seek to subvert or submerge humanist and other feminist and critical theories which are arguably fundamental in exploring the role of emotions (Clegg and David, 2006; Hey and Leathwood, 2009). Beard et al. suggest that

> The question is not whether emotion should be introduced into the curriculum; our argument is that the affective and embodied are already aspects of all pedagogical encounters but that in higher education, in particular, emotion is rarely acknowledged and is under- or mis-theorised.
>
> (Beard et al., 2007, p. 235)

The fundamental role of emotions within learning means that the discourses should now be around how to acknowledge and theorise this, and how to incorporate this insight into practice.

When considering how far emotions have already, or have the potential to, become integrated within learning theories in higher education, a good starting point is the 2002 literature review on pedagogy and post-compulsory education by Cullen et al. Their analysis of two key educational databases found that literature on this topic was "not enormous", with empirical evidence found to be "thin on the ground" (2002, pp. 24–25). Based on the evidence available, their conclusions largely reflect the general shifts in learning theories discussed earlier. They point to the traditional academic view of knowledge as "abstract, disciplinary based and valued for its own sake" but suggest that this has been more recently challenged by concepts such as constructivism and experiential learning. In particular, constructivism is said to be "widely favoured" in higher education pedagogy (Cullen et al., 2002, p. 45). It is unsurprising, then, that the learning experience is said to be increasingly "student-centred" (Cullen et al., 2002, p. 38). Ertl and Wright's meta-analysis of work on the student learning experience mirrors Cullen et al.'s conclusions in this regard, finding that:

> Many of the developments and innovations discussed fit within a broadly constructivist framework, with the underlying assumption that students should take an active role in constructing knowledge and creating learning environments, though this is often not discussed explicitly and has to be inferred from the text.
>
> (Ertl and Wright, 2008, p. 203)

However, there also appear to be a dichotomy within Cullen et al.'s findings. Despite the prevalence of constructivist theories, the role of neo-liberalism is referred to obliquely, with a reference to a shift towards "knowledge utilisation" and "accountability" rather than "critical enquiry" and "personal transformation" (Cullen et al., 2002, pp. 38, 39). This emphasises the tensions in higher education that were touched on in Chapter 4.

Cullen et al. did find that the use of learning theory in higher education was eclectic, with theories often used as "technologies" rather than being grounded in philosophical or theoretical examination (2002, p. 39). This mirrors the criticism of Malcom and Zukas who, the previous year, had concluded that the majority of literature on teaching and learning in higher education focused on a mainstream form of psychology, demonstrating an over-reliance on behaviourist notions and an over-emphasis on cognitive theories with an underlying assumption that students are "rational, autonomous, unified, consistent beings" (2001, p. 39; see also Ertl and Wright, 2008). The move towards constructivist theory indicates an implicit acknowledgement of the role of emotions, given their part within individuals' experiences, but the tendencies within higher education to focus on the practical, and revert to traditional norms, is a potential barrier to this becoming explicit.

In relation to law schools, there is a lack of generalised discussion of the interrelationship of emotions and learning within law schools. As Bromberger (2010, p. 47) suggests, the majority of literature on the role of emotions focuses on the negative impact it has on law students. Traditionally discussion has tended to focus on "the political, the practical and the methodological" rather than "the theoretical or the analytical" (Sherr, 1998, p. 37). This has led to educational theory being largely disregarded or dismissed outside the legal skills tradition (Cownie, 2000, p. 230). Nevertheless, Cownie argues that an understanding of both educational philosophy and educational theory is important to increase the quality of teaching and to enable legal academics to make (and justify) informed choices over the strategies and techniques to employ in the curriculum. Ferris (2009) also suggests that educational theory is required to provide a foundation for new approaches as the changing nature of higher education, and the pressures on it, mean that reproducing traditional teaching and learning models is no longer appropriate.

More recent debate demonstrates that the importance of educational theory within legal education is still contested. For example, in the Australian context, Svantesson argues that "we can do what we do, and be great at what we do, without detailed knowledge of the science behind what we do" (2011, p. 255). However, in arguing that only four attributes are required to be a good teacher (knowledge of the subject, creativity, interpersonal skills and showmanship) he is in fact (and seemingly unknowingly) already ascribing to a particular theoretical view which draws on behaviourist traditions as viewing the teacher as the transmitter of knowledge (see previously). Gray, in a direct response to Svantesson, argues that educational theory is necessary to enable legal academics to ask fundamental questions about the purpose of the law school and to engage in genuinely interdisciplinary work. However, he suggests that within law:

> Theory is perceived as not only external to law but as something of an irrelevance clinging parasitically to the 'real world' core law subjects.
>
> (Gray, 2012, p. 172)

In terms of individual learning theories, there is little literature on their specific application to legal education. There are occasional articles advocating the adoption (or adaptation of) the work of a particular theorist (see, for example, Ferris, 2009; Maharg, 2007). A greater body of literature exists on specific forms of learning which are (often implicitly) linked to particular learning theories. In particular, problem-based learning has recently been discussed quite widely with both explicit and non-explicit links to constructivism and experiential learning (Grimes, 2015; Sylvester, 2015). This does appear to reflect the general focus of higher education on constructivist theories, once again indicating an implicit acknowledgement of the value of emotions. However, perhaps the most interesting development when considering the role of emotions in law schools is a small body of literature based around the concept of a humanist form of legal education. As discussed earlier, humanist learning theory is the only one which explicitly includes emotions as central influences within learning. In the context of European legal education, Vanistendael argues that the humanist part of higher education is a part which is often lost:

> It is that part of education that allows the student to discover their own personality, their own relative position in time, in space and in relation to other humans. It is the part that permits students to study and reflect on cultural and moral values so as to enable them to weigh the pros and cons in moral and social questions in order to make a balanced judgment which can carry them through the increasing uncertainties of the times. . . . An education that develops the human side of a person's intellectual capabilities is as important as total technical mastery of a scientific discipline.
>
> (Vanistendael, 2006, p. 63)

Somewhat confusingly, he argues that this opportunity for personal development should be restricted to fifteen to twenty-five year olds, assuming mature students can focus solely on the technical mastery. This appears to contradict the basis of much UK adult education in humanist theory. He also appears to see this humanist thread as running alongside the substantive law curriculum, rather than integrated into it. However, he does indicate that socio-legal studies (looking at the impact of legal rules) could act as a bridge between the two. Interestingly, Vanistendael suggests that the English undergraduate law degree "has a strong humanistic flavour" (2006, p. 72), possibly suggesting some conflation between the law as a liberal subject and a humanistic approach to law, which is difficult to justify given the liberal tradition's lack of engagement with emotions.

A more persuasive argument is put forward by Maharg (2000) who argues that the work of Rogers (1983) sits well with constructivist learning theories. He highlights that both question the value of didactic, instructional forms of teaching and instead emphasise the importance of "self-discovered, self-appropriated learning" (Rogers, 1957, p. 242). The epistemology of both is grounded in experience and practice. This once again suggests that constructivist learning theories can accommodate an inclusion and examination of emotions within the learning process. Incorporating elements of humanistic learning theories within the dominant paradigm of constructivism is likely to be an important tool in this accommodation within legal education.[2]

Conclusion: broadening legal learning

Arguments that learning and emotions can be separated fail to acknowledge the significant philosophical and scientific weight of evidence that views emotions and cognition as, at the least, interlinked or even possible as integral (Damasio, 2006; Nussbaum, 1997). This has been increasingly acknowledged and illustrated within work on learning in compulsory schooling (Pekrun and Linnenbrink-Garcia, 2014). It is also clearly demonstrated through empirical evidence from social and emotional learning programmes where evidence indicates they have the potential to impact significantly on academic achievement (Durlak et al., 2011, p. 417). In terms of learning theories, the only theory not to include any engagement with the emotions is that of behaviourism. However, this is now commonly viewed as incomplete as an explanation of learning (Pritchard, 2009; Illeris, 2009). There is an implicit role for emotions within both cognitivist and constructivist theories (Powell and Kalina, 2009; Garrison, 1998) and it holds an explicit and central place within humanist theory (Maharg, 2000; Knowles, 1984; Rogers, 1983).

Within higher education, for Ecclestone, an increased acknowledgement of emotions and a consequent focus on therapeutic interventions can lead to learners being characterised as vulnerable in a way which diminishes their autonomy and reduces their aspirations, leading to an eventual lack of purpose (Ecclestone, 2004; Furedi, 2002). There are also concerns that emotions are being exploited as a tool to promote the neo-liberal agenda in society (Clegg and David, 2006; Burke, 2015). These concerns are valid and should be acknowledged and understood, but they cannot and should not detract from the core proposition that emotions play an important role within learning. If legal education fails to include emotions within its conception of learning, and instead focuses on a narrow, outdated concept of "thinking like a lawyer" and a purely intellectual form of cognitivism, then it is failing its students in their processes and experiences of learning.

Notes

1 Conditioning is the process by which a person's response to a stimuli can be changed. For behaviourists, this change is what constitutes learning and the results of the change can then be objectively measured to assess what learning has taken place (Curzon, 2004).

2 For an interesting practical attempt to integrate humanistic legal education with the demands of the US Bar system see Steffey and Wunsch (1991).

References

Ahmed, W., van der Werf, G., Minnaert, A. and Kuyper, H. (2010) "Students' Daily Emotions in the Classroom: Intra-individual Variability and Appraisal Correlates", *British Journal of Educational Psychology*, 80, 583–597.

Armitage, A., Bryant, R., Dunnill, R., Flanagan, K., Hayes, D., Hudson, A., Kent, J., Lawes, S. and Renwick, M. (2007) *Teaching and Training in Post-Compulsory Education*, Maidenhead, Open University Press.

Aubrey, K. and Riley, A. (2016) *Understanding and Using Educational Theories*, London, Sage Publications.

Bannerjee, R., Weare, K. and Farr, W. (2014) "Working with "Social and Emotional Aspects of Learning" (SEAL): Associations with School Ethos, Pupil Social Experiences, Attendance and Attainment", *British Educational Research Journal*, 40(4), 718–742.

Barr, R. and Tagg, J. (1995) "From Teaching to Learning – A New Paradigm for Undergraduate Education", *Change*, 26(6), 13–26.

Beard, C., Clegg, S. and Smith, K. (2007) "Acknowledging the Affective in Higher Education", *British Educational Research Journal*, 33(2), 235–252.

Boghossian, P. (2006) "Behaviorism, Constructivism, and Socratic Pedagogy", *Educational Philosophy and Theory*, 38(6), 713–722.

Bowers, C. A. (2005) "Is Transformative Learning the Trojan Horse of Western Globalization?", *Journal of Transformative Education*, 3(2), 116–125.

Bredo, E. (1997) "The Social Construction of Learning", in Pyhe, G. D. (ed), *Handbook of Academic Learning*, London, Academic Press Ltd, 3–45.

Bromberger, N. (2010) "Enhancing Law Student Learning – The Nurturing Teacher", *Legal Education Review*, 20(1–2), 45–57.

Burke, P. J. (2015) "Re/imagining Higher Education Pedagogies: Gender, Emotion and Difference", *Teaching in Higher Education*, 20(4), 388–401.

Burridge, R. (2002) "Learning Law and Legal Expertise by Experience", in Burridge, R., Hinett, K., Paliwala, A. and Varnava, T. (eds), *Effective Learning & Teaching in Law*, London, Kogan Page Limited, 25–51.

Clegg, S. and David, M. (2006) "Passion, Pedagogies and the Project of the Personal in Higher Education", *Twenty-First Century Society*, 1(2), 149–165.

Collaborative for Academic, Social and Emotional Learning (2018) About CASEL, https://casel.org/about-2/ (accessed 9 October 2018).

Cownie, F. (2000) "The Importance of Theory in Law Teaching", *International Journal of the Legal Profession*, 7(3), 225–238.

Cullen, J., Hadjivassiliou, K., Hamilton, E., Kelleher, J., Sommerlad, E. and Stern, E. (2002) *Review of current pedagogic research and practice in the fields of post-compulsory education and lifelong learning. Final report for ESRC by the Tavistock Institute*, www.tlrp.org/pub/acadpub.html (accessed 6 October 2018).

Curzon, L. B. (2004) *Teaching in Further Education: An Outline of Principles and Practice*, 3rd edn, London and New York, Continuum.

Damasio, A. (2006) *"Descartes" Error*, London, Vintage.

Durlak, J. A., Weissberg, R. P., Dymnicki, A. B., Taylor, R. D. and Schellinger, K. B. (2011) "The Impact of Enhancing Students' Social and Emotional Learning: A Meta-Analysis of School-Based Universal Interventions", *Child Development*, 82(1), 405–432.

Ecclestone, K. (2004) "Learning or Therapy? The Demoralisation of Education", *British Journal of Educational Studies*, 52(2), 112–137.

Ecclestone, K. (2011) "Emotionally-vulnerable Subjects and New Inequalities: The Educational Implications of an 'Epistemology of the Emotions'", *International Studies in Sociology of Education*, 21(2), 91–113.

Elias, M. J. (2003) *Academic and Social-Emotional Learning. Educational Practices Series – 11*, Chicago, International Academy of Education and International Bureau of Education.

Ertl, H. and Wright, S. (2008) "Reviewing the Literature on The Student Learning Experience in Higher Education", *London Review of Education*, 6(3), 195–210.

Ertmer, P. A. and Timothy, J. N. (2013) "Behaviorism, Cognitivism, Constructivism: Comparing Critical Features from an Instrumental Design Perspective", *Performance Improvement Quarterly*, 26(2), 43–71.

Ferris, G. (2009) "The Legal Educational Continuum that is Visible Through a Glass Dewey", *The Law Teacher*, 43(2), 102–113.

Fleming, T. (2011) "Models of Lifelong Learning: An Overview", in London, M. (ed), *The Oxford Handbook of Lifelong Learning*, www.oxfordhandbooks.com.libezproxy.open.ac.uk/view/10.1093/oxfordhb/9780195390483.001.0001/oxfordhb-9780195390483-e-003?print=pdf (accessed 15 January 2016).

Furedi, F. (2002) "The Silent Ascendancy of Therapeutic Culture in Britain", *Society*, 39(3), 16–34.

Garrison, J. (1998) "Toward a Pragmatic Social Constructivism", in Larochelle, M., Bednarz, N. and Garrison, J. (eds), *Constructivism and Education*, Cambridge, Cambridge University Press.

Gates, G. S. (2000) "The Socialization of Feelings in Undergraduate Education: A Study of Emotional Management", *College Student Journal*, 34(4), 485–504.

Grams, S. L. and Jurowetzki, R. (2015) "Emotions in the Classroom: The Powerful Role of Classroom Relationships", in Lund, B. and Chemi, T. (eds), *Dealing with Emotions. A Pedagogical Challenge to Innovative Learning*, Rotterdam, Sense Publishers.

Gray, J. (2012) "Thawing out the Law School: Why We Need Legal Education Theory", *Alternative Law Journal*, 37(3), 171–174.

Gregory, J. (2006) "Experiential Learning", in Jarvis, P., Holford, J. and Griffin, C. (eds), *The Theory and Practice of Teaching*, 2nd edn, Abingdon and New York, Routledge, 114–129.

Grimes, R. (2015) "Problem-based Learning and Legal Education – A Case Study in Integrated Experiential Study", *REDU: Revista de Docencia Universitaria*, 13(1), 361–375.

Hey, V. and Leathwood, C. (2009) "Passionate Attachments: Higher Education, Policy, Knowledge, Emotion and Social Justice", *Higher Education Policy*, 22(1), 101–118.

Humphrey, N., Lendrum, A. and Wigelsworth, M. (2010) *Social and Emotional Aspects of Learning (SEAL) Programme in Secondary Schools: National evaluation*, Research Report RR049, Department for Education, www.gov.uk/government/uploads/system/uploads/attachment_data/file/181718/DFE-RR049.pdf (accessed 9 October 2018).

Hutchinson, T. and Duncan, N. (2012) "Defining and Describing What We Do: Doctrinal Legal Research", *Deakin Law Review*, 17(1), 83–119.

Illeris, K. (2009) "Introduction", in Illeris, K. (ed), *Contemporary Theories of Learning*, Abingdon, Routledge.

Immordio-Yang, M. H. and Damasio, A. (2011) "We Feel, Therefore We Learn: The Relevance of Affective and Social Neuroscience to Education", *Learning Landscapes*, 5(1), 115–131.

James, C. (2008) ""Lawyers" Wellbeing and Professional Legal Education", *The Law Teacher*, 42(1), 85–97.

Jarvis, P. (2003) "Teaching in a Changing World", in Jarvis, P., Holford, J. and Griffin, C. (eds), *The Theory and Practice of Learning*, 2nd edn, London and Sterling, Kogan Page.

Jonassen, D. H. (1991) "Objectivism Versus Constructivism: Do We Need a New Philosophical Paradigm?", *Educational Technology Research and Development*, 39(3), 5–14.
Knowles, M. (1984) *The Modern Practice of Adult Education: From Pedagogy to Andragogy*, Engelwood Cliffs, Cambridge Adult Education.
Kolb, D. A. (1984) *Experiential Learning. Experience as the Source of Learning and Development*, Engelwood Cliffs, Prentice-Hall Inc.
Kotzee, B. (2010) "Seven Posers in The Constructivist Classroom", *London Review of Education*, 8(2), 177–187.
Leathwood, C. and Hey, V. (2009) "Gender/ed Discourses and Emotional Subtexts: Theorising Emotion in UK Higher Education", *Teaching in Higher Education*, 14(4), 429–440.
Linnenbrink-Garcia, L., Patall, E. A. and Pekrun, R. (2016) "Adaptive Motivation and Emotion in Education: Research and Principles for Instructional Design", *Policy Insights from the Behavioral and Brain* Sciences, 3(2), 228–236.
Lund, B. and Chemi, T. (2015) "Introduction", in Lund, B. and Chemi, T. (eds), *Dealing with Emotions. A Pedagogical Challenge to Innovative Learning*, Rotterdam, Sense Publishers.
Lynch, K. (2006) "Neoliberalism and Marketisation: The Implications for Higher Education", *European Education Research Journal*, 5(1), 1–12.
Maharg, P. (2000) "Rogers, Constructivism and Jurisprudence: Educational Critique and the Legal Curriculum", *International Journal of the Legal Profession*, 7(3), 189–203.
Maharg, P. (2007) *Transforming Legal Education. Learning and Teaching the Law in the Early Twenty-First Century*, Aldershot, Ashgate Publishing.
Malcolm, J. and Zukas, M. (2001) "Bridging Pedagogic Gaps: Conceptual Discontinuities in Higher Education", *Teaching in Higher Education*, 6(1), 33–42.
McIntosh, A. (2010) "Humanist Learning Theories", in McKintosh-Scott, A., Gidman, J. and Mason-Whitehead, E. (eds), *Key Concepts in Healthcare Education*, London, Sage Publications Ltd.
Nussbaum, M. (1997) *Cultivating Humanity: A Classical Defense of Reform in Liberal Education*, Cambridge, Massachusetts, Harvard University Press.
O'Donnell, E., Lawless, S., Sharp, M. and O'Donnell, L. (2015) "Learning Theories: e-Pedagogical Strategies for Massive Open Online Courses (MOOCs) in Higher Education", in McKay, E. and Lenarcic, J. (eds), *Macro-Level Learning through Massive Open Online Courses (MOOCs): Strategies and Predictions for the Future*, Hershey, Information Science Reference.
Op 'T Eynde, P., De Corte, E. and Verschaffel, L. (2007) "Students' Emotions: A Key Component of Self Regulated Learning?", in Schutz, P. and Pekrun, R. (eds), *Emotion in Education*, Burlington, San Diego and London, Elsevier Inc.
Pekrun, R. and Linnenbrink-Garcia, L. (2014) "Introduction to Emotions in Education", in Pekrun, R. and Linnenbrink-Garcia, L. (eds), *International Handbook of Emotions in Education*, London and New York, Routledge.
Phillips, D. C. (1995) "The Good, the Bad and the Ugly: The Many Faces of Constructivism", *Educational Researcher*, 24(7), 5–12.
Pons, F., de Rosnay, M and Cuisinier, F. (2011) "Cognition and Emotion", in Aukrust, V. G. (ed), *Learning and Cognition in Education*, Oxford, Elsevier Limited.
Powell, K. C. and Kalina, C. J. (2009) "Cognitive and Social Constructivism: Developing Tools for an Effective Classroom", *Education*, 130(2), 141–150.

Pritchard, A. (2009) *Ways of Learning. Learning Theories and Learning Styles in the Classroom*, 2nd edn, London and New York, Routledge.
Ramsden, P. (2003) *Learning to Teach in Higher Education*, Abingdon and New York, Routledge Falmer.
Rogers, C. (1957) "Personal Thoughts on Teaching and Learning", *Merrill-Palmer Quarterly*, 3, 241–243.
Rogers, C. R. (1983) *Freedom to Learn for the 80's*, New York, Macmillan.
Romasz, T. E., Kantor, J. H. and Elias, M. J. (2004) "Implementation and Evaluation of Urban School-wide Social – Emotional Learning Programs", *Evaluation and Program Planning*, 27, 89–103.
Sherr, A, (1998) "Legal Education, Legal Competence and Little Bo Peep", *The Law Teacher*, 32(1), 37–63.
Shuman, V. and Scherer, K. R. (2014) "Concepts and Structures of Emotions" in Pekrun. R. and Linnenbrink-Garcia, L. (eds) *International Handbook of Emotions in Education*, New York and London, Routledge.
Skinner, B. F. (1975) "The Steep and Thorny Way to a Science of Behavior", *American Psychologist*, 30(1), 42–49.
Skinner, B. F. (2014) *Science and Human Behaviour*, The B. F. Skinner Foundation, file://userdata/documents2/ejj62/Downloads/ScienceHumanBehavior%20(1).pdf (accessed 3 October 2018).
Staats, A. W. (1988) "Skinner's Theory and the Emotion-behavior Relationship: Incipient Change with Major Implications", *American Psychologist*, 43(9), 747–748.
Steffey, M. S. and Wunsch, P. (1991) "A Report on CUNY's Experiment in Humanistic Legal Education: Adrift Towards Mainstream (City University of New York Law School at Queens College)", *UMKC Law Review*, 59(2), 155–179.
Steiner, C. M. and Perry, P. (1979) *Emotional Literacy: A Personal Program to Increase your Emotional Intelligence*, New York, Avon Books.
Svantesson, D. J. B. (2011) "The Emperor's New Legal Education Theory", *Alternative Law Journal*, 36(4), 255–257.
Sylvester, C. (2015) "More Questions than Answers? A Review of the Effectiveness of Inquiry-Based Learning in Higher Education", *Journal of Commonwealth Law and Legal Education*, 10(1), 21–29.
Tyng, C. M., Amin, H. U., Saad, M. N. M. and Malik, A. S. (2017) "The Influence of Emotions in Learning and Memory", *Frontiers in Psychology*, 8, 1–22.
Universities UK (2014) *Patterns and trends in UK Higher Education*, www.universitiesuk.ac.uk/highereducation/Documents/2014/PatternsAndTrendsInUKHigherEducation2014.pdf (accessed 5 October 2018).
Vanistendael, H. (2006) "Designing a Humanistic Legal Education", *European Journal of Legal Education*, 3(1), 59–73.
Vygotsky, L. (1929) *The Problem of the Cultural Development of the Child*, www.marxists.org/archive/vygotsky/works/1929/cultural_development.htm (accessed 4 October 2018).
Wangerin, P. T. (1988) "Objective, Multiplistic and Relative Truth in Developmental Psychology and Legal Education", *Tulane Law Review*, 62(6), 1237–1301.
Watson, J. (1913) "Psychology as the Behaviorist Views It", *Psychological Review*, 20, 158–177.
Weare, K. and Gray, G. (2003) *What Works in Developing Children's Emotional and Social Competence and Wellbeing?*, Research Report RR456, Department for Education

and Skills, http://webarchive.nationalarchives.gov.uk/20130401151715/www.education.gov.uk/publications/eOrderingDownload/RR456.pdf (accessed 9 October 2018).

Yilmaz, K. (2011) "The Cognitive Perspective on Learning: Its Theoretical Underpinnings and Implications for Classroom Practices", *The Clearing House: A Journal of Educational Strategies, Issues and Ideas*, 84(5), 204–212.

Zins, J. E., Bloodworth, M. R., Weissberg, R. P. and Walberg, H. J. (2007) "The Scientific Base Linking Social and Emotional Learning to School Success", *Journal of Educational and Psychological Consultation*, 17(2–3), 191–210.

6 Healthy, wealthy and wise? Law student wellbeing

Introduction: wellbeing and emotions

Students' emotions will influence all aspects of their learning and this learning will also generate further emotions which will impact on their wider experience within the law school (Tyng et al., 2017; Bromberger, 2010). Emotions are experienced individually by every student, in every learning environment, as part of their own learning processes and experience (Pekrun and Linnenbrink-Garcia, 2014). The presence of emotions can be discerned at a relatively abstract level through an examination of learning theories and broader empirical data. However, it is also crucial to explore the realities of how emotions manifest themselves within each individual's lived experience of law school. If it is accepted that emotions are integral to cognition and learning, and therefore each student's experience of legal education, it is necessary for law schools to be aware of the emotional aspects of legal education and consider the impact the law school experience has upon psychological health.

At the same time, students' emotional engagement and responses in other aspects of their lives, including family and friends, accommodation, romantic entanglements, events from their past and plans for the future, will also interplay with their learning and law school experience in a myriad of ways (Tett et al., 2017). These impacts and influences will further be mediated by broader economic, social and cultural factors (Leathwood and Hey, 2009), which will again impact emotionally on the individual student. For law schools to be able to provide a positive and productive experience for their key stakeholder, they must be concerned with the psychological and emotional wellbeing of their students.

Within the literature on wellbeing and legal education, there is no single definition of the term "wellbeing". It is sometimes used broadly, including referring to physical health (Skread and Rogers, 2014) and even spiritual health (Siptroth, 2007). However, the term is generally used to refer to subjective wellbeing, in other words, the way in which the individual experiences their life (Diener, 1984). In addition, the main focus tends to be on psychological health (Sheldon and Krieger, 2007), although there is clear evidence that physical, psychological and other forms of wellbeing are, in fact, interconnected and cannot therefore be considered in total isolation (Skread and Rogers, 2015). In the general psychological literature on wellbeing, there is also considerable debate over its definition (Dodge et al., 2012). This can be traced in part back to arguments over the Aristotelian notion of "eudaimonia", which is commonly translated as wellbeing, and whether this stems from the parts of the soul dealing with reason or emotions. However, its key contemporary definitions largely (implicitly or explicitly) include emotions as a key component of wellbeing. Thus a reference to psychological wellbeing effectively encompasses both emotional and cognitive processes (Diener et al., 2003).

Causes, culture and competition

> Students entering law school expect to be intellectually challenged, but few realize that they are also beginning an emotionally hazardous journey.
>
> (Dresser, 2005, p. 42)

This quotation neatly encapsulates the conclusions of the range of empirical research into law student wellbeing in both the USA and Australia. In the USA context, a number of studies have taken place since the 1960s (Solkoff, 1968; Hedegard, 1979), leading Shanfield and Benjamin (1985) to conclude that "there is general agreement among legal educators that the stress of legal education is high" (1985, p. 65). Benjamin et al.'s 1986 study of 320 law students and law graduates of the University of Arizona focused specifically on the question of whether such stress was linked to the pre-existing personalities of students who chose to study law, or whether it was created by the law school experience. Their findings were that prior to entering law school, students exhibited symptoms of psychological distress similar to those found in the general population (3% to 9% at that time). However, between 20% and 40% of all law students demonstrated such symptoms, for example, obsessive compulsive behaviour, anxiety and depression.

These findings were supported by later studies from Pritchard and McIntosh (2003) in the Canadian context and Sheldon and Krieger (2004; 2007) in the USA context. Pritchard and McIntosh's longitudinal study was conducted amongst first year law students at the University of Denver's College of law (2003, p. 731). It indicated that "health problems" increased during the students' first year with an increase in negative affect and a decrease in positive affect. By the end of the year, 12% of students scored high enough to indicate depression and another 30% reported "significant dysphoria" (a state of dissatisfaction or anxiety) (Pritchard and McIntosh, 2003, p. 735). Their findings also indicated that such negative effects were not linked to prior academic ability, suggesting that "something about the law school experience" causes the stress (Pritchard and McIntosh, 2003, p. 740). In the USA, the seminal studies are Sheldon and Krieger's longitudinal exploration of the wellbeing of law students within two law schools in the USA. The first of these followed a single student cohort through three years of their (postgraduate) legal study (Study 1), whilst the second explored the effect of law school on a first year cohort at another law school by comparing scores at the beginning and the end of the first year (Study 2). In Study 1, a survey of first-year law students found that they experienced "declining happiness and well-being" during their first year at law school (Sheldon and Krieger, 2004, p. 275) with a reduction in wellbeing and increase in both psychological and physical symptoms of ill-health. These effects continued throughout years 2 and 3 of law school for the students who completed the follow-up questionnaires. Similar results were demonstrated within Study 2, with a commensurate decline in psychological wellbeing. Sheldon and Krieger's 2007 study was a longitudinal three-year study, again with cohorts from two USA law schools (Sheldon and Krieger, 2007, p. 885) which once again indicated similar results and demonstrated a decline in subjective wellbeing during the students' time at law school (Sheldon and Krieger, 2007, p. 889).

In Australia, interest in law student wellbeing appears to have been ignited in part by the USA studies and also due to the tragic suicide of Christian Jepson, a young lawyer and former law student, whose parents set up a foundation (now known as the "Minds Count Foundation") to raise awareness of psychological health issues amongst law students and the legal profession (Council of Australian Law Deans, 2013). The first detailed study into depression and psychological distress amongst both law students and the legal profession was conducted across thirteen universities and nearly 2,000 members of the legal profession (Kelk et al., 2009). This concluded "that law students and members of the legal profession exhibit higher levels of psychological distress and depression than do community members of a similar age and sex" (Kelk et al., 2009, p. 42). The questionnaire administered identified that 35.4% of the law students surveyed reported suffering high or very high levels of psychological distress in the last thirty days, compared to 13% of eighteen to thirty-four year olds overall in the Australian population. Of law students surveyed, 46.9% also reported that they had experienced depression, although 39.4% stated that they would not seek help from a professional if they were depressed. Of those students who had suffered depression, 80.6% viewed their study as a contributing factor; the next highest factor was work at 54%.

When discussing their findings, Kelk et al. (2009, p. 42) did note that this did not equate with law students being "severely dysfunctional" due to the general levels of psychological distress and depression amongst Australian young people. However, it did show them to be more distressed than the norm. This finding was supported in a more recent study at the Monash University Law School which found that there was a "statistically significant" increase in depression over law students' first year. At the start of the year, 6% of students reported symptoms of mild depression and 8.5% of students reported symptoms of moderate to very high depression. By the end of the year these figures had risen to 12% and 15% respectively (Lester et al., 2011). While these figures were lower than those identified by Kelk et al. they were still substantially higher than levels of depression in the general population at that time. Similarly, following a study of 647 undergraduate students across three universities in south-east Queensland, Bergin and

Pakenham concluded that "a significant proportion of Australian law students are sufficiently stressed to warrant intervention" (2015, p. 401).

Another reported Australian study took a different approach to previous surveys, which have largely compared law students with either medical students or the general population. This study included a range of law, non-law, undergraduate and postgraduate students at the University of Melbourne, spanning six disciplines in total (Larcombe et al., 2015). The findings confirmed that law students did experience significant levels of psychological distress. While over half of law students fell within the "normal" range of symptoms, around 30% were in the "moderate to higher severity categories". Around 16.8% demonstrated symptoms of anxiety, with 13.2% showing signs of severe stress and 12.3% showing symptoms of severe depression at a point in the semester where there were no significant assessment demands (Larcombe et al., 2015, p. 256). Interestingly, Larcombe et al. did not find that law students demonstrated higher levels of psychological distress than other students overall, with similar levels reported amongst undergraduate engineering and postgraduate science, nursing and psychology students. Conversely, in their study of 188 undergraduate students from both the law and psychology schools of the University of Western Australia, Skread and Rogers found "that law students experience higher levels of stress, anxiety and depression than university students in other disciplines, particularly psychology" (2015, p. 89). This therefore leaves the question of how much the specific law school experience contributes to psychological distress open to debate. There is also the caveat that the evidence is based on self-report by law students who, it has been suggested, may be trying to comply with cultural norms which view the law as requiring hard work and stress (Glenn, 1995). However, an overview of the various studies suggests, in the USA and Australia at least, clear indicators that aspects of the law school experience in particular do influence the level of psychological distress experienced. Overall, it is clear that the emotional responses and reactions of law students are being influenced by their time in law school in a way which can be potentially damaging and distressing.

Within the UK, there has been very little reported research conducted on law student wellbeing, although anecdotally it appears likely that this will change within the next few years. In a study focused on undergraduate law student autonomy, Childs (2004) found that 65% of the 114 students surveyed described their first year at law school in positive terms (in particular, as "enjoyable" and "interesting"). However, 32% used less positive terms, including " 'intimidating', 'difficult', 'frightening' 'exhausting' and 'stressful' ". Of the nine who described it as stressful, five attributed this to workload. This was reflected in other parts of the survey with workload also identified as the biggest challenge in making the transition to university (24 respondents), although this does indicate that not everyone who found the workload challenging also found it stressful. The age, small size and restricted focus of this survey makes it of limited value. More recently, Jones et al. (2018) conducted an empirical study of law students studying via distance learning at the Open University in the UK involving applying two standardised self-report measures, the Depression Anxiety and Stress Scales 21

(DASS-21) and the World Health Organisation's Well-Being Index (WHO-5), to 344 participants. The results of these indicated that the participants' levels of stress, anxiety and depression were higher than those of the general UK population. Whilst the majority fell within the "normal" range, around 12–15% displayed symptoms within the severe or very severe range, with a further 7–14% falling within the moderate range (Jones et al., 2018, p. 25). Therefore, there were interesting parallels with the previous studies undertaken in both the USA and Australia, despite the open nature of the institution (with no previous qualifications required for study), the format of learning involved (online, at a distance) and the difference in demographics (participants' mean age was 40.6 years). Once again, this highlights the potential emotional impact of law school upon all students, regardless of differences between institutions and modes of learning.

There is a fuller body of work on student wellbeing overall in the UK (see, for example, Thorley, 2017; Student Minds, 2017; Universities UK, 2015). Thorley, in his report for the Institute of Public Policy Research, notes the importance of this issue, stating that:

> Poor psychological health and wellbeing can affect students' academic performance and desire to remain in higher education. In the most severe and tragic circumstances, it can contribute to death by suicide – levels of which have also increased among students in recent years.
>
> (Thorley, 2017, p. 3)

This report concluded that students experienced lower levels of wellbeing than the general population of young adults and noted that five times as many students had been reported as disclosing a psychological health condition in 2015/16 than in 2006/07 (from 0.4% of first year students to 2%). Of course, a psychological health condition does not necessarily equate to poor levels of wellbeing (or vice versa). However, in 2011 the Royal College of Psychiatrists also emphasised the need for long-term research into psychological disorders amongst students in higher education, suggesting that around 4% of university students are seen each year by counsellors for a range of emotional and psychological issues (Royal College of Psychiatrists, 2011). It suggests that factors influencing this may include the larger and more diverse student cohort now entering higher education, as well as external societal factors, such as economic pressures and family breakdown (Royal College of Psychiatrists, 2011).

Within the academic literature, Macaskill (2013) undertook a study of 1,197 undergraduate students at a post-1992 English university, studying a range of 10 courses (including law). She found an overall instance of "psychiatric caseness"[1] amongst these students of 17.3%, comparing with 17.6% in the UK population overall, with the figure peaking midway through the second year at 23.1%. Macaskill argues that this represents a historical increase in relation to students, which can be explained by the widening of participation in higher education. Ansari et al. conducted a wider study of 3,706 students across seven universities throughout England, Wales and Northern Ireland. This found a total of 34%

of those surveyed had experienced depression in the past academic year. Their conclusion was that

> Although health awareness was quite high and the use of the health services relatively was low in this sample of students from different universities in the UK, their level of health complaints and psychological problems/burdens fell within the same high range as observed in other student populations across Europe.
>
> (Ansari et al., 2013, p. 1320)

Similarly, a meta-analysis by Ibrahim et al. (2013) of twenty-four articles (15 from Western countries) demonstrates that almost a third of students are affected by depression overall (2013, p. 10). This suggests that the issue of student wellbeing is one that is widespread and cannot be solely attributed to the law school. Nevertheless, a number of causes specific to legal education have been identified in the literature on this topic. These are key to understanding the lived emotional experience of the law school, which in turn must influence the overall role of emotions within legal education. Therefore, it is necessary to consider these factors in detail to begin to consider how law schools can and should respond.

Although the causes of deteriorating law student wellbeing are multi-factorial (Skread and Rogers, 2014), the academic pressures and workload involved have commonly featured in discourses on wellbeing (Bergin and Pakenham, 2015; Skread and Rogers, 2014). The USA literature in particular emphasises the academically competitive nature of law, with students competing to earn honours, status and sought-after professional opportunities (Dresser, 2005). Krieger refers to "the top-ten-percent tenet", suggesting that there is an "entirely obvious" belief that to succeed at law school you must fall within the top 10% of your cohort (Krieger, 2002a, p. 117). This can lead to students associating their future happiness and security with their position in the hierarchy of academic success. Towness O'Brien et al. (2011a) also refer to academic competition in the Australian context, whilst emphasizing that it also applies to other disciplines, such as medicine and engineering. However, Tani and Vines' study indicated that law students were "significantly less interested" than medical and other students in participating in group work and assessment, implying a form of individualistic competitiveness (2009, p. 21). Skread and Roger's survey of students also noted that one of the "stand out" sub-scales for causes of stress was external pressures, including "competition (on grades and work), deadlines, and work overload", with a higher reported mean than demonstrated in a range of studies of other disciplines (2014, pp. 572–573).

In the UK context, a recent study indicated that 79.1% of law students at the start of the degree intended to enter the legal profession, either in the UK or elsewhere (Hardee, 2012, p. 34; see also Hardee, 2016). Previous surveys have also identified a majority (usually significant) of law students wishing to enter the legal profession (Childs et al., 2014, p. 55). Despite this emphasis on a career in law, there is evidence that less than half of all law graduates actually train as solicitors (Boon and Whyte, 2010, p. 189). This suggests that the competitive element present in USA and Australian law schools is also a feature of UK legal education. In addition, Hardee's survey identified that law students believe the most important factor to prospective employers seeking law graduates is degree classification, which suggests a sense of academic pressure. This is also reflected in the LETR's reference (2013) to the demands for reform generated by "escalating costs of qualification and difficulties in finding employment". With the competitive and demanding nature of qualification into the legal profession, alongside an increasing emphasis on employability within higher education (as discussed in Chapter 4), it is unsurprising if students are absorbing tacit messages about the nature of academic success which place competition in their studies above their own personal wellbeing and the need for self-care.

The issue of workload appears to be inter-related with the academic pressures noted previously, with law students feeling the need to work hard to compete (Dresser, 2005; Allen and Baron, 2004). There are also suggestions that the type of work law students are engaged in can be detrimental to their wellbeing, with a large amount of activities revolving around what Brown refers to, in the Australian context, as the "cult of individualism" (Brown, 2000, p. 279). This involves large class sizes which limit student-teacher involvement, a focus on individualistic learning tasks and rigid, exam-based forms of assessment (Larcombe et al., 2013; Allen and Baron, 2004). Within the UK, Bone's 2009 survey found 81% of respondents (1156 of 1428 from across nine UK universities) agreed or agreed strongly with the statement "Lectures are the most important part of my learning experience at university" and 93% of respondents agreed or strongly agreed with the statement "Seminars are an effective way of improving my understanding" (Bone, 2009, p. 231). Therefore, Bone concludes lectures and seminars are seen as of "fundamental importance" to students' learning (2009, p. 244). There does appear to have been increased interested in the benefits of group work and collaborative assessment. For example, in the UK context, Berry (2007) discusses the use of group work on two legal jurisprudence undergraduate modules, motivated by a lack of tutor time and resources. However, as recently as 2014, Steel et al. suggested (in an Australian context) that there was still a lack of familiarity with this approach. In their survey of law students at the University of New South Wales they found an appreciation of the benefits of group work, but students were resistant to it being subject to summative assessment (Steel et al., 2014; see also Tani and Vines, 2009). Once again, the image given is of the driven, competitive law student who is eschewing more collaborative ways of working to pursue a rigidly defined form of academic success.

Aligned to this traditionally individualistic approach, another element of legal education highlighted as impacting on the wellbeing of law students is a failure to allow adequate autonomy (Huggins, 2012; Sheldon and Krieger, 2007). Autonomy refers to "self-rule or self-determination" (Holm, 2012, p. 229). It can be defined as "ability to take control of one's life" (Tani and Vines, 2009, p. 26). However, Krieger prefers to characterise it as "authenticity", suggesting it incorporates the need for a person to express their true selves and their true values and interests (2002a, p. 119).

In the USA, Sheldon and Krieger's 2004 paper found that decreases in psychological wellbeing were accompanied by decreases in the relative importance of law students' intrinsic values (for example, prosocial values such as helping others and personal growth) compared to their extrinsic values (such as achieving status or impressing others). The students also indicated that their sense of self-determination (the capacity to autonomously pursue goals or interests) has decreased. This led to the conclusion that there was a link between changes in psychological wellbeing and in student values and motivation (Sheldon and Krieger, 2004). This is supported by the theory of self-determination, which posits that individuals require the appropriate balance of autonomy, relatedness and competence to enable them to thrive; thus if they are unable to act autonomously they struggle to grow (Ryan and Deci, 2000). Although this has not fully been explored in the UK context, there is some evidence of law students taking an instrumental, extrinsically motivated approach to their studies (Hardee, 2012; Sherr and Webb, 1989).

In the context of Australian legal education, Huggins, drawing on self-determination theory, also argues that a lack of autonomy amongst law students contributes to higher levels of psychological distress. She suggests that "some law students may perceive that their actions are not self-governed, volitional, and congruent with their true beliefs, values and interests" (2012, pp. 692–693). Interestingly, this has resonances of Ecclestone's (2011) comments from Chapter 3, where she warns of the dangers of therapeutic interventions in higher education diminishing students' sense of autonomy. It is clear that any interventions or shifts towards acknowledging emotions must acknowledge the importance and value of autonomy. It is also interesting to speculate whether requiring students to suppress or ignore their emotions within the law schools contributes to the sense of a lack of autonomy, particularly as a key factor in this appears to be the emphasis on a particular way of "thinking like a lawyer" which has traditionally been prized within the law school environment (Huggins, 2012; Krannitch et al., 2009).

As briefly discussed in Chapter 1, there is now a considerable body of literature on the negative effects of the doctrinal approach and its focus on "thinking like a lawyer". For example, in the Australian context, James argues that rather than being correctly perceived as "a form of linear analysis in a restrictive paradigm" it has become elevated to a prized way of thinking within the law school which largely disregards broader notions of problem-solving, providing a service and trying to help people (2008, p. 91). In the same context, Allen and Baron (2004) argue that the focus on teaching content that is abstract, rather than connected to real-life experience, and the focus on a particular type of reasoning and rationality, may lead students to lose their sense of connection to their personal values, feelings and sense of morality, stifling their creative and moral development. In the USA context, Krieger has described "thinking like a lawyer" as encompassing a frame of mind which is "critical, pessimistic and depersonalizing" (2002a, p. 117).

One of the key characteristics associated with this form of "thinking like a lawyer" is identified by Towness O'Brien et al. (2011b) as adversarialism. Common law justice systems are classified as adversarial because of their focus on the representative of each party pursuing that party's interest, by defeating or undermining those of an opponent. Hence in court cases there is a clearly defined victor and loser. Sturm (1998, p. 121) argues that legal education also follows a "gladiatorial" model, with successful performance defined as being the victor within a case or argument. Students are socialised into this model at a very early stage – from the competition for admission to the content of the curriculum (including a focus on appellate cases) and the individualistic forms of assessment used. This approach discourages students from engaging with the messier, more emotionally involved aspects of the law, focusing instead on abstract problem-solving (Towness O'Brien et al., 2011b; Dresser, 2005). It may also raise obstacles to the progress of women (who are often excluded in this model), as well as failing to prepare students for the evolving landscape of the legal profession where alternative dispute resolution and negotiation are often key (Sturm, 1998). Sturm and Guinier do suggest that attempts are being made to reform the USA law school and make it more pluralistic and diverse in its approach. However, they suggest that there is competitive and conformist culture, "remarkably static, non-adaptive, and resistant to change" (Sturm and Guinier, 2007, p. 120).

It has been argued that the impact of "thinking like a lawyer" is sufficiently embedded in law schools to generate a shift in law students' thinking styles. Towness O'Brien et al. suggest that:

> We believe there is sufficient evidence to support the hypothesis that a change towards, or a reinforcement of, rational thinking styles can occur in law school. In our experience, emphasizing the rational mode while neglecting the experiential mode of thinking is consonant (p. 56) with the approach to law that teachers often refer to as *thinking like a lawyer.* [authors' italics]
>
> (Towness O'Brien et al., 2011a, pp. 56–57)

In a study of over 300 law students, involving surveying a Australian National University College of Law cohort at the end of their first year of the law degree and another cohort at the start and end of their first year, Towness O'Brien et al. applied a rational-experiential inventory. A rational way of thinking is "conscious and deliberative", involving a focus on analysis, logic and reasoning. An experiential way of thinking is founded on "effortless intuition", with a holistic, emotionally orientated focus (Towness O'Brien et al., 2011a, p. 155). Indeed, Norris and Epstein (2011) suggest that emotion is fundamental to the experiential style of thinking. The study by Towness O'Brien et al. found "significant differences" between the scores at the start and end of the first year, with scores on the rational thinking scale becoming "significantly higher" and scores on the experiential thinking scale becoming "significantly lower". A higher score on the rational thinking scale was "consistently associated" with a more positive anticipated and actual experience of law school (Towness O'Brien et al., 2011a, p. 163). However, students who were higher than the average in rational thinking but lower than the average in experiential thinking demonstrated "a significant increase in depressive symptoms" over the course of the first year, and a "clear association" was identified between lower levels of depressive symptoms and higher levels of experiential thinking (Towness O'Brien et al., 2011a, p. 165).

Towness O-Brien et al. suggest that higher levels of experiential thinking may enable students to more successfully encounter new motivations, beliefs and goals and navigate the competitive law school environment without succumbing to the pressures to conform that can generate cognitive dissonance and psychological distress. They also point to the possibility that, rather than just developing their rational thinking, law students "may trade one mode of thinking for another, rather than using both" (Towness O'Brien et al., 2011a, p. 167). In other words, they begin to place less value and importance on experiential ways of thinking that utilise emotions. If emotions are not seen as valued or relevant, in the competitive environment of the law school they will become hindrances that are to be overcome. The survey by Towness O'Brien et al. was followed up by an additional dialogue with eighteen law students and ten faculty members. The results of this appear to correspond with the previous findings, as students indicated that law school was making them "more rational, objectifying, analytical and logical" (Towness O'Brien et al., 2011a, p. 177). At the same time, they reported feeling "more competitive, adversarial, arrogant and elitist" with increased feelings of "feelings of isolation, disconnection and intolerance" (Towness O'Brien et al., 2011a, p. 177).

The manner in which "thinking like a lawyer" is prized is also viewed as contributing to shifts in the motivations, values and goals of law students during their time at law school. In the USA context, Sheldon and Krieger's study of cohorts at two law schools found there was a decline in students' intrinsic motivation and "community service values" throughout their first year at law school which correlated with a decline in psychological wellbeing (2004, pp. 275–276). Their later studies indicated that the effect persisted throughout the second and third year of law school (Sheldon and Krieger, 2007, p. 884). More recently, they conducted further research which identified that "walking" such values (taking action to adhere to them) had a greater correlation with wellbeing than simply "talking" (claiming to adhere to them) (Sheldon and Krieger, 2014, p. 616). Hall (2009, p. 8), applying cognitive dissonance theory, argues that when law students are introduced to the law school culture and the idea of "thinking like a lawyer" they may find it conflicts with their previous experiences and beliefs. As it is impossible to reconcile both these previous and new experiences and beliefs, students are more likely to reject or reappraise their previous ideals and instead adopt the extrinsic values which they see perpetuated within the environment around them. Granfield had earlier explained this as a transition from "idealism to cynicism" with the idea of "thinking like a lawyer" forming a major contribution factor (1986, p. 515). It is viewed as effectively supplanting the sense of self which with students arrive at law school and also as leading to a diminished sense of autonomy (Sheldon and Krieger, 2007, p. 884; Krieger, 2002a, p. 125).

Interestingly, Tani and Vines' Australian survey of students at the University of New South Wales indicated that law students were more likely than students in any other discipline to be doing the course for external reasons, most notably due to parental influence (Tani and Vines, 2009, p. 15). They were also less intrinsically interested in the subject matter than any other cohort of students (Tani and Vines, 2009, p. 13; Allen and Baron, 2004, p. 288). This does appear to contradict Sheldon and Krieger's findings that students started law school with more intrinsic values then their comparator group (2004, p. 280).

The final factor often referred to as influencing law student wellbeing is a lack of social connectedness, an issue closely related to each of the other elements discussed previously and which appears to sometimes be identified as a cause of psychological distress and sometimes as a consequence of it (Bergin and Pakenham, 2015, p. 400; Tani and Vines, 2009, p. 31). Tani and Vines suggest that a lack of social connectedness is a key risk factor in incidences of depression. Skread and Rogers' data on Australian law students supports this, indicating that students who had a "greater sense of belonging" to their institution and year group had lower incidences of depression, anxiety and stress (2014, p. 565). Similarly, Bergin and Pakenham identified social isolation as the "strongest predictor of all adjustment outcomes" and one which indicated lower levels of autonomy (2015, p. 400). Worryingly, Tani and Vines identified that law students were more likely than other students to view their friendships in terms of networking opportunities for future career gain (2009, p. 25). It appears that larger intakes and bigger class sizes may also lead to students finding it harder to form friendships with peers or relationships with their teachers (Larcombe et al., 2015, p. 245). Overall, this means that, at a time when law students may be struggling to cope with academic demands, they have isolated themselves from their usual network of support (Iijima, 1998, p. 527).

Results and (possible) resolutions

> As legal education encourages a mind that thrives, grows, and evolves, the soul of the law student atrophies, withers, and disappears in a fog of dysfunction.
>
> (Siptroth, 2007, p. 181)

The very fact that there is the potential for a significant number of law students to experience a decline in wellbeing and an increase in psychological and emotional distress is in itself a compelling reason to argue that there is a need for emotional and other facets of wellbeing to be more widely acknowledged and explored within legal education. However, in addition, these psychological issues can create further, negative consequences, including inhibiting learning (Galloway et al., 2011; Bromberger, 2010), promoting disengagement (Bromberger, 2010; Dresser, 2005) and causing long-term damage to those whose wellbeing is affected (Grover, 2008).

With regard to learning, we once again return to the growing acknowledgement that it is "limiting and inaccurate" to focus on the role of cognition in learning when, in fact, the process is intertwined with emotions and other aspects of affect (Bromberger, 2010, p. 47). Chapter 5 has already emphasised the importance of emotions to effective learning and academic achievement. This relationship between wellbeing, emotions and academic achievement has significant implications for stakeholders in the law school, with Glesner pointing out that:

> Even if one sees our responsibility as solely to impart a body of knowledge, then one must necessarily address those factors within our control that impede that goal, including the psychological climate of the law school.
>
> (Glesner, 1991, p. 641)

There is evidence that people learn most effectively when in a moderate state of arousal (Bromberger, 2010). This state "maximizes the biochemical processes that drive the protein synthesis necessary for modifying neural structures" (Cozolino and Sprokay, 2006, p. 13). It is this modification process, known as neural plasticity, which enables people to learn. Although there may be some situations where a certain level of stress can enhance learning, there is evidence that high levels of stress and stress over a longer duration can result in memory impairment (Joels et al., 2006) and also inhibit neural plasticity (Rager, 2009; Cozolino and Sprokay, 2006). Dresser also argues it detracts focus from learning as it causes students to "worry more than learn" and encourages them to narrow their focus, to try and cope with the demands being placed on them (2005, p. 46). For example, a student given reading for a tutorial may focus on learning the legal rules, but fail to engage with what is perceived as the incidental task of case analysis, with the attitude that if they do the reading they have completed the task (Glesner, 1991). This means that the high levels of stress identified in law students throughout their studies are likely to have a direct impact on their academic performance. Iijima suggests that "because emotional state and academic performance are so closely related, and because law school contributes to emotional dysfunction, students may get caught in a downward spiral of emotional and academic problems" (1998, p. 527). She argues that academic support programmes alone will not be able to resolve this issue, because of the emotional aspects involved (Iijima, 1998, p. 527). Equally, simply putting in place pastoral support will not be sufficient, because it is the interplay of the academic and the emotional which is causing these issues.

In addition, there is some evidence that such stress can also lead to students disengaging from their studies (Bromberger, 2010; Do and Schallert, 2004). Dresser suggests that:

> Students also cope with stress by distancing themselves from the tasks of law school, reducing their involvement in these tasks. They begin to practice "avoidance tactics," which include skipping class, requesting the professor not to call on them, saying they are "not prepared" when they are called on, and not returning to class after a break.
>
> (Dresser, 2005, pp. 46–47)

Bromberger (2010, pp. 49–50) relates this to self-efficacy, arguing that, when given a task, students with low self-efficacy will focus on avoiding potentially unwelcome consequences instead of engaging with it positively. It therefore becomes a "self-fulfilling prophecy" as they put in less effort and the negative consequences confirm their belief that they are unable to succeed in it. The effects of this can impact on students' perception of law as a whole, causing them to become disengaged. Glesner (1991) describes such distancing from tasks as a coping mechanism. She also suggests other such mechanisms may include the setting of unachievable goals and putting off work. The findings of Sheldon and Krieger's study (2004) appear to support this. It was identified that there was a general decrease in both intrinsic and extrinsic values in law students between the end of their first year and the middle of the second year (which remained from then onwards). The authors suggest that this is consistent with a general "numbing" of values and emotions caused by "excessively analytical legal processes" (Sheldon and Krieger, 2004, p. 282).

In terms of long-term impact, at worst, law students suppressing values and personality traits which they view as inappropriate in a law school environment can lead to the "disintegration or fragmentation of the whole person" (Grover, 2008, p. 422). More prosaically, the harmful pattern of pursuing extrinsically motivated activities at the expense of time spent with family and friends (social connectedness) is likely to have become a habit which will be carried forward in future (Krieger, 2002b). As well as impacting on students' personal lives, Sheldon and Krieger (2007) argue that whether students begin their legal career with intrinsic or extrinsic motivations can determine their long-term ability to thrive in the legal profession (assuming this is their career goal). A focus on extrinsic motivations has been linked to psychological disorders and substance abuse issues within the legal profession (Jolly-Ryan, 2009). Somewhat ironically, in light of these potential effects, despite law students with higher levels of intrinsic motivation achieving better academically, those who obtained higher grades were found to then shift their motivation away from "'service-'orientated and potentially more satisfying law careers" towards more "'lucrative' and higher-stress" jobs (Sheldon and Krieger, 2004). Conversely, there is some data to suggest students who achieve lower grades shift their focus towards different, less-stressful legal careers (Sheldon and Krieger, 2004).

Closely related to the preceding issues, there are also arguments that students are leaving law school without the emotional skills required to succeed in the legal profession or elsewhere (James, 2005; Dresser, 2005). In relation to the legal profession, James argues that law schools need to inculcate students with a form of "ethical resilience" to enable them to act appropriately in a commercial setting. He argues that law schools have a "duty of care" to promote personal development and the "soft skills" (in which category he includes emotional intelligence) required to navigate personal relationships (James, 2008, pp. 85–87). This form of emotional stress can impair lawyers' competence and lead them to suffer from burnout, an extreme state of emotional exhaustion. More generally,

Kelk et al. (2009) suggest that the competitive style adopted in law schools is unlikely to be appropriate if applied to everyday life.

However, these arguments are not accepted by all commentators, for example, Wangerin suggests that increased levels of worry and stress may be a necessary part of students' intellectual development and not a specific consequence of the study of law:

> The education part of legal education, and not the legal part, forces students to move from dualistic to multiplistic and relativistic thinking. . . . Thus, any student who studies a subject taught in the same manner as law may experience enormous intellectual pain.
>
> (Wangerin, 1988, p. 1259)

The suggestion that this is a consequence common to all students seems to have subsequently been largely disproved by the USA and Australian studies previously discussed which demonstrate that law students do suffer significantly higher levels of distress than students in other disciplines. However, other commentators have also focused on the idea that it is necessary for law to challenge students to ensure that they are capable of dealing with the pressures of legal life as a member of the profession (Galloway et al., 2011), an argument that is particularly pertinent in the USA given the postgraduate nature of the law degree. Dresser (2005) refers to the argument that the rigours of a law degree will help to identify and remove unsuitable candidates for the legal profession. However, it appears significant numbers of students who do experience negative impacts on wellbeing at law school are not removed from the pool of candidates in this way, but instead join the legal profession where they are at risk of depression and other potentially damaging consequences. There is also a danger that those who are discarded or damaged will be those who do not fit within the "traditional" modes of thinking and being that are prized within the law school. Grover suggests that "outsiders are the canaries in the coal mine when it comes to law" (2008, p. 419; see also Sturm, 1998). In other words, their wellbeing is likely to be most affected. This is contrary to the focus on widening participation and diversity which has become an increasingly important part of the agenda in higher education (Macaskill, 2013; Royal College of Psychiatrists, 2011).

This discussion highlights the negative consequences arising from declines in law student wellbeing. These can be potentially far-reaching both in terms of time and impact. The possibility of emotional harm, or an inability to manage emotions successfully, underlies many of these issues (James, 2008, pp. 85–87). Therefore, it is necessary to briefly consider the suggestions made by commentators to ameliorate these consequences and enhance wellbeing.

Several commentators suggest that preparatory work needs to begin even prior to students beginning their degree, with more effort being made to prepare and educate potential law students (Glenn, 1995), admission criteria being amended to try and recruit those students with an intrinsic motivation and interest (Tani and Vines, 2009) and the orientation process for new law students being developed to emphasise the importance of wellbeing (Skread and Rogers, 2014). It is also crucial to embedding approaches to teaching and learning which emotionally support students appropriately and foster social connectedness. This is one of the guidelines proposed by the Council of Australian Law Deans, who state:

> It is good practice for law schools to engage in curriculum renewal to integrate strategies for the promotion of law student well-being into their teaching and learning practices.
>
> (Council of Australian Law Deans, 2013, p. 6)

Larcombe et al. (2013) echo this guideline, arguing that measures introduced to improve the law school experience are unlikely to be successful while the underlying culture in relation to teaching and assessment remains intact. They refer to the need for a "whole school" approach which integrates wellbeing into the design of both the curriculum and its assessment, as well as throughout the wider law school environment. In other words, wellbeing is not construed as a simply pastoral manner, but is pro-actively fostered and developed through teaching and learning. The benefits of this are also emphasised by Galloway et al., discussing their own work to embed student support within their teaching, who point to both quantitative evidence demonstrating effective learning as well as positive student feedback which is "unequivocal" in highlighting the impact of this approach on "feelings of connectedness, resilience and motivation" (2011, p. 246). Specific suggestions to incorporate such an approach include the use of relational forms of teaching and scaffolding (Galloway et al., 2011), creating a collaborative learning environment with interactive teaching techniques (Skread and Rogers, 2014), using variety in teaching methods to address multiple learning styles and drawing on concepts of experiential learning (Dresser, 2005), giving students the opportunity to take greater control of their own learning (Tani and Vines, 2009) and varying assessment techniques (Dresser, 2005). Tani and Vines (2009) also argue that more should be done to increase the intrinsic interest that students have in law as a subject, for example, by focusing on developing students understanding of the broader role of legal education and legal practice within society. Field et al. also echo this, suggesting that the first year of the LLB should be used to encourage students to develop a "positive professional identity" (2013, p. 15).

The overall focus of the preceding shifts in teaching and learning is on engaging and nurturing each law student's existing abilities and gifts (Jolly Ryan, 2009). These may range from written and oral communication to bringing order to a complicated issue to being compassionate with others. Grover argues that "to the extent that law school extinguishes any of these gifts, law school exerts a destructive force on those who entrust their education to the school" (2008, p. 424).

Another key element of a more holistic approach appears to be on fostering social connectedness and preserving and developing relationships (Iijima, 1998).

The use of peer mentors, group work and the fostering of closer relationships between staff and students can shift the focus from competition and grades and facilitate social connectedness (Tani and Vines, 2009). A further possibility is that of including some form of programme dealing with social learning, echoing the use of social and emotional learning programmes discussed in Chapter 5 (Tani and Vines, 2009). Bergin and Pakenham (2015) refer to the possibility of "buddy" systems between year groups. They also suggest that students should be provided with the option to engage in a range of meaningful activities within the law school and wider community, for example, through volunteering in law centres. However, the solution does not lie wholly within the environs of the law school and the legal community. There is also a need for law students to make wider adjustments in lifestyle (or, perhaps, to avoid discarding previously held good habits in this regard, for example, participating in sports and other extracurricular activities (Skread and Rogers, 2014)). It should also be noted that there may be interventions used in other disciplines which can be adapted to assist within the law school. In their meta-analysis of twenty-four studies across various university disciplines, Regehr et al. (2013) conclude that cognitive, behavioural and mindfulness interventions all have value in stress reduction, for example, using cognitive therapies to pinpoint and alter potentially harmful beliefs and teaching relaxation techniques.

This discussion demonstrates that improving law student wellbeing is not simply a pastoral task, or one that can be discretely parcelled off into a single intervention or initiative, webpage or pamphlet, or even a discrete course. Instead, there is a need for law schools to provide a more holistic form of legal education, to address "systemic stressors" and ensure a form of intervention that is "sufficiently intense and sustained" to improve the "educational climate" (Glesner, 1991, p. 645; see also Galloway et al., 2011; Krieger, 2008). This requires a transformative approach in which the term "curriculum" is perceived as a form of organising concept which spans both the academic, the social and the emotional (Duffy et al., 2011; Galloway et al., 2011). Legal education must draw on the learning of compulsory education (Bannerjee et al., 2014; Durlak et al., 2011) in taking a whole-law-school approach to emotional wellbeing, embedded guidance, support and insights throughout the entire law school experience, including the curriculum, but also in terms of the wider culture, values and mission which they (impliedly or explicitly) foster.

Individuals, resilience and emotional sticking plasters

Whilst the issues with wellbeing which arise in law schools impact on the lived experience of individual students, it is the broader cultural norms and expectations within law schools (often encapsulated in the term "thinking like a lawyer") which create an environment in which stress, anxiety, depression and poor levels of emotional and psychological wellbeing can proliferate. Mirroring the discussion of the neo-liberal university in Chapter 4, there is a danger that discussions of, and interventions around, wellbeing may focus on individuals, medicalising issues of psychological health and disregarding the way in which neo-liberalism has fostered a political and economic climate which is (at least in part) the creator of the perceived crisis in wellbeing. As Thornton describes it:

> Neoliberalism sloughs off responsibility for stress, leaving such problems to be borne by the individual or resolved by the market.
>
> (Thornton, 2016, p. 48)

The type of contradictions inherent in neo-liberalism are once again present within this debate as, on the one hand, the consumerisation of students has led to an increased concern with their feelings and overall university experience. On the other hand, the dominance of the market and the demands for productivity and accountability have all militated against the development of stronger relationships and better pastoral provision for students (Tett et al., 2017; Universities UK, 2015). There is a danger that law schools will seek to resort to relatively quick fix solutions (for example, the training of mental health first-aiders and the introduction of some form of wellbeing week) without challenging the causes of the issues at a policy level. Parker suggests that this form of approach is insufficient and instead argues that those involved in legal education must:

> Engage our own and our students' 'sociological imagination' and critical faculties to connect private experiences of psychological distress with a recognition that legal education and the practice of law is only good when it is pursued for the public good.
>
> (2014, p. 1105)

In other words, lessons must be learnt from the lived experience of law students which can be taken forward to shape the wider law school environment as a whole.

Conclusion: shaping law's graduates

Emotions are ever-present within the law school in the lives and welfare of its students, but at present the emotional and psychological wellbeing of law students is potentially at risk. The studies conducted in the USA and Australia indicate that the law school experience itself is contributing to significant levels of psychological distress. The causes of this are multi-factorial, but the concept of "thinking like a lawyer" contributes to the distress through prizing a narrow and impersonal form of legal reasoning (James, 2008). It is arguable that this also has an impact on the motivation of students and even on their thinking style (Towness O'Brien et al., 2011a; Krieger, 2002a).

Although the reported research on law student wellbeing in the UK is limited, the evidence available on undergraduate students generally suggests that they do suffer from higher levels of psychological distress than the general population (Macaskill, 2013; Royal College of Psychiatrists, 2011), therefore psychological wellbeing should be of concern to law schools. Evidence from the USA and Australia demonstrates that failure to acknowledge this issue can impact on students' learning, engagement and long-term psychological health (Bromberger, 2010; Grover, 2008; Dresser, 2005). One of the key themes that arises from discussions of ways to promote law student wellbeing is the need to provide a more holistic form of legal education (Galloway et al., 2011; Tani and Vines, 2009; Krieger, 2002a). The acknowledgement and incorporation of emotions within law schools has a fundamental role to play in achieving this. By incorporating insights from humanist, feminist and other perspectives, it could move beyond the use of emotions as a form of soft skill and develop a richer conception, designed to promote wellbeing amongst law students by fostering broader cultural and environmental changes within legal education.

Note

1 "Caseness" refers to the number meeting the criteria for a psychiatric disorder to be diagnosed (Oxford University Press, 2010).

References

Allen, J. and Baron, P. (2004) "Buttercup Goes to Law School. Student Wellbeing in Stressed Law Schools", *Alternative Law Journal*, 29(6), 285–288.

Ansari, W. E., Stock, C., the UK Student Health Group, Snelgrove, S., Hu, X., Parke, S., Davies, S., John, J., Adetunje, H., Stoate, M., Deeny, P., Phillips, C. and Mabhala, A. (2011) "Feeling Healthy? A Survey of Physical and Psychological Wellbeing of Students from Seven Universities in the UK", *International Journal of Environmental Research and Public Health*, 8(5), 1308–1323.Bannerjee, R., Weare, K. and Farr, W. (2014) "Working with "Social and Emotional Aspects of Learning" (SEAL): Associations with School Ethos, Pupil Social Experiences, Attendance and Attainment", *British Educational Research Journal*, 40(4), 718–742.

Benjamin, G. A. H, Kaszniak, A., Sales, B. and Shanfield, S. B. (1986) "The Role of Legal Education in Producing Psychological Distress Among Law Students and Lawyers", *Law & Social Inquiry*, 11(2), 225–252.

Bergin, A. and Pakenham, K. (2015) "Law Student Stress: Relationships Between Academic Demands, Social Isolation, Career Pressure, Study/Life Imbalance and Adjustment Outcomes in Law Students", *Psychiatry, Psychology and Law*, 22(3), 388–406.

Berry, E. (2007) "Group Work and Assessment – Benefit or Burden?", *The Law Teacher*, 41(1), 19–36.

Bone, A. (2009) "The Twenty-First Century Law Student", *The Law Teacher*, 43(3), 222–245.

Boon, A. and Whyte, A. (2010) "Will there be Blood? Students as Stakeholders in the Legal Academy", in Cownie, F. (ed), *Stakeholders in the Law School*, Oxford and Portland, Oregon, Hart Publishing, 185–224.

Bromberger, N. (2010) "Enhancing Law Student Learning – The Nurturing Teacher", *Legal Education Review*, 20(1–2), 45–57.

Brown, H. (2000) "The Cult of Individualism in Law School", *Alternative Law Journal*, 25(6), 279–287.

Childs, P. (2004) *Autonomy and the Ability to Learn Project Report*, Warwick, England, *UK Centre for Legal Education.*

Childs, P., Firth, N. and de Rijke, H. (2014) "The Gap Between Law Student Career Aspirations and Employment Opportunities", *The Law Teacher*, 48(1), 51–68.

Council of Australian Law Deans (2013) *Promoting Law-Student Well-being. Good Practice Guidelines for Law Schools*, www.cald.asn.au/assets/lists/Resources/Promoting%20Law%20Student%20Well-Being%20Good%20Practice%20Guidelines%20for%20Law%20Schools.pdf (accessed 7 January 2018).

Cozolino, L. and Sprokay, S. (2006) "Neuroscience and Adult Learning", *New Directions in Adult Continuing Education*, 110, 11–20.

Diener, E. (1984) "Subjective Well-being", *Psychological Bulletin*, 95, 542–575.

Diener, E., Oishi, S. and Lucas, R. E. (2003) "Personality, Culture, and Subjective Well-Being: Emotional and Cognitive Evaluations of Life", *Annual Review of Psychology*, 54, 403–425.

Dodge, R., Daly, A., Huyton, J. and Sanders, L. (2012) "The Challenge of Defining Wellbeing", *International Journal of Wellbeing*, 2(3), 222–235.

Do, S. L. and Schallert, A. L. (2004) "Emotions and Classroom Talk: Toward a Model of the Role of Affect in Students' Experiences of Classroom Discussions", *Journal of Educational Psychology*, 96(4), 619–634.

Dresser, L. (2005) "Promoting Psychological Health in Law Students", *Legal Reference Services Quarterly*, 24(1–2), 41–72.

Duffy, J., Field, R. and Shirley, M. (2011) "Engaging Law Students to Promote Psychological Health", *Alternative Law Journal*, 36(4), 250–254.

Durlak, J. A., Weissberg, R. P., Dymnicki, A. B., Taylor, R. D. and Schellinger, K. B. (2011) "The Impact of Enhancing Students' Social and Emotional Learning: A Meta-analysis of School-based Universal Interventions", *Child Development*, 82(1), 405–432.

Ecclestone, K. (2011) "Emotionally-vulnerable Subjects and New Inequalities: The Educational Implications of an 'Epistemology of the Emotions'", *International Studies in Sociology of Education*, 21(2), 91–113.

Field, R., Duffy, J. and Huggins, A. (2013) "Supporting Transition to Law School and Student Well-being: The Role of Professional Legal Identity", *The International Journal of the First Year in Higher Education*, 4(2), 15–25.

Galloway, K., Bradshaw, R., Dunbar, N. and Fellows, J. (2011) "Approaches to Student Support in the First Year of Law School", *Legal Education Review*, 21(2), 235–249.

Glenn, P. (1995) "Some Thoughts About Developing Constructive Approaches to Lawyer and Law Student Distress", *Journal of Law & Health*, 10(1), 69–77.

Glesner, B. A. (1991) "Fear and Loathing in the Law Schools", *Connecticut Law Review*, 23(3), 627–668.

Grover, S. (2008) "Personal Integration and Outsider Status as Factors in Law Student Well-Being", *Washburn Law Journal*, 47, 419–452.

Hall, K. (2009) "Do We Really Want to Know? Recognising the Importance of Student Psychological Wellbeing in Australian Law Schools", *Queensland University of Technology, Law and Justice Journal*, 9(1), 1–12.

Hardee, M. (2012) *Career Expectations of Students on Qualifying Law Degrees in England and Wales*, The Higher Education Academy, www.heacademy.ac.uk/resources/detail/disciplines/law/Hardee_InterimReport_2014FINAL (accessed 5 October 2018).

Hardee, M. (2016) *The Cohort Study of the Career Expectations of Students on Qualifying Law Degrees in England and Wales* http://ials.sas.ac.uk/sites/default/files/

files/About%20us/Leadership%20%26%20Collaboration/LERN/LERN_Hardee.pdf (accessed 18 July 2018).

Hedegard, M. (1979) "The Impact of Legal Education: An In-Depth Examination of Career-relevant Interests, Attitudes, and Personality Traits Among First-Year Law Students", *American Bar Foundation Research Journal*, 4(4), 791–868.

Holm, S. (2012) "Autonomy" in Chadwick, R. (ed) (2012) *Encyclopaedia of Applied Ethics*, 2nd edn, Burlington, San Diego and London, Elsevier.

Huggins, A. (2012) "Autonomy Supportive Curriculum Design: A Salient Factor in Promoting Law Students' Wellbeing", *University of New South Wales Law Journal*, 35(3), 683–716.

Ibrahim, A. K., Kelly, S. J., Adams, C. E. and Glazebrook, C. (2013) "A Systematic Review of Studies of Depression Prevalence in University Students", *Journal of Psychiatric Research*, 47, 391–400.

Iijima, A. (1998) "Lessons Learned: Legal Education and Law Student Dysfunction", *Journal of Legal Education*, 48(4), 524–538.

James, C. (2005) "Seeing Things as We Are. Emotional Intelligence and Clinical Legal Education", *International Journal of Clinical Legal Education*, 9, 123–149.

James, C. (2008) "'Lawyers' Wellbeing and Professional Legal Education", *The Law Teacher*, 42(1), 85–97.

Joels, M., Pu, Z., Wiegert, O., Oitzl, M. S. and Krugers, H. J. (2006) "Learning Under Stress: How Does It Work?", *Neuroscience & Biobehavioral Reviews*, 10(4), 152–158.

Jolly-Ryan, J. (2009) "Promoting Mental Health in Law School: What Law Schools Can Do for Law Students to Help Them Become Happy, Mentally Healthy Lawyers", *University of Louisville Law Review*, 48(1), 95–137.

Jones, E., Samra, R. and Lucassen, M. (2018) "The World at Their Fingertips? The Mental Wellbeing of Online Distance Learning Students", *The Law Teacher*, [early online access].

Kelk, N., Luscombe, G., Medlow, S. and Hickie, I. (2009) *Courting the Blues: Attitudes Towards Depression in Australian Law Students and Lawyers*, Sydney, Brain & Mind Research Institute.

Krannitch, J. M., Holbrook, J. R. and McAdams, J. J. (2009) "Beyond 'Thinking Like a Lawyer' and the Traditional Legal Paradigm: Towards a Comprehensive View of Legal Education", *Denver University Law Review*, 86(2), 381–404.

Krieger, L. S. (2002a) "Institutional Denial About the Dark Side of Law School and Fresh Empirical Guidance for Constructively Breaking the Silence", *Journal of Legal Education*, 52(1–2), 112–129.

Krieger, L. S. (2002b) "Psychological Insights: Why Our Students and Graduates Suffer and What We Might Do About It", *Journal of the Association of Legal Writing Directors*, 1(1), 258–265.

Krieger, L. S. (2008) "Human Nature as a New Guiding Philosophy for Legal Education and the Profession", *Washburn Law Journal*, 47(2), 247–312.

Larcombe, W., Finch, S. and Sore, R. (2015) "Who's Distressed? Not Only Law Students: Psychological Distress Levels in University Students Across Diverse Fields of Study", *Sydney Law Review*, 37(2), 243–273.

Larcombe, W., Tumbaga, L., Malkin, I., Nicholson, P. and Tokatlidis, O. (2013) "Does am Improved Experience of Law School Protect Students against Depression, Anxiety and Stress? An Empirical Study of Wellbeing and the Law School Experience of LLB and JD Students", *Sydney Law Review*, 35(2), 407–432.

Leathwood, C. and Hey, V. (2009) "Gender/ed Discourses and Emotional Subtexts: Theorising Emotion in UK Higher Education", *Teaching in Higher Education*, 14(4), 429–440.

Legal Education and Training Review (2013) *Setting Standards. The Future of Legal Services Education and Training Regulation in England and Wales*, http://letr.org.uk/the-report/index.html (accessed 29 September 2018).

Lester, A., England, L. and Antolak-Saper, N. (2011) "Health and Wellbeing in the First Year. The Law School Experience", *Alternative Law Journal*, 36(1), 47–49.

Macaskill, A. (2013) "The Mental Health of University Students in the United Kingdom", *British Journal of Guidance and Counselling*, 41(4), 426–441.

Norris, P. and Epstein, S. (2011) "An Experiential Thinking Style: Its Facets and Relations with Objective and Subjective Criterion Measures", *Journal of Personality*, 79(5), 1043–1080.

Oxford University Press (2010) *Oxford Dictionary of English*, 3rd edn, Oxford, Oxford University Press.

Parker, C. (2014) "The 'Moral Panic' Over Psychological Wellbeing in the Legal Profession: A Personal or Political Ethical Response?", *University of New South Wales Law Journal*, 2014, 37(3), 1103–1141.

Pekrun, R. and Linnenbrink-Garcia, L. (2014) "Introduction to Emotions in Education", in Pekrun, R. and Linnenbrink-Garcia, L. (eds), *International Handbook of Emotions in Education*, London and New York, Routledge.

Pritchard, M. E. and McIntosh, D. N. (2003) "What Predicts Adjustment Among Law Students? A Longitudinal Panel Study", *The Journal of Social Psychology*, 143(6), 727–745.

Rager, K. B. (2009) "I Feel, Therefore I Learn: The Role of Emotion in Self-directed Learning", *New Horizons in Adult Education and Human Resource Development*, 23(2), 22–33.

Regehr, C., Glancy, D. and Pitts, A. (2013) "Interventions to Reduce Stress in University Students: A Review and Meta-analysis", *Journal of Affective Disorders*, 148(1), 1–11.

Royal College of Psychiatrists (2011) *Mental Health of Students in Higher Education*, College Report CR166.

Ryan, R. M. and Deci, E. L. (2000) "Self-determination Theory and the Facilitation of Intrinsic Motivation, Social Development, and Well-being", *American Psychologist*, 55(1), 68–78.

Shanfield, S. and Benjamin, G. A. H. (1985) "Psychological Distress Among Medical and Law Students", *Journal of Legal Education*, 35, 65–75.

Sheldon, K. M. and Krieger, L. S. (2004) "Does Legal Education Have Undermining Effects on Law Students? Examining Changes in Motivation, Values, and Well-being", *Behavioral Sciences and the Law*, 22(2), 261–286.

Sheldon, K. S. and Krieger, L. S. (2007) "Understanding the Negative Effects of Legal Education on Law Students: A Longitudinal Test of Self-Determination Theory", *Personality and Social Psychology Bulletin*, 33(6), 883–897.

Sheldon, K. S. and Krieger, L. S. (2014) "Walking the Talk: Value Importance, Value Enactment, and Well-being", *Motivation and Emotion*, 38(5), 609–619.

Sherr, A. and Webb, J. (1989) "Law Students, the External Market and Socialization: Do We Make Them Turn to the City?", *Journal of Law and Society*, 16(2), 225–249.

Siptroth, S. M. (2007) "Forming the Human Person: Can the Seminary Model Save the Legal Profession?", *Brigham Young University Education and Law Journal*, 1, 181–198.

Skread, N. K. and Rogers, S. L. (2014) "Stress, Anxiety and Depression in Law Students: How Student Behaviours Affect Student Wellbeing", *Monash University Law Review*, 30(2), 564–587.

Skread, N. K. and Rogers, S. L. (2015) "Do Law Students Stand Apart from Other University Students in their Quest for Mental Health: A Comparative Study on Wellbeing and Associated Behaviours in Law and Psychology Students", *International Journal of Law and Psychiatry*, 42–43, 81–80.

Solkoff, N. (1968) "The Use of Personality and Attitude Tests in Predicting the Academic Success of Medical and Law Students", *Journal of Medical Education*, 43, 1250.

Steel, A., Huggins, A. and Laurens, J. (2014) "Valuable Learning, Unwelcome Assessment: What LLB and JD Students Really Think about Group Work", *Sydney Law Review*, 36, 291–322.

Student Minds (2017) *Student Voices*, www.studentminds.org.uk/uploads/3/7/8/4/3784584/170901_student_voices_report_final.pdf (accessed 12 October 2018).

Sturm, S. P. (1998) "From Gladiators to Problem-Solvers: Connecting Conversations About Women, the Academy and the Legal Profession", *Duke Journal of Gender Law and Policy*, 4, 119–147.

Sturm, S. P. and Guinier, L. (2007) "The Law School Matrix: Reforming Legal Education in a Culture of Competition and Conformity", *Vanderbilt Law Review*, 60(2), 515–553.

Tani, M. and Vines, P. (2009) ""Law Students" Attitudes to Education: Pointers to Depression in the Legal Academy and the Profession?", *Legal Education Review*, 19, 3–39.

Tett, L., Cree, V. E., Mullins, E. and Christie, H. (2017) "Narratives of Care Amongst Undergraduate Students", *Pastoral Care in Education*, 35(3), 166–178.

Thorley, C. "Not by Degrees. Improving Student Mental Health in the UK's Universities", Institute of Public Policy Research, September 2017, www.ippr.org/files/2017-09/1504645674_not-by-degrees-170905.pdf (accessed 13 October 2018).

Thornton, M. (2016) "Law Student Wellbeing: A Neo-liberal Conundrum", *Australian Universities' Review*, 58(2), 42–50.

Towness O'Brien, M., Tang, S. and Hall, K. (2011a) "Changing our Thinking: Empirical Research on Law Student Wellbeing, Thinking Styles and the Law Curriculum", *Legal Education Review*, 21(1–2), 149–182.

Towness O'Brien, M., Tang, S. and Hall, K. (2011b) "No Time to Loose: Negative Impact on Law Student Wellbeing May Begin in Year One", *The International Journal of the First Year in Higher Education*, 2(2), 49–60.

Tyng, C. M., Amin, H. U., Saad, M. N. M. and Malik, A. S. (2017) "The Influence of Emotions in Learning and Memory", *Frontiers in Psychology*, 8, 1–22.

Universities UK (2015) *Student Mental Wellbeing in Higher Education*. Good Practice Guide, www.universitiesuk.ac.uk/policy-and-analysis/reports/Documents/2015/student-mental-wellbeing-in-he.pdf (accessed 12 October 2018).

Wangerin, P. T. (1988) "Objective, Multiplistic and Relative Truth in Developmental Psychology and Legal Education", *Tulane Law Review*, 62(6), 1237–1301.

7 Creating an emotionally engaged legal academy

Introduction: the work of legal academics

No examination of the role of emotions within legal education is complete without reference to the role of legal academics. Previous chapters have demonstrated that the acknowledgement and inclusion of emotions within legal education can be characterised as a form of soft skill, an integral part of learning or a component of psychological wellbeing. Legal academics have a key role in influencing which characterisation (if any) is accepted and perpetuated within the law degree. In addition, not only do they mediate the learning experience of students and the design of the curriculum and wider learning environment, they also bring to the law school their own emotions. These may be generated by, and impact upon, each facet of their role, namely (for most), teaching, research and administration (Guth, 2009; Cownie, 2004). As such their own lived experience within the law school, together with the emotional experiences within their wider lives, all play a role in the varied and complex interplay between emotions and other aspects of legal education.

Nevertheless, despite this interconnectedness, there is some resistance to the notion of teaching having an emotional component. This argument is perhaps best captured by Fish within his argument that it is inappropriate for college and university teachers to involve themselves in trying to impart values to students or develop character:

> So what is it that institutions of higher learning are supposed to do? My answer is simple. College and university teachers can (legitimately) do two things: (1) introduce students to bodies of knowledge and traditions of inquiry that had not previously been part of their experience; and (2) equip those same students with the analytical skills – of argument, statistical modeling, laboratory procedure – that will enable them to move confidently within those traditions and to engage in independent research after a course is over.
>
> (Fish, 2008, pp. 12–13)

He argues that these two things provide teachers with objectives that they are trained for and which are achievable. Trying to do more, such as developing students' character or instilling particular values (or, in the context of this book, acknowledging and utilising emotions), will distract them from their core responsibilities and involve them in areas where they are untrained, inexperienced and are likely to do "a bad job at a job they shouldn't be doing at all" (Fish, 2008, p. 14). Fish acknowledges that it may be that along the way a teacher does in some way touch on a value or help shape a character (or gain some emotional understanding), but argues that this is merely a "contingent effect" and not something that should be aimed for, as such issues can become a subject for impartial analysis, but nothing more than that (Fish, 2008, p. 25). To explore the validity of this argument in relation to emotions, it is necessary to consider their relationship with teaching.

Teaching as an emotional occupation

> Good teachers are not just well-oiled machines. They are emotional, passionate beings who connect with their students and fill their work and their classes with pleasure, creativity, challenge and joy.
>
> (Hargreaves, 1998, p. 835)

Teaching, often through the delivery of lectures or seminars (Bone, 2009, p. 244) is a core component of the role of most legal academics. However, the role of emotions in teaching generally is under-acknowledged and under-theorised (Hyland, 2014). This is particularly the case in relation to higher education and most certainly in relation to legal education (Bromberger, 2010). In relation to teacher training, Rosiek mirrors the criticisms of the doctrinal tradition within legal education discussed in Chapter 1 when he refers to "a corrosive Cartesian assumption, a fantasy of an individual mind that acquires a mastery of certain concepts independent of any emotional, social, and cultural context" (2003, p. 399). In other words, the form of Cartesian dualism discussed in relation to legal education also pervades other areas of education and may well, therefore, be absorbed by educators (Sutton and Wheatley, 2003).

Despite the arguably fledgling nature of research into this area, a strong argument has been developed for the importance of the way teachers handle emotions within the classroom in relation to compulsory schooling, much of which can be translated into the higher education environment. The way teachers understand, regulate and utilise emotions within the classroom has been identified as playing a role in academic achievement, standards of behaviour and student wellbeing (Rosiek, 2003, p. 400). For example, Curci et al., in their study of junior high students in the USA, found that teachers' abilities in emotional intelligence were correlated to students' success in school, seemingly through their ability to "enhance the student's self-esteem and self-reported ability" (2014, p. 440). Meyer and Turner suggest that teachers can perform "emotional scaffolding" (2007, p. 244). Drawing on the constructivist concept of scaffolding learning they argue that providing positive emotional support can be used to encourage the students to attain a number of goals, including increased autonomy and wellbeing. The role of teaching in generating, influencing and managing emotions amongst students within higher education has also been recognised (Titsworth et al., 2010, 2013). In the law school setting, the importance of balancing the students' experience so that their emotions are stimulated, but not over-simulated, has been emphasised, in order to provide challenge within a safe space (Bromberger, 2010, p. 51).

As well as the role teachers and the classroom environment have in mediating the emotions of students, there is also increasing recognition of the role of teachers' own emotions within their work and wellbeing. In relation to compulsory schooling, Nias identifies three ways in which affect, including emotions, is "of fundamental importance in teaching and to teachers" (1996, p. 293). Firstly, Nias argues that the inter-relationship between cognition and emotions means that teachers can only fully develop their management skills and abilities within the classroom if they address their "emotional reactions and responses" and the underlying "attitudes, values and beliefs" which influence these (1996, p. 294). Sutton and Wheatley's (2003) discussion of the role of emotions in teaching also emphasises this point, suggesting that emotions can impact on teachers' cognitive functioning; for example, negative emotions can cause them to become distracted from their educational goals. It is also argued that emotions can affect memory, for example, prompting teachers to recall memories involving an emotional stimuli (such as an angry confrontation) more clearly. Conversely, teachers experiencing more positive emotions could be more productive in generating plans and strategies. More broadly, the weight of scientific evidence, discussed in Chapter 3, demonstrates that emotions and cognition are intertwined in all aspects of life, including compulsory schooling, higher education generally and the law school specifically (Damasio, 2006; Nussbaum, 2001; Lazarus, 1984; Arnold, 1960).

Harking back to Fish's argument (2008), to view emotions as irrelevant to teaching implies that teaching is a wholly cognitive process, in which emotions have no necessary or desirable role. However, the weight of scientific and educational evidence demonstrates that emotions and cognition are intertwined in a way which makes them inseparable. It also indicates that there are positive benefits to acknowledging and utilising emotions. Therefore, it is arguable that to seek to artificially separate emotions from cognition would impact on the very intellectual development of students which Fish views as the proper role of the academic. Cozolino and Sprokay suggest that the most successful educators are, in fact, "unwitting neuroscientists" who are able to use their skills to foster rich and supportive learning environments (2006, p. 11).

The second way in which Nias (1996) identifies that emotions are important in teaching is as a result of the way that teachers' feelings are engaged in their job – in the way they interact with pupils and colleagues, in their perception of educational policies and structures and in their views of professionalism. Hargreaves echoes this, referring to teaching as an "emotional practice" which "activates, colors, and expresses teachers own feelings, and the actions in which those feelings are embedded" (1998, p. 839; see also Meyer and Turner, 2007). In their study of ninety-seven higher education teachers in Finland, Postareff and Lindblom-Ylänne found that in interviews regarding teaching issues, where emotion was not explicitly raised as an issue, ninety-two of the teachers "described emotions in some way" during their interviews (2011, p. 803). The "*irretrievably* emotional" [author's italics] nature of teaching (Hargreaves, 2000, p. 812) will impact both on the teacher and on their students. For example, when students are asked to describe which teachers most influenced them, the qualities referred to are likely to include those with an emotional component, such as empathy and the ability to discern social cues (Jones et al., 2013). Nonverbal signals, competency in verbal communication and clarity displayed by teachers can all influence the levels of emotional support that students perceive as present, feeding into the notion that teachers must understand the role that feelings and emotions are playing in order to be able to utilise them and enable students to feel supported (Titsworth et al., 2010, 2013). Doing this can influence the overall classroom environment (such as by creating a calm, supportive space) and model appropriate behaviour and responses to students (Jones et al., 2013).

Within the law school, Juergens argues that legal academics have an important role to play in modelling the types of behaviour that will demonstrate to their students how to handle both "the emotional and rational aspects of lawyers' work" (2005, p. 414). Although this suggestion is being made in the more vocational USA context, the point that students are absorbing implicit messages about handling emotions appears applicable elsewhere as well, particularly in light of the changes in values identified by studies of law student wellbeing discussed in Chapter 6 (Sheldon and Krieger, 2004, 2007). Once again, the theme of suppressing emotions to "think like a lawyer" emerges with Juergens suggesting that students are taught "that it is better to be smart than passionate, that people who feel too deeply tend not to think too clearly, that a fine intellect can rationalise any position or state of affairs, no matter how outrageous or indecent or unjust" (2005, p. 417). Juergens suggests that developing well-rounded students requires the members of the legal academy to be more open with their emotions, for example, showing delight at a good result or showing sadness at a harrowing topic (see also Akinbode, 2013; Gates, 2000).

Building on the idea of emotional engagement, Akinbode (2013), in the context of teacher training, argues that it is important for teachers to be able to identify and explore the emotional experience of teaching, to enable them to reflect on their teaching practice. Although she acknowledges that it contradicts traditional notions of professionality and objectivity, she suggests that understanding the influence of emotions on responses can enable resulting subjectivities to be identified and avoided as appropriate. However, as such emotional literacy is usually not measurable, it may not be highly prized by policymakers (O'Connor, 2008). Teachers may instead feel the need to focus on content and performance measurement within the contemporary neo-liberal climate, but this can lead to emotional misunderstandings in relation to students (and also parents and colleagues) (Hargreaves, 1998). Such misunderstandings, and a failure to connect emotionally with others, can potentially lead to lower engagement and academic attainment amongst students (Jones et al., 2013), as well as a reduction in the intrinsic motivation of teachers (Sutton and Wheatley, 2003). Mirroring the discussion of the impact of extrinsic versus intrinsic motivation in Chapter 6, if teachers have less intrinsic motivation, this may impact on their performance, their level of engagement and their wellbeing (Ryan and Deci, 2000).

In relation to the possible link between emotions and the quality of teaching, a number of studies have taken place within higher education (Trigwell, 2012; Su and Wood, 2012; see also Moore and Kuol, 2007; Martin and Lueckenhausen, 2005). Trigwell's study of 175 Australian higher education teachers suggests there are "significant relations" between teachers' emotional experience of teaching and their chosen approach to teaching (2012, p. 607). Positive emotions were associated with a "student-focused approach" which could generate "more meaningful or deeper approaches to learning", whereas negative emotions were associated with a shallower "teacher-focused approach" (Trigwell, 2012, pp. 608, 617). It was acknowledged that this did not demonstrate a causality between the two factors (for example, the use of a more student-focused approach could itself generate the positive emotions). However, Trigwell speculates that this link could help determine the success or failure of the implementation of educational initiatives, reflecting the reference in Chapter 5 to staff buy-in as a determinant in the success of social and emotional learning programmes.

In the UK context, Su and Wood reported on the results of a qualitative study looking at essays submitted to the Higher Education Authority which demonstrate the perceptions undergraduate students have of a "good university lecturer" (2012, p. 142). As well as "being authoritative and expert in knowledge and skills" and other content-focused skills, the students also identified a number of attributes involving, or linked to, emotions, including "being passionate and inspiring" and "having a sense of humour (Su and Wood, 2012, pp. 147–149). As a result, Su and Wood conclude:

> There is, we argue, an elusive aspect to great teaching which is felt and experienced as much as seen. It is in part to do with passion . . . and also with a capacity to forge meaningful connectedness with students through empathy and, some would argue, love.
>
> (Su and Wood, 2012, p. 151)

This is an aspect of teaching which Fish's argument fails to capture. However, without this element, teaching appears to be more of a behaviourist construct, about mechanically meeting learning objectives, bereft of the richer, more valuable experience that emotions can provide. If teaching is an emotional experience, then a decision to ignore emotions in teaching is, in fact, a fundamental statement about the nature and form of teaching to be provided. By ignoring something that is present, it is not a case of avoiding including something, but of suppressing or disregarding something. In the case of emotions, it is something that has importance and value throughout teaching, learning and the wider educational experience.

A third way in which Nias (1996; see also Zembylas, 2007) argues that emotion is key in teaching within compulsory schooling is due to the way both emotions and cognition are closely inter-related with wider social and cultural factors which shape teachers' views of themselves and which, in turn, influence the social and cultural context within which they work. Hargreaves (1998) broadens this last point out further, referring to political factors which may influence the policies and practices of education and the lived experience of individual teachers. This point echoes the discussion of the neo-liberal university in Chapters 4 and 5 and the tensions between the focus on the personal and affective which is encouraged within a neo-liberal society and the instrumental manner in which this is characterised, focused on meeting the demands of the market (Clegg and David, 2006; Burke, 2015). For example, in relation to "employability" Clegg and David refer to the prevalence of Personal Development Planning (PDP) within higher education and its focus on developing generic skills for future life. Overall, they caution that:

> The project of the 'personal' and 'personalisation' cannot be read as ideologically neutral.
>
> (Clegg and David, 2006, p. 158)

However, rather than this leading to emotions being once again disregarded within teaching, this instead suggests that there is a need for a more detailed and nuanced examination of the role of affect (including emotions) which can draw on broader feminist, critical and humanist theories (Hey and Leathwood, 2009; Beard et al., 2007).

Examination of the social and cultural context of teaching also highlights the organisational confines of particular educational settings. This is a key factor which may influence the way in which teachers acknowledge and utilise emotions and it is an element which, previous chapters have demonstrated, legal academics have to navigating within the neo-liberal university. Hargreaves (2000), in a study of Canadian elementary and secondary school teachers, found that organisational patterns and professional norms around student-teacher interactions within these environments were problematic in terms of developing teachers' emotional understanding. The demands of a content-driven curriculum, the timetabling involving different teachers for each subject and notions of professionalism which prize emotional distance all appear to contribute to this. It is arguable that these points could all equally be applied to higher education where subjects are modularised and taught by different academics who are juggling a range of other commitments (Guth, 2009; Twining, 1997). Therefore, returning once more to Fish's argument, the remaining rationale for ignoring or suppressing emotions is that it is simply the most practically expedient approach given the pressures and time constraints placed on academics, a point which appears to fit in with Fish's suggestion that simply imparting knowledge is "at least a full time job" (2008, p. 13). However, this seeming expedience needs to be measured against the benefits of acknowledging and responding to emotions, which could potentially include a richer learning experience, higher rates of retention and improved student wellbeing (Galloway and Bradshaw, 2010; Sutton and Wheatley, 2003; Hargreaves, 1998; Nias, 1996).

Although the literature on emotions and teaching within the law school is very limited, one example of how the teaching role can be expanded upon to acknowledge and utilise emotions in practice is given by Galloway and Bradshaw in their report on the LLB at James Cook University in Australia and the work that has been done on integrating pastoral care into the curriculum to create a "student-centered, holistic approach to student welfare" (2010, p. 8). This includes tangible elements such as offering a workshop on legal writing during orientation week, referring to student support mechanisms in early lectures, allocating a personal tutor, using peer mentors (including a peer-assisted learning programme involving final year students, sending regular emails to develop social connectedness and providing detailed formative assessment. However, it also includes a "care factor" in the relationship between academics and students. Galloway and Bradshaw emphasise that this is not the same as expecting academics to undertake a counselling role, but "First Year Co-ordinators" from amongst the academic staff are identified to assist with students' practical needs (2010, p. 12). They argue that "in the authors' experience, the supportive aspect of the teacher's role is integral to success as a teacher" (Galloway and Bradshaw, 2010, p. 13). This approach mirrors the argument of Jacklin and Le Riche who argue for a change in the culture of legal education so that support for students becomes embedded into the curriculum (2009, p. 744). They argue that this enables the support provided to be "inclusive and proactive" rather than an add-on service for individual students (Jacklin and Le Riche, 2009, p. 744).

There is perhaps a valid argument that many academics within higher education are, at present, poorly equipped to take on such a role and to handle issues relating to emotions (Hughes et al., 2018; Moore and Kuol, 2007; Nelmes, 2000). This could particularly be the case in legal education because of its traditional suppression of, and disregard for, emotions (Maharg and Maughan, 2011; Abrams and Keren, 2010; Bromberger, 2010). Cownie (2011) discusses the traditional lack of formal training in teaching within the legal academy and questions the effectiveness of the training now provided (which does not appear to address emotions in any event). She argues that including discipline-specific training could assist in raising the profile of teaching amongst academics. There are possibilities for training to be offered and for academics to learn to equip themselves with such skills. For example, Baron when discussing the principles of humanist teaching theory espoused by Rogers (1983) argues that the required qualities are "not difficult to learn", although they do run counter to much existing academic staff development (Baron, 2002, p. 136). Postareff and Lindblom-Ylänne (2011, p. 804) note that a majority of the ninety-seven higher education teachers in their survey who had undertaken pedagogical training had positive emotions towards it, particularly in relation to the peer support involved, suggesting it could be a valuable avenue to explore. At the same time, if such training is going to be an expected part of the academic role, the personal investment in terms of the time, energy and resources individual academics must be acknowledged, and in some way repaid, to avoid a detrimental impact on wellbeing (Hughes et al., 2018). Once again, the notion of a more holistic form of legal education is important here, one which fosters a culture where such work and training is valued and nurtured.

Teaching, at any level and in any environment, is not a wholly cognitive activity as Fish (2008) appears to suggest. Instead it is one which engages the emotions of both the teacher and the students. To separate out cognition and emotion in teaching is to construct an artificial divide which may impact on the quality of teaching as well as teacher and student wellbeing. The institutional restraints on academics generally, and the culture of the legal academy which has traditionally disregarded emotions, may militate against the acknowledgement and inclusion of emotions on occasion, but there are also possible solutions to be found.

Administration and research: tensions and triumphs

Alongside teaching, research and administration form the nexus of academic life both generally and within the law school (Guth, 2009; Cownie, 2004; Bradney, 2003). Within the neo-liberal university, with its focus on auditing and measuring performance, research in particular has become increasingly important in terms of how law schools measure academic performance and outputs, with Collier suggesting that:

> What can be said with some confidence about law schools, however, is that for all institutions whose ambition is to be seen as part of a research-led university in the United Kingdom, it is now beyond question that the performance and research productivity of all legal academic staff has become crucial to the status, financial health and, perhaps, the very future of the law school itself.
>
> (Collier, 2002, p. 15)

There is an increasing acknowledgement that both the research and administration required in legal education have an emotional impact on legal academics, both in terms of the shifting focus of the law school as a whole and the pressures neo-liberalism engenders on individual academics. This strand of literature contextualises the emotions involved in such wider aspects of the academic role by characterising the university as a workplace, with all the accompanying potential for "pain, pleasure, frustration and fulfilment" (Woods, 2010, p. 172). In relation to the law school, Thornton argues that the pressure on academics to perform leads them to focus on work with measurable outputs, such as the publication of research and the supervision of PhD students. This leads to "pastoral care, including student advising and emotional management, work" becoming devalued and ignored (Thornton, 2001, p. 17; see also Collier, 2002). Thornton and Collier argue that this division is gendered, with the expectation that women will be involved in the caring, pastoral side leading to their role becoming increasingly invisible (Thornton, 2001; Collier, 2002; see also Lynch, 2010; Galloway and Bradshaw, 2010). The findings of Wells, based on her interviews with a number of female law professors, support this argument. She found that the "strongest theme" in interviews was "that women *believe that they take on more pastoral work* in universities" [author's italics] (Wells, 2002, p. 16). Cownie's survey of legal academics also found evidence of this with a fifth of respondents suggesting that "administrative burdens fell unfairly on women", particularly at the post-1992 universities (2004, p. 146). If this pastoral work (including the forms of personal tutoring suggested by Galloway and Bradshaw, 2010) is devalued it is arguable that this has potentially negative consequences for both the students who are seeking such support and guidance and the morale of those who are providing it without recognition (Thornton, 2011; Cownie, 2004). This leads Galloway and Bradshaw to argue that such work needs to be formally recognised and defined within the law school (2010), part of which would be appropriate training and guidance for legal academics performing this role.

With regard to the neo-liberal university's emotional impact on individual academics, Lynch argues that the neo-liberal focus on performance has led to "a type of Orwellian surveillance of one's everyday work by the university institution that is paralleled in one's personal life with a reflexive surveillance of the self" (2006, p. 11; see also Ball, 2003; Baron, 2007). In other words, people internalise the external focus on measurable, market-driven outputs and measure themselves against that criterion in a way which leads to "feelings of personal inauthenticity" (Lynch, 2006, p. 11). This argument reflects that of Ball, who argues that:

> The new vocabulary of performance renders old ways of thinking and relating dated or redundant or even obstructive. We must become adept at presenting and representing ourselves with this new vocabulary and its prescribed signifiers and the possibilities of being 'otherwise' to or within it are extremely limited.
>
> (Ball, 2003, p. 218)

Collier (2013) views this new way of presenting the self as one which has significant emotional consequences. Burrows suggests there is a "deep, affective, somatic crisis" in higher education, which he attributes to the new focus on metrics and accountability within higher education and the ensuing transformation of academic values into market-driven processes. He suggests that as a result academics are subject to a range of emotions, including shame, aggression and anxiety (Burrows, 2012, pp. 355–356). Leath and Heywood (2009) also identify similar emotions as being generated by the REF, emphasising the feelings of shame felt by academics whose work was not submitted, but also their retaliatory use of emotion to generate pride in their status as non-conformists, for example, by the formation of a social media group.

As well as the negative emotions engendered by neo-liberalism, Rowland also refers to the stifling of more positive emotions, in particular the "intellectual love" which an academic feels for their subject (2008, p. 353). His description of this is akin to the liberal conception of knowledge as holding value in itself, focused on love of knowledge and of the subject involved and of a collegiate working environment (Rowland, 2008; Bradney, 2003). He suggests that increased focus on accountability has undermined this love by forcing academics to focus on measurable outputs and performance as well as damaging the collegiality generated by a shared, intellectual focus, arguing that:

> The collegial relationships that sustain research are also perverted, becoming characterized by competition, greed and acquisitiveness rather than the kind of sociality that is a necessary part of intellectual love.
>
> (Rowland, 2008, p. 356)

As previously discussed, in relation to teaching, this could impact on the intrinsic motivation of academics. Ryan and Deci argue that "not only tangible rewards, but also threats, deadlines, directives, pressured evaluations and imposed goals diminish intrinsic motivation" (2000, p. 70). A focus on performance and outputs could therefore lead to a lessening of intrinsic motivation and an increase in extrinsic motivation, with similar detrimental consequences to academic wellbeing as discussed in relation to students (Allen and Baron, 2004, p. 288; Krieger, 2002, pp. 118, 125).

Grummell et al. argue that the type of academic prized in the new conditions of higher education is one who is "care-less" (2009, p. 192). In other words, one who has the freedom to attend conferences nationally and internationally and work whatever hours are required without commitments to family and friends (Collier, 2002). They argue that this disadvantages women, who are "significantly less likely" than men to be "care-less" (Grummell et al., 2009, p. 192). Lynch, in support of this view, argues that the origins of this "carelessness" in fact stems from the notion of Cartesian dualism which separates reason from emotions and prizes rationality in a way which fails to acknowledge the importance of "relationality" within academics lives (2010, p. 59). She suggests it has, therefore, previously formed an implicit part of liberal notions of higher education, but that under the dominant, neo-liberal ideology it is now the new norm – demanded and endorsed within higher education. Lynch argues that, to combat this focus on performativity, there is a need to build a "counter-hegemonic discourse" which creates a new vision for universities (2006, p. 16). Lynch's vision for this discourse focuses on notions of equality and democracy. Within the law school, it is arguable that the concepts of liberal and post-liberal legal education discussed in Chapter 1 could (and do) serve this purpose (see, for example, Guth and Ashford, 2014; Cownie and Bradney, 2005). However, this would seem at present to do little to acknowledge and include emotions, suggesting that relying on this alone would not take account of the affective impact of neo-liberalization as internalised by legal academics.

Interestingly, mirroring Ecclestone's (2004) concerns around the therapeutic agenda in relation to student learning, Hargreaves does suggest that an overly indulgent focus on emotional and personal dimensions of teaching could detract attention from important changes in the way their work is organised and structured. He argues that it is important to be "critical" in engagement with emotion to avoid sentimental and inauthentic diversions (Hargreaves, 2000, p. 812). Rosiek suggests that emotion has often been conflated with sentiment in critiques of teaching as a way of portraying teaching as "feminised" and, therefore, lower status (2003, p. 411). He argues that thinking and research on emotions in teaching needs to be documented to avoid this occurring. In addition, the types of humanist, feminist and critical discourses around emotions that can add nuance and depth to discussions on its role must continue to be incorporated (Beard et al., 2007; Clegg and David, 2006).

Although the preceding discussion of neo-liberalism and the changes in academic identity raises important issues in relation to the emotional experience and wellbeing of legal academics, certain qualifications must be made to the bleak picture presented herein. Both higher education generally, and law schools specifically, remain a diverse stratum, both within individual institutions, nationally and internationally (Jones, 2017; Fanghanel, 2012), meaning that the impact and practical effect of contemporary neo-liberal policies and expectations may vary considerably. In addition, as discussed in Chapter 4, Cownie and Bradney have characterised the response of the legal academy as one of "resistance" (2005, p. 278). Bradney has also argued that "thus far, legal academic culture has proved to be more important than market forces in decisions about the development of law as an academic discipline" (2003, p. 63). This may ameliorate some of the affective consequences discussed previously, although the only way to be certain of this will be for further work to be done in acknowledging and exploring the potentially emotionally damaging effects of the dominant discourses around research and administration.

Despite suggestions of resistance, there are clear indications that the contemporary discourse on research and administration is impacting on the wellbeing of academics. In the UK context, Kinman and Wray's "Survey of Stress and Well-Being Among Staff in Higher Education"[1] conducted for the University and College Union found that nearly three quarters of the sample surveyed strongly agreed or agreed with the statement "I find my job stressful" and over a half had high or very high general levels of stress (2013, p. 3). Overall, Kinman and Wray concluded that:

> On all but one of the Health and Safety Executive stressor categories, UCU members in higher education reported lower well-being than the average for those working in the target group industries (including education). The biggest 'well-being gaps' related to work demands, change management, management support and role clarity.
>
> (Kinman and Wray, 2013, p. 3)

In the USA context, Watts and Robertson's survey (2011) of literature on stressors in higher education supports the idea that increased student numbers can cause burnout, with other stressors identified including research, pressures on time and a diminishing sense of collegiality.

In relation to law schools specifically, Wilson and Strevens' 2015 survey of legal academics found that the large majority of the 185 participants fell within the normal range for stress, anxiety and depression using the DASS-21 (one of four self-report standardised measures applied). However, between 13% and 16% fell within the severe or very severe range, with a further significant minority displaying mild or moderate symptoms (the highest being 29% in that range in relation to stress) (Wilson and Strevens, 2018). Using the framework of self-determination theory, open-ended items identified factors impacting on psychological wellbeing to include a lack of autonomy, difficulties in living out their values and a sense of self-blame, which the authors indicate are linked to the shifting focus of higher education, including the consumerization of students, competition between institutions, demands for curriculum redesign, and increased requirements for accountability and high levels of performance in terms of both teaching and research (as well as income generation) (Wilson and Strevens, 2018; see also Franco-Santos and Doherty, 2017).

Perhaps unsurprisingly, given these demands and the lack of recognition of the relevance of broader relationships, many legal academics appear to have increasing issues with maintaining work-life balance. In relation to staff in higher education generally, Kinman and Wray identified that work-life balance was "poor" with a majority of survey respondents "unable to set an acceptable boundary between their home and work life" (2013, p. 3). Those staff in academic roles were found to have higher levels of stress, lower levels of wellbeing and more difficulties with work-life balance than those staff in academic-related roles. This mirrors the discussion of the increasing requirement for academics to be "care-less" as discussed previously (Lynch, 2010; Grummell et al., 2009). Indeed, Kinman and Wray attribute the problems suffered by workers in higher education to its massification and the pressures of market forces, as well as the use of fixed-term and casual contracts causing job insecurities (2013; see also Heath et al., 2017).

Cownie's earlier survey of legal academics found that they were split evenly in relation to the question "Do you find it easy to balance the demands of work and the rest of your life?" Those who agreed with the question either prioritised their family, had partners with equally demanding careers or felt that the flexibility involved in the role enabled them to manage their time. Those who did not find it easy to find a balance were again split, between those who attributed this issue to heavy workloads and those who viewed their work as a vocation which therefore "permeated the majority of their existence" (Cownie, 2004, pp. 113, 116). This suggests there may be dangers in a vocation becoming all-consuming. Just as law students may lose their sense of social connectedness and fail to make time for family and friends, the same could also apply to legal academics.

Emotional labour in teaching and learning

One way of interpreting these difficulties with work-life balance relates to the concept of emotional labour. This is an often-ignored element of academic life which spans teaching, administration and research and provides a theoretical lens for interpreting the role of emotions within the academy. The concept of emotional labour has been applied to both academics in higher education generally, and legal academics particularly (Heath et al., 2017; Bellas, 1999). It was originated by Hochschild who describes it as "the management of feeling to create a publically observable facial and bodily display" (2003, p. 7). She categorises this either as "surface acting", where a person deliberately and knowingly will "deceive others about what we really feel" and "deep acting", where a person also "deceives oneself" by altering their actual feelings (Hochschild, 2003, p. 34). Hochschild views both these forms of acting as having negative consequences in estranging people from their true feelings and relinquishing their "healthy sense of wholeness" (2003, p. 183). This could lead them either to separate their sense of self from their job role in a way which leads them to view their role as inauthentic or to burn out (Hochschild, 2003, p. 187).

Hochschild (2003) argues that for a job to include emotional labour it will have three key characteristics. Firstly, it will involve face-to-face (or voice-to-voice) contact with the public; secondly, it will require the worker to produce an emotional reaction in the other person; and thirdly, it will enable the employer (through training and supervision) to exercise a degree of control over the emotional activities of employees. Interestingly, although much of her focus is on non-professional occupations, she gives the example of lawyers as people who meet the first two criteria in their interaction with clients, but suggests they don't meet the third as their emotional work is not directly supervised, but moderated via professional norms and client expectations.

In relation to teaching generally, Schutz et al. (2006) argue that emotional labour is present as teachers "express, repress, or manufacture emotions based on a perceived need during particular transactions. . . . For instance, if a teacher's felt emotions and pedagogically desired emotions are not congruent, then the teacher needs to put forth great effort to display the desired emotions". They also link this to social and cultural factors, as discussed by Nias (1996) by suggesting that the perception of pedagogically desirable emotions will be influenced by these factors and that teachers need to be able to identify and understand this to deal with emotions in a way that is empowering.

Bellas (1999), discussing university professors generally, argues that they meet Hochschild's criteria as they have face-to-face contact with students (and others) and often seek to elicit an emotional reaction from them. This latter argument is not developed further in her work, and its validity arguably rests on whether or not emotions are accepted as a part of the academic's teaching practice. In relation to Hochschild's third criteria, Bellas suggests that although professors do have a degree of autonomy, their work is to some extent supervised by administrators, for example, through performance evaluations. It is arguable that this analysis could be extended to all academics who may, in fact, be subjected to more supervision at a more junior level, particularly within the neo-liberal university environment. In any event, it has now become an established pattern to treat self-supervision as adequate to fulfil this criteria (Kruml and Geddes, 2000).

Gates (2000) in interviews with nine USA professors, found that they often used "surface acting" in their interaction with students. For example, by displaying enthusiasm for a particular topic or when dealing with student disturbances in lectures they "frequently masked their feelings by the display of other emotions such as humor or by using actions and statements which convey emotional neutrality". He also identified that "deep acting" was used as well, for example, by attributing a display of anger by a student over a low grade to youth and immaturity, to enable them to deal with it calmly. Gates suggests that by managing their emotions in this way, professors are accepting the traditional view of emotion and reason as separate and privileging reason by "modeling the neutral, non-emotional, or rational response". Interestingly, however, he also found that whilst the professors interviewed explicitly ascribed to the preceding view of emotions, in actuality their use of emotions often resembled what he terms as a "constructivist" model of emotion, which intertwines emotions and cognition (Gates, 2000; see also Zembylas, 2007), for example, by seeking to create a supportive and caring environment and assisting students in dealing with uncomfortable feelings.

In their study of 164 English instructors at ten universities in China, Zhang and Zhu (2008) found that the participants engaged in "deep acting" the most and "surface acting" the least. They identified that surface acting was a contributing factor towards burnout, decreasing levels of satisfaction with their work, but that deep acting and authenticity had positive implications for participants. However, they note that "in Chinese culture, emotion and reason are conceived as continuous processes, with emotion entwining inextricably and equitably with rationality" (Zhang and Zhu, 2008, p. 109). Therefore, it is debateable whether this different philosophical approach to emotions will have influenced these results.

An analysis of more general discussions of their work by legal academics suggests that forms of emotional labour can arguably be perceived in a variety of aspects of their role. For example, in relation to teaching, Guth (discussing her first year as a law lecturer) states that:

> Lecturing is scary. Standing up in front of a lecture theatre full of students is daunting. I have met colleagues who are not at all fazed by it and others who, like me, get extremely nervous. Lecturing is undoubtedly a performance. I am not a natural performer.
>
> (Guth, 2009, p. 189)

Similarly, James's survey of legal academics in their first year of teaching identified two key pieces of advice to others. Firstly, the need to prepare carefully, and secondly, the importance of having (or being able to project) a "confident, relaxed" demeanour (James, 2009, p. 206). Thomas in his guide to law lecturing also advises, when giving a lecture, to "remember you are going onto a stage and giving a public presentation" one which, he argues "demands considerable entertainment skills" (Thomas, 2000, pp. 29, 33). In their interviews with a small number of the South African legal academy, Kotzé and Gravett noted that their questions designed to ascertain what individuals wanted to achieve when teaching students usually obtained responses relating to the emotional experience of teaching and the development of relationships with students. Their findings mirrored Cownie's 2004 conclusions by showing a focus on socio-legal studies, but also highlighted a "display of emotion and passion" in teaching practice (Kotzé and Gravett, 2013, p. 95). More recently, Heath et al.'s focus groups and interviews with (a relatively small sample) of sessional staff in Australian law schools identified emotional labour as being important within legal education, particularly in interactions between staff and students, in delivering content of the curriculum and in dealing with students' own wellbeing issues. The precarious nature of sessional employment was also identified as exacerbating this labour, for example, due to a lack of institutional support and professional development opportunities. Aligned to this, Constanti and Gibbs have also highlighted the use of emotional labour as a strategy for academics to conceal their true feelings, quoting an interview they conducted with a Cypriot faculty member who states:

> Somehow I feel that we are not allowed to be stressed, frustrated, it is the job and we have to do it and not complain about it.
>
> (Constanti and Gibbs, 2004, p. 246)

Although such emotional labour is usually portrayed as damaging to psychological wellbeing (Constanti and Gibbs, 2004; Hochschild, 2003), Hargreaves (in the context of compulsory schooling) suggests that the positive facets of emotional labour are often overlooked. He argues that "for many teachers, it is a labor of love. Classrooms would be (and sometimes are) barren and boring places without it" (1998, p. 840). He argues that emotional labour being used meaningfully to do the best job possible is rewarding and pleasurable. However, he acknowledges that it can become "negative and draining" when it is being used as a mask to comply with the demands of others (Hargreaves, 2000, p. 814). Therefore, the question of emotional labour and the legal academy is one which warrants further attention, to ascertain its consequences and ensure it does not become detrimental to wellbeing. This form of examination is particularly important given the way in which legal academics are (knowingly or unknowingly) modelling forms of behaviour to their students (Juergens, 2005).

Conclusion: leading by (emotional) example

The role of a legal academic is imbued with emotions in relation to teaching, research and administration. As such, it is inter-related with the emotional aspects of student learning and wellbeing and the emotional impact of wider changes within higher education. Failing to acknowledge the challenges to emotional and psychological wellbeing and the emotional labour currently embedded within law schools means that there is a lack of understanding and examination of these issues and an inability to challenge the potentially damaging demands and expectations currently impacting upon the legal academy. Although there is an increasing body of work considering how legal academics are "surviving" within law schools, conversations need to had around how to facilitate "thriving", promoting the wellbeing of individual members (Baron, 2007, p. 28). This in turn would impact on law student wellbeing by influencing the culture of legal education, promoting a more holistic and emotionally literate approach.

Within the existing literature, possible approaches to developing the emotional understanding and wellbeing of legal academics have included institutions incorporating a focus on the affective domain as a part of academics' professional development, for example, through the use of mentoring and mindfulness techniques and by encouraging individuals to develop daily reflective practices (Jones et al., 2013; Weare and Gray, 2003). At an institutional level, better workload management and changes in the educational culture are also likely to be required, drawing on humanist, feminist and critical insights (Naude et al., 2014; Kinman and Wray, 2013; Maharg, 2000). In terms of individual legal academics, Bradney argues that a liberal legal education requires "a personal response from the people engaged in it" due to the difficulty in separating work and life when engaged in a vocation (2003, p. 199). Such habits of self-reflection and self-examination are valuable and relevant (Galloway et al., 2011; Bradney, 2003). However, as discussed in Chapter 6, there is always the danger of solutions then being sought solely at the level of individuals, demanding that the "care-less" academic becomes the caring academic without sufficient training, support and encouragement being put in place to facilitate this (Grummell et al., 2009, p. 192). Once again, therefore, there is a need for emotions to be acknowledged and utilised at a broader level, throughout the law school, as part of a more holistic overall approach to legal education.

Note

1 Out of 24,030 surveyed, 14,667 primarily worked in higher education (Kinman and Wray, 2013, p. 10).

References

Abrams, K. and Keren, H. (2010) "Who's Afraid of Law and the Emotions?", *Minnesota Law Review*, 94(6), 1997–2074.

Akinbode, A. (2013) "Teaching as Lived Experience: The Value of Exploring the Hidden and Emotional Side of Teaching Through Reflective Narratives", *Studying Teacher Education*, 9(1), 62–73.

Allen, J. and Baron, P. (2004) "Buttercup Goes to Law School. Student Wellbeing in Stressed Law Schools", *Alternative Law Journal*, 29(6), 285–288.

Arnold, M. B. (1960) *Emotion and Personality. Volume 1 Psychological Aspects*, London, Cassell & Company.

Ball, S. J. (2003) "The Teacher's Soul and the Terrors of Performativity", *Journal of Education Policy*, 18(2), 215–228.

Baron, P. (2002) "Deep and Surface Learning: Can Teachers Really Control Student Approaches to Learning in Law?", *The Law Teacher*, 36(2), 123–139.

Baron, P. (2007) "Thriving in the Legal Academy", *Legal Education Review*, 17(1–2), 27–52.

Beard, C., Clegg, S. and Smith, K. (2007) "Acknowledging the Affective in Higher Education", *British Educational Research Journal*, 33(2), 235–252.
Bellas, M. L. (1999) "Emotional Labor in Academia: The Case of Professors", *The Annals of the American Academy of Political and Social Science*, 561, 96–110.
Bone, A. (2009) "The Twenty-First Century Law Student", *The Law Teacher*, 43(3), 222–245.
Bradney, A. (2003) *Conversations Choices and Chances the Liberal Law School in the Twenty-First Century*, Oxford and Portland, Oregon, Hart Publishing.
Bromberger, N. (2010) "Enhancing Law Student Learning – The Nurturing Teacher", *Legal Education Review*, 20(1–2), 45–57.
Burke, P. J. (2015) "Re/imagining Higher Education Pedagogies: Gender, Emotion and Difference", *Teaching in Higher Education*, 20(4), 388–401.
Burrows, R. (2012) "Living with the h-index: Metric Assemblages in the Contemporary Academy", *Sociological Review*, 60(2), 355–372.
Clegg, S. and David, M. (2006) "Passion, Pedagogies and the Project of the Personal in Higher Education", *Twenty-First Century Society*, 1(2), 149–165.
Collier, R. (2002) "The Changing University and the (Legal) Academic Career – Rethinking the Relationship Between Women, Men and the 'Private Life' of the Law School", *Legal Studies*, 22(1), 1–31.
Collier, R. (2013) "Privatizing the University and the New Political Economy of Socio-Legal Studies: Remaking the (Legal) Academic Subject", *Journal of Law and Society*, 40(3), 450–467.
Constanti, P. and Gibbs, P. (2004) "Higher Education Teachers and Emotional Labour", *International Journal of Educational Management*, 18(4), 243–249.
Cownie, F. (2004) *Legal Academics Culture and Identities*, Oxford and Portland, Oregon, Hart Publishing.
Cownie, F. (2011) "Twining, Teachers of Law and Law Teaching", *International Journal of the Legal Profession*, 18(1–2), 121–138.
Cownie, F. and Bradney, T. (2005) "Gothic Horror? A Response to Margaret Thornton", *Social & Legal Studies*, 14(2), 277–285.
Cozolino, L. and Sprokay, S. (2006) "Neuroscience and Adult Learning", *New Directions in Adult Continuing Education*, 110, 11–20.
Curci, A., Lanciano, T. and Soleti, E. (2014) "Emotions in the Classroom: The Role of Teachers' Emotional Intelligence Ability in Predicting Students' Achievement", *The American Journal of Psychology*, 127(4), 431–445.
Damasio, A. (2006) *"Descartes" Error*, London, Vintage.
Ecclestone, K. (2004) "Learning or Therapy? The Demoralisation of Education", *British Journal of Educational Studies*, 52(2), 112–137.
Fanghanel, J. (2012) *Being an Academic*, Abingdon and New York, Routledge.
Fish, S. (2008) *Save the World on your Own Time*, New York, Oxford University Press.
Franco-Santos, M. and Doherty, N. (2017) "Performance Management and Well-being: A Close Look at the Changing Nature of The UK Higher Education Workplace, *The International Journal of Human Resource Management*, 28(16), 2319–2350.
Galloway, K. and Bradshaw, R. (2010) "Responding to Changed Parameters of the Law Student: A Reflection on Pastoral Care in the Law School", *Journal of the Australasian Law Teachers Association*, 3(1–2), 101–112.
Galloway, K., Bradshaw, R., Dunbar, N. and Fellows, J. (2011) "Approaches to Student Support in the First Year of Law School", *Legal Education Review*, 21(2), 235–249.

Gates, G. S. (2000) "The Socialization of Feelings in Undergraduate Education: A Study of Emotional Management", *College Student Journal*, 34(4), 485–504.

Grummell, B., Devine, D. and Lynch, K. (2009) "The Care-less Manager: Gender, Care and New Managerialism in Higher Education", *Gender and Education*, 21(2), 191–208.

Guth, J. (2009) "The Case for Time Turners – The Practicalities of Being a New Law Lecturer", *The Law Teacher*, 43(2), 185–199.

Guth, J. and Ashford, C. (2014) "The Legal Education and Training Review: Regulating Socio-legal and Liberal Legal Education", *The Law Teacher*, 48(1), 5–19.

Hargreaves, A. (1998) "The Emotional Practice of Teaching", *Teaching and Teacher Education*, 14(8), 835–854.

Hargreaves, A. (2000) "Mixed Emotions: Teachers' Perceptions of Their Interactions with Students", *Teaching and Teacher Education*, 16(8), 811–826.

Heath, M., Galloway, K., Skead, N., Steel, A. and Israel, M. (2017) "Learning to Feel Like a Lawyer: Law Teachers, Sessional Teaching and Emotional Labour in Legal Education", *Griffith Law Review*, 26(3), 430–457.

Hey, V. and Leathwood, C. (2009) "Passionate Attachments: Higher Education, Policy, Knowledge, Emotion and Social Justice", *Higher Education Policy*, 22(1), 101–118.

Hochschild, A. R. (2003) *The Managed Heart: Commercialization of Human Feeling*, Berkeley, University of California Press.

Hughes, G., Panjwani, M., Tulcidas, P. and Byrom, N. (2018) *Student Mental Health: The Role and Experiences of Academics*, www.studentminds.org.uk/uploads/3/7/8/4/3784584/180129_student_mental_health__the_role_and_experience_of_academics__student_minds_pdf.pdf (accessed 14 October 2018).

Hyland, T. (2014) "Mindfulness-based Interventions and the Affective Domain of Education", *Educational Studies*, 40(3), 277–291.

Jacklin, A. and Le Riche, P. (2009) "Reconceptualising Student Support: From 'Support' to 'Supportive'", *Studies in Higher Education*, 34(7), 735–749.

James, H. (2009) "Supporting New Law Teachers – A Study to Determine Needs", *The Law Teacher*, 43(2), 200–208.

Jones, E. (2017) "One Size Fits All? Multiple Intelligences and Legal Education", *The Law Teacher*, 51(1), 56–68.

Jones, S. M., Bouffard, S. M. and Weissbourd, R. (2013) "Educators' Social and Emotional Skills Vital to Learning", *Kappan Magazine*, 94(8), 62–65.

Juergens, A. (2005) "Practising What We Teach: The Importance of Emotion and Community Connection in Law Work and Law Teaching", *Clinical Law Review*, 11(2), 413–424.

Kinman, G. and Wray, S. (2013) *Higher Stress. A Survey of Stress and Well-being Among Staff in Higher Education, University and College Union*, www.ucu.org.uk/media/5911/Higher-stress-a-survey-of-stress-and-well-being-among-staff-in-higher-education-Jul-13/pdf/HE_stress_report_July_2013.pdf (accessed 12 October 2018).

Kotzé, G. and Gravett, S. J. (2013) "Law Teaching: A True Vocation or Mere Prostration?", *The Law Teacher*, 47(1), 83–96.

Krieger, L. S. (2002) "Institutional Denial About the Dark Side of Law School and Fresh Empirical Guidance for Constructively Breaking the Silence", *Journal of Legal Education*, 52(1–2), 112–129.

Kruml, S. M. and Geddes, D. (2000) "Exploring the Dimensions of Emotional Labor: The Heart of Hochschild's Work", *Management Communication Quarterly*, 14(1), 8–49.

Lazarus, R. S. (1984) "On the Primacy of Cognition", *American Psychologist*, 39(2), 124–129.

Lynch, K. (2006) "Neoliberalism and Marketisation: The Implications for Higher Education", *European Education Research Journal*, 5(1), 1–12.

Lynch, K. (2010) "Carelessness: A Hidden Doxa in Higher Education", *Arts & Humanities in Higher Education*, 9(1), 54–67.

Maharg, P. (2000) "Rogers, constructivism and jurisprudence: educational critique and the legal curriculum", *International Journal of the Legal Profession*, 7(3), 189–203.

Maharg, P. and Maughan, C. (2011) "Introduction", in Maharg, P. and Maughan, C. (eds), *Affect and Legal Education. Emotion in Learning and Teaching the Law*, Aldershot, Ashgate Publishing, 1–10.

Martin, E. and Lueckenhausen, G. (2005) "How University Teaching Changes Teachers: Affective as Well as Cognitive Challenges", *The International Journal of Higher Education and Educational Planning*, 49(3), 389–412.

Meyer, D. K. and Turner, J. C. (2007) "Scaffolding Emotions in Classrooms", in Schutz, P. and Pekrun, R. (eds) (2007) *Emotion in Education*, Burlington, San Diego and London, Elsevier.

Moore, S. and Kuol, N. (2007) "Matters of the Heart: Exploring the Emotional Dimensions of Educational Experience in Recollected Accounts of Excellent Teaching", *International Journal for Academic Development*, 12(2), 87–98.

Naude, L., van den Bergh, T. J. and Kruger, L. S. (2014) "'Learning to Like Learning': An Appreciative Inquiry Into Emotions in Education", *Social Psychology of Education*, 17(2), 211–228.

Nelmes, P. (2000) *The role of the emotions in the discourse of teaching and learning*, EdD thesis, The Open University.

Nias, J. (1996) "Thinking about Feeling: The Emotions of Teaching", *Cambridge Journal of Education*, 26(3), 293–306.

Nussbaum, M. (2001) *Upheavals of Thought: The Intelligence of Emotions*, Cambridge, Cambridge University Press.

O'Connor, K. E. (2008) "'You Choose to Care': Teachers, Emotions and Professional Identity", *Teaching and Teacher Education*, 24(1), 117–126.

Postareff, L. and Lindblom-Ylänne, S. (2011) "Emotions and Confidence Within Teaching in Higher Education", *Studies in Higher Education*, 36(7), 799–813.

Rogers, C. R. (1983) *Freedom to Learn for the 80's*, New York, Macmillan.

Rosiek, J. (2003) "Emotional Scaffolding: An Exploration of the Teacher Knowledge at the Intersection of Student Emotion and the Subject Matter", *Journal of Teacher Education*, 54(5), 399–412.

Rowland, S. (2008) "Collegiality and Intellectual Love", *British Journal of Sociology of Education*, 29(3), 353–360.

Ryan, R. M. and Deci, E. L. (2000) "Self-determination Theory and the Facilitation of Intrinsic Motivation, Social Development, and Well-being", *American Psychologist*, 55(1), 68–78.

Schutz, P., Hong, J. Y., Cross, D. I. and Osbon, J. N. (2006) "Reflections on Investigating Emotion in Educational Activity Settings", *Educational Psychology Review*, 18(4), 343–360.

Sheldon, K. M. and Krieger, L. S. (2004) "Does Legal Education Have Undermining Effects on Law Students? Examining Changes in Motivation, Values, and Well-being", *Behavioral Sciences and the Law*, 22(2), 261–286.

Sheldon, K. S. and Krieger, L. S. (2007) "Understanding the Negative Effects of Legal Education on Law Students: A Longitudinal Test of Self-Determination Theory", *Personality and Social Psychology Bulletin*, 33(6), 883–897.

Su, F. and Wood, M. (2012), "What Makes a Good University Lecturer? Students' Perceptions of Teaching Excellence", *Journal of Applied Research in Higher Education*, 4(2), 142–155.

Sutton, R. and Wheatley, K. (2003) "Teachers; Emotions and Teaching: A Review of the Literature and Directions for Future Research", *Educational Psychology Review*, 15(4), 327–358.

Thomas, P. (2000) *Learning about law lecturing*, Warwick, National Centre for Legal Education.

Thornton, M. (2001) "Among the Ruins: Law in the Neo-Liberal Academy", *Windsor Yearbook of Access to Justice*, 20, 3–24.

Thornton, M. (2011) *Privatising the public university: The case of law*, Abingdon and New York, Routledge.

Titsworth, S., McKenna, T. P., Mazer, J. P. and Quinlan, M. M. (2013) "The Bright Side of Emotion in the Classroom: Do Teachers' Behaviors Predict Students' Enjoyment, Hope and Pride?", *Communication Education*, 62(2), 191–209.

Titsworth, S., Quinlan, M. M. and Mazer, J. P. (2010) "Emotion in Teaching and Learning: Development and Validation of the Classroom Emotions Scale", *Communication Education*, 59(4), 431–452.

Trigwell, K. (2012) "Relations Between Teachers' Emotions in Teaching and Their Approaches to Teaching in Higher Education", *Instructional Science*, 40, 607–621.

Twining, W. (1997) "Pericles and the Plumber", in Twining, W. (ed), *Law in Context: Enlarging a Discipline*, Oxford, Oxford University Press.

Watts, J. and Robertson, N. (2011) "Burnout in University Teaching Staff: A Systematic Literature Review", *Educational Research*, 53(1), 33–50.

Weare, K. and Gray, G. (2003) *What Works in Developing Children's Emotional and Social Competence and Wellbeing?*, Research Report RR456, Department for Education and Skills, http://webarchive.nationalarchives.gov.uk/20130401151715/www.education.gov.uk/publications/eOrderingDownload/RR456.pdf (accessed 9 October 2018).

Wells, C. (2002) "Women Law Professors – Negotiating and Transcending Gender Identities at Work", *Feminist Legal Studies*, 10(1), 1–38.

Wilson, J. C. and Strevens, C. (2018) "Perceptions of Psychological Wellbeing in UK Law Academics", *The Law Teacher*, 52(3), 335–349.

Woods, C. (2010) "Employee Well-being in the Higher Education Workplace: A Role for Emotional Scholarship", *Higher Education*, 60, 171–185.

Zembylas, M. (2007) "Emotional Ecology: The Intersection of Emotional Knowledge and Pedagogical Content Knowledge in Teaching", *Teaching and Teacher Education*, 23, 355–367.

Zhang, Q. and Zhu, W. (2008) "Exploring Emotion in Teaching: Emotional Labor, Burnout, and Satisfaction in Chinese Higher Education", *Communication Education*, 57(1), 105–122.

Conclusion

Feeling our way towards transformation

A holistic vision for the future

If this book were a journey, it would be more of a long haul flight than a hike through the local hills. The chapters have spanned varied and diverse terrains including the philosophical bases of the law, its practical applications, shifts within legal education in the UK and beyond, theories of emotions, the policies and politics of higher education (with a particular emphasis on neo-liberal discourses), learning theories, social and emotional learning and the mental wellbeing of both students and academics. However, at the core of this book is a key theme that remains constant throughout: *Emotions are important within legal education.* In fact, despite the inclusion of such potentially disparate topics, there is an amazing level of synchronicity in the way in which philosophy, neuroscience, psychology and educational theory all support this message. Wherever cognition is used, emotions are interacting with, and influencing, it. Where emotions appear not to be present it is because they have been actively suppressed or (knowingly or unknowingly) disregarded. Given the weight of scientific evidence, this is not the rational or reasoned approach to take. Instead, law schools should be considering how emotions can be acknowledged and utilised to provide a richer experience for all its stakeholders.

The law in its theoretical underpinnings, practical application and the roles played by legal actors frequently characterises itself as the embodiment of reason and rationality (Maroney, 2006), yet it is signally failing to acknowledge, let alone accept, the vast (and ever increasing) body of evidence that emphasises the value and importance of emotions. Within law schools, the doctrinal tradition epitomises law's suppression and disregard for emotions. Given that this has been the dominant approach to legal education since the nineteenth century (Sugarman, 1986), at least until recently, it has therefore largely characterised the treatment of emotions within legal education as a whole. This doctrinal approach evolved from a both pragmatic and ideological desire to give law, as an academic discipline, credibility and standing. To do this, it concentrated on developing a set of coherent and orderly legal principles as a form of scientific endeavour (Bartie, 2010; Sugarman, 1983). Its focus is on an (allegedly) neutral analysis of the law as it stands (Twining, 1997a), one which excludes emotions as being in opposition to reason and rationality. In recent years, the doctrinal tradition has come under sustained attack, with key critiques suggesting that the doctrinal tradition both relies on a flawed scientific basis and obscures hidden subjectivities and partiality (Conoghan, 2013; McCrudden, 2006; Bradney, 1998; Naffine, 1990). Its suppression of and disregard for emotions to preserve the so-called science of law has also been demonstrated to have a detrimental impact on law students (Goodrich, 1996; Kennedy, 1982). Nevertheless, despite these criticisms, many commentators still characterise the doctrinal tradition as being at the heart of the discipline of law (Hutchinson and Duncan, 2012).

Alongside the doctrinal tradition, the other key approach to legal education can be found in the liberal tradition. This views law as an independent intellectual discipline which is not defined by its relationship to the legal profession and which believes "knowledge is capable of being its own end" (Newman, 1994, p. 103). For proponents of a liberal legal education, it is the development of law students' intellectual faculties that are at the core of the law schools' mission. Knowledge will enrich and shape understanding, reasoning and intellect (Bradney, 2003; Nussbaum, 1997). A key characteristic of the liberal tradition is its critique of the narrow, inward focus of the doctrinal tradition (Cotterrell, 2002; Bradney, 1998). It also distances itself from the legal profession and the vision of undergraduate legal education as vocational preparation, although some commentators call for a form of compromise in this area (Hepple, 1996). Within some strains of liberal thought, an interest in the development of good citizens is expressly articulated (Burridge and Webb, 2009; Johnstone, 1999; Brownsword, 1999), whilst other liberal commentators focus on the development of individuals as critical thinkers (Bradney, 2003; Nussbaum, 1997). Although there have also been calls for a form of post-liberalism with a greater focus on ethics and values and, by implication, emotions (Burridge and Webb, 2007), overall, the liberal tradition echoes the doctrinal tradition in prizing what it perceives as neutrality and objectivity and emphasizing the importance of what the law characterises as reason and rationality (Burridge and Webb, 2009; Green and Lim, 1987).

Therefore, despite the significant differences that have been highlighted between the doctrinal tradition and the liberal tradition's views of the use and purpose of legal education, it is perhaps unsurprising that there is a striking similarity in their treatment of emotions. Although Bradney speaks of the liberal tradition as allowing law students to explore their "humanity" (1995), in fact, the focus appears to largely be on developing forms of rationality and reason which do not acknowledge or value emotions (Hyland, 2014; Lynch, 2010). The commentator who has moved closest to acknowledging the potential role of emotions is Webb, in his discussion of the "care why" of the law degree (Webb, 2006, p. 149). However, overall, the liberal approach has offered little to challenge the suppression and disregard of emotions by law schools. Instead, both the doctrinal and liberal traditions have steadfastly subscribed to the concept of Cartesian dualism by portraying emotions as irrational and potentially dangerous impulses, with cognition, characterised by reason and rationality, being required to keep them firmly in check (Descartes, 1989; Solomon, 2000). Emotions and reason are dichotomised and reason is valued at the expense of emotions.

That legal education can adapt and change in its approach to emotions is demonstrated by the development of the socio-legal studies movement. As we have seen, defining the term "socio-legal" has proved contentious. Its origins lie in the application of the social sciences to legal topics (Harris, 1983). However, it is now most commonly associated with a multi-disciplinary approach which looks at the "law in context" (Twining, 1997a, p. 23). The extent of socio-legal studies assimilation into the law degree, and its relationship with the doctrinal tradition have been widely debated (Sanders, 2015; Siems and Mac Sithigh, 2012; Cownie, 2004). Overall, the evidence appears to suggest that many academics have moved towards a more pluralistic approach, although the doctrinal tradition still plays an important role, even if its form has somewhat evolved (Siems and Mac Sithigh, 2012; Hutchinson and Duncan, 2012). The ability of law schools to encompass new approaches suggests a potential for insights regarding the role of emotions to be acknowledged and incorporated within their remit. In terms of the relationship between socio-legal studies and emotions, if a narrow definition of the socio-legal is taken then there appears to be little difference from a doctrinal or liberal approach. Although it allows for a wider curriculum and field of research, the only real acknowledgement of emotions appears to be in relation to eliminating subjectivities within empirical research projects (McCosker et al., 2001). However, if a broader definition of the socio-legal is taken then it could be viewed as encompassing a much wider spectrum, including critical legal studies, feminist jurisprudence and scholarship on law and emotions.

Both critical legal studies and feminist legal studies are based on an epistemology which challenges the mainstream acceptance of Cartesianism and relies on a constructivist viewpoint (Conoghan, 2013; Hey and Leathwood, 2009; Williams, 1993). In terms of legal education, this challenges its focus on neutrality and objectivity in a way which implies that emotions (alongside other forms of subjective experience and knowledge) do have value. However, these arguments are highly contested and there is no clear method to translate these to legal studies (Sherry, 1996). Nevertheless, both critical legal studies and feminist legal scholars have contributed to debates on legal education. Although the critical legal studies movement has had little impact in the UK overall, its critique of the emotional impact of the doctrinal tradition on students has been significant (Goodrich, 1996; Stanley, 1988; Kennedy, 1982). The feminist legal studies movement appears to have had a wider impact in the UK and, in particular, offers a fuller critique of education generally (Menkel-Meadow, 1988). The different phrases of feminist thought (as characterised by Naffine, 1990) each demonstrate different challenges to mainstream legal practices and legal education (Bromberger, 2010; Sturm, 1998; Rhode, 1993). Overall, they recognise education, pedagogy and agency as having passionate components and thus fundamentally question the traditional binary split between emotions and reason. In doing so they challenge the Cartesian formulation which has conventionally underpinned the foundations of Western rationality (Hey and Leathwood, 2009, p. 22).

In terms of law schools, these feminist critiques have led to some individual and useful suggestions for reform but, more importantly, it has also fed into a growing body of scholarship on law and emotions. Law and emotions scholarship is based on the premise that emotions can and should be studied in the legal context and takes the approach of applying a perspective grounded in the theory or study of emotions. This scholarship has considered a variety of aspects of law such as decision-making and the application of emotion to specific legal doctrines (Maroney, 2006). As we have seen, Abrams (2009) traces the different trends or currents within scholarship on law and emotions and considers potential objections to the use of emotions within law. Both her survey and Grossi's later discussion suggest that there is still no universal acceptance of emotions as a suitable topic for legal scholarship (Grossi, 2015; Abrams, 2009). This is reflected in the context of legal education by the way in which both the doctrinal tradition and liberal tradition largely disregard or suppress emotions. It is also illustrated by the fact that there is very little writing on the role of emotions within law schools, suggesting that the scholarship in this area is still at the stage of seeking recognition of its validity and worth (Maharg and Maughan, 2011; Bromberger, 2010; Abrams, 2009). Therefore, although socio-legal studies, defined as encompassing critical legal studies, feminist legal studies and scholarship on law and emotions, offers the potential for a far greater acknowledgement and use of emotions within legal education, at present the literature on this topic is too sparse to provide a full (or even partial) justification for this. It is this gap which this book aims, at least in part, to fill by demonstrating the relevance, importance and value of emotions to law schools.

What the critical, feminist and law and emotions literature acknowledges, sometimes explicitly, sometimes implicitly, is the evolving philosophical and scientific conceptualisations of emotions. The clearest manifestation of Cartesian dualism can be seen within basic emotions theory from its development via James (1884) and Darwin (1890) to its contemporary framing by Ekman (1992). The emphasis on the universal nature of emotions, their evolutionary origins and physiologically programmed nature has echoes of Cartesian dualism. It also mirrors traditional notions of a form of hierarchy within the brain with emotions (in the limbic system) being regulated by reason and rationality in the cortex (Damasio, 2006; MacLean, 1949). However, even basic emotions theorists demonstrate an acknowledgement that emotions may be influenced by social or cultural factors, suggesting an increasingly nuanced understanding (Coplan, 2010). The concept of appraisal theory has also challenged the dominance of Cartesian dualism (Gendron and Feldman Barrett, 2009). This theory views an emotion as generated as a result of an individual's perception and appraisal of an object or situation (Moors, 2014). Some forms of appraisal theory mirror Cartesian dualism in viewing emotions as non-cognitive. However, the contrast lies in their argument that emotion and cognition (including reason and rationality) are inter-related (Ellsworth, 2013; Oatley et al., 2006). An emotion viewed as having a cognitive element in their generation and as being a necessary influence on cognition which assists with decision-making and other processes (Bandes and Blumenthal, 2012; Damasio, 2006). Drawing on appraisal theory, several commentators have developed the idea of an inter-relationship between emotions and cognition further and have instead suggested that emotions can be perceived as an actual part of cognition: in other words, that emotions consist of cognitive, evaluative judgements (Nussbaum, 2001; Lazarus, 1984). For social constructivists these are judgements that are constructed through the social environment an individual is part of (Feldman Barrett, 2017; Averill, 2004).

Much contemporary philosophical and scientific work focuses on the idea of emotions as either intertwined with, or even part of, cognition. It is clear and well-evidenced that emotions are more than irrational impulses and have a value and worth within processes of reasoning and rationality (Coplan, 2010). As Oatley et al. explain:

> To be functioning members of society, our emotions need to be in working order in relation to each other, so that they may guide our reasoning and action wisely. One of the most striking qualities of emotion is how they influence our reasoning.
>
> (Oatley et al., 2006, p. 259)

Getting the key stakeholders in legal education to consider and accept this form of "emotions and reason" approach is key to the acknowledgement of emotions in law schools. As the purveyors of reason and rationality, if law schools fail to explore, analyse and evaluate the role of emotions within legal education then they are failing in their cherished function.

Perhaps some acceptance of this argument can be found within movements towards some limited acknowledgements of emotions within legal education, particularly within the USA (see, for example, Silver, 1999). However, to date, the limited and partial ways that legal education has recognised the potential of emotions demonstrates several ironies. Firstly, in that discussion around emotions will often revolve around the concept of "emotional intelligence" (Goleman, 1996). This disregards the widespread criticism of this concept in the scientific community and the differing models it encompasses (Murphy and Sideman, 2006). Secondly, through the shifting perceptions which mean that the doctrinal tradition, (originally a way to set the study of law apart from its messy, real-life practice) is now commonly linked to vocational forms of legal education (Stropus, 1996) which are more likely to acknowledge, and even perhaps, ascribe a form of value to emotions, as a form of so-called soft skill.

The notion of "soft skills" is one that lacks definitional clarity, but tends to encompass those skills which are not formally incorporated into, or assessed within, the curriculum (Chamorro-Premuzic et al., 2010, p. 211). These commonly have some form of vocational quality, linking them to employability (Andrews and Higson, 2008, p. 419). The changing landscape of higher education from an elite to a mass system, and the growth and dominance of a neo-liberal ideology which prizes market forces above all else whilst imposing strict controls and forms of standardisation upon the public sector (Bessant et al., 2015; Blalock, 2014; Ball, 2009), have all raised the profile of such soft skills within higher education. This is important because it once again demonstrates the relevance of emotions as part of a contemporary skillset within both higher education and also the workplace (Pertegel-Felices et al., 2014). More than that, it raises the possibility of emotional competencies being included within the growing skills agenda as neo-liberalism views emotions as expedient tools in creating attachment to neo-liberal ideology and increasing productivity (D'Aoust, 2014; Kiersey, 2014).

Whilst this potential should not be ignored, its ideological basis is problematic. Although the law degree has shifted towards the inclusion of more vocational "lawyering" skills, there is a lack of consensus and uniformity over which skills should be incorporated, and to what extent (Harris and Beinart, 2005). Overall, the response of universities to neo-liberalism is contested (Shore and Davidson, 2014; McArthur, 2011). Within law schools there is evidence of resistance to neo-liberal initiatives amongst the legal academy (Bradney, 2011; Cownie and Bradney, 2005). The focus of neo-liberalism on market forces is more likely to fit with forms of legal education which focus on vocational training, rather than those with more liberal ends (Cownie, 2010; Collier, 2004). Therefore, although skills should not automatically be equated with vocationalism, if emotions are to be incorporated into the law school as a form of skill, the implications for the overall direction of legal education need to be considered. The use of emotions in this way also appears to disregard broader conceptualisations of emotions by failing to acknowledge their role in developing or nurturing relationships (Burke, 2015; Lynch, 2006). The neo-liberal individual is characterised as autonomous and self-reliant, using cognition to manage emotions for greater productivity in a way which does little to challenge the notion of Cartesian dualism (Lynch, 2006).

It may be that some law schools who favour a vocationally orientated provision could seek to use the notion of "soft skills" as a way to begin the acknowledgement of emotions. However, the ideological underpinning and shallow characterisation of emotions usually involved means that in order to incorporate a wider vision of the role and value of emotions, it is necessary to consider other ways in which they play an (often unacknowledged) role within legal education. The shift away from traditional, transmissional forms of teaching in law schools towards student learning and student-centred models (Davies, 1998) lends fresh impetus for a theoretical examination of how learning occurs, and a broad literature has developed on the links between emotions and learning generally, often with a focus on social and emotional aspects of learning in compulsory schooling (Pekrun and Linnenbrink-Garcia, 2014; Schutz et al., 2007). In terms of specific learning theories, there are clear parallels between both classical and neo-behaviourist theories and the doctrinal tradition of legal education, with both upholding notions of Cartesian dualism and perceiving emotions as, therefore, irrelevant (Boghossian, 2006; Curzon, 2004). However, this focus solely on measurable outputs and disregard for the cognitive processes involved is now marginalised and viewed as being of very limited application (Illeris, 2009; Boghossian, 2006). Cognitive theories, considering how individuals process and interpret information (Yilmaz, 2011), have commonly focused on the mental activity involved in learning, viewing such cognitive processes as detached from emotions and physicality (Bredo, 1997). Constructivist learning theories are closely aligned to these, but their key distinction is in the constructivist conceptualisation of knowledge as created, rather than acquired (Ertmer and Timothy, 2013). In other words, it is the learner's experiences, and their perception of these experiences, which have value in an educational setting (Boghossian, 2006). Despite criticism of their epistemological basis (see, for example, Kotzee, 2010) these have now become dominant within higher education (Cullen et al., 2002).

Although there is a limited amount of literature linking cognitive and constructivist learning theories to emotions (Pons et al., 2011), it has been suggested that both cognitivist and constructivist theories of learning currently continue to uphold the notion of Cartesian dualism by separating the cognitive from the emotional (Immordino-Yang and Damasio, 2011). It is extremely questionable how feasible it is for this to continue when faced with the increasing evidence that cognition and emotions are inter-related, for this implies that emotions must have a role to play within the student's construction of their experience and mental processing (Garrison, 1998). To date, the learning theories which have most clearly acknowledged emotions are those within the humanist tradition (Knowles, 1984; Rogers, 1957). Their perception of learning as a holistic process involving the whole being explicitly accords a value and importance to the role of emotions (McIntosh, 2010; Krieger, 2008). Therefore, although the notion of incorporating emotions into learning within formal education can still be viewed as "curious and potentially risky" (Gregory, 2006, p. 115), there are theoretical foundations to draw on in doing so, and there are also signs that both cognitivist and constructivist learning theories can (and should) include a role for it.

Overall, there appears to be an acceptance within higher education that emotions play an inescapable role in learning (Hey and Leathwood, 2009; Beard et al., 2007). What is more contentious is how they should be conceptualised, given the dominance of the neo-liberal paradigm (Hey and Leathwood, 2009; Clegg and David, 2006). It is also questionable whether this acceptance has yet permeated the law school (Maharg and Maughan, 2011). This is despite the narrow conception of legal education focused around "thinking like a lawyer" (Krannitch et al., 2009, p. 381) increasingly being challenged as inadequate and insufficient (Cownie, 2004; Bradney, 1998). Within the law schools, there has traditionally been a lack of regard for educational theory (Cownie, 2000), exacerbating the danger of emotions solely being characterised as a form of soft skill. However, there is a small amount of literature arguing for the incorporation of humanist learning theories (Vanistendael, 2006; Maharg, 2000) suggesting an increasing openness to the acknowledgement of relevant ideas. It is important for these richer, humanist insights to be drawn upon, alongside feminist and critical perspectives, to avoid a shallow or inadequate conceptualisation of emotions.

As well as the integral part emotions play within learning, they are also present within the law school through the embodied, living experience of its students both inside and outside the learning environment (Towness O'Brien, 2011a; Hall, 2009; Jolly-Ryan, 2009; Grover, 2008). Studies in the USA and Australia have largely demonstrated that law students suffer from disproportionately high levels of psychological distress which appears to be specifically linked to their law school experience (Sheldon and Krieger, 2004, 2007; Bergin and Pakenham, 2015). The sparser evidence in the UK context points to similar findings (Jones et al., 2018). The emotions students experience in their individual learning, their wider university experience and through their personal circumstances will all impact on levels of wellbeing. Their ability to regulate and manage their emotions will also influence their longer-term mental health. Factors identified as influencing law student wellbeing in the USA and Australian contexts are varied, but include, amongst others, issues such as academic pressure, a reliance on extrinsic motivation and a lack of social connectedness (Skread and Rogers, 2014; Galloway et al., 2011; Tani and Vines, 2009). The idea of "thinking like a lawyer" appears to contribute towards a decline in wellbeing, with evidence suggesting that it can lead to a form of detachment and de-personalisation which suppresses creativity, emotions and the acknowledgement of values and moral issues (James, 2008; Allen and Baron, 2004; Krieger, 2002). It has also been argued that this idea is sufficiently deeply embedded within law schools to generate a shift in law students' thinking patterns, in a way which can lead to emotions being disregarded and can cause students to become isolated and depressed (Towness O'Brien et al., 2011b). The consequences of such a decline can include learning being inhibited (Galloway et al., 2011), increased disengagement (Bromberger, 2010) and long-term psychological damage (Grover, 2008).

> There is an urgent need to raise the profile of emotion in the learning and teaching of law to bring the topic into mainstream teaching and to build capacity amongst all law teachers to engage in emotional work in a sustainable way. We must look beyond the traditional thinking like a lawyer, to embed within law teaching feeling like a lawyer in a way that might genuinely break with tradition.
>
> (Heath et al., 2017, p. 451)

If learning is inherently emotional in nature, then so is teaching. Emotions are intertwined with cognition in relation to teachers' classroom and management skills (O'Connor, 2008; Schutz et al., 2007). The act of teaching also engages teachers' feelings and requires emotional understanding from them (Jones et al., 2013; Zembylas, 2007). Emotions interact with social, cultural and political factors shaping teachers' views of themselves and the context in which they work (Hargreaves, 1998; Nias, 1996). In addition, within higher education, there is an increasing recognition of the emotional components of both administration and research. The neo-liberal focus on measurable outputs has led to a devaluing of pastoral work which is gendered in nature, and damaging to wellbeing

(Lynch, 2010; Thornton, 2001). The pressure to perform in terms of research productivity can generate a range of negative emotions and a stifling of more positive emotions (Burrows, 2012; Rowland, 2008), and lead to feelings of personal inauthenticity (Ball, 2003). The emphasis is on the academic as "care-less" in a way which disregards emotion and relationships (Grummell et al., 2009, p. 192). Whilst the evidence of resistance to neo-liberalism within the academy may ameliorate some of these impacts (Cownie and Bradney, 2005), research into the wellbeing of members of the academy indicate high levels of stress (Wilson and Strevens, 2018; Kinman and Wray, 2013; Watts and Robertson, 2011). There is also a growing recognition of the emotional labour involved within the role of the academic (Schutz et al., 2006; Gates, 2000; Bellas, 1999). It appears likely that these findings relating to the wider academy are also replicated in the legal academy (Heath et al., 2017) and that issues with work-life balance permeate both the academy generally and the legal academy in particular (Kinman and Wray, 2013; Cownie, 2004).

Anecdotally, within the legal academy, there are suggestions that emotions are irrelevant to the role; that they form part of pastoral initiatives which belong to the shadowy remit of Central Services or the Students Union. This is akin to Fish's argument (2008) that wider issues such as character development are not part of a teacher's role. Once again, this returns to the comfort of Cartesian dualism with its assumption that emotions are irrational and misleading. It does not acknowledge the body of evidence which demonstrates that emotions are present in all aspects of the life of the law school. Legal education, by design or by default, has made a series of choices in relation to emotions which have impacted on, and continue to influence, law schools' teaching and learning, management and policy, staff and students, wellbeing and values. This impact and influence has often been detrimental and damaging. At best, it leads to a shallower experience for its key stakeholders as the importance and value of emotions is not engaged with and utilised. At worst, it is damaging to those involved in legal education and provides an incomplete and inadequate experience. A shift towards a holistic form of legal education which acknowledges and values emotions would require a far greater change than the incorporation of emotions as just forms of a vocationally orientated soft skill. However, this type of holism would allow for a far richer conceptualisation of emotions within the law school. One which draws on insights from humanist, feminist, critical and other explorations of emotions and is not reliant on neo-liberal discourse for its rationale. One which is transformational in both institutional and individual experiences.

What, why and how?

Some years ago, William Twining (1998; 1994) memorably created the University of Rutland, a fictitious institution whose law school, from secretaries to curriculum to library resources, held a mirror up to many of legal education's strengths and weaknesses. If such an institution still exists, it is no doubt now wrestling with the intricacies of REF and TEF. However, I would question whether it has changed its approach to one key area, that of emotions. There is, quite probably, a counselling service offered to all students, which would warrant a one-sentence mention in the law school's myriad webpages (somewhat obscured by the images of students mooting and conducting valuable work experience). Perhaps also a student video which touches on the great support they have received from friends or lecturers, to show the "human face" of the law school. So far so conventional and familiar, but also so very lacking.

Law schools are offering an impoverished and shallow version of legal reality to their students. By failing to acknowledge and incorporate emotions they are failing to engage with the essence of law's subject matter, the deluge of affect that swirls around legal offences, transactions, rhetoric and actors. They are ignoring (or perhaps ignorant of) the plethora of scientific evidence demonstrating that emotions and cognition are intertwined and are instead seeking refuge in the certainty of Cartesian dualism. To work for change and recognition there needs to be an awareness that this approach, this choice, is becoming increasingly unfeasible and unsustainable. It may well be that the increasing evidence of poor wellbeing across law students and the legal academy is the catalyst for this realisation, but the danger still remains that such "touchy feely" elements will be relegated to the realm of the administrative and pastoral and carefully compartmentalised to avoid tainting what is perceived as the pure rationality and reason of law.

So, what is the alternative? The solution will not be the same for each law school – instead it will need further discussion and debate at both theoretical and practical levels; between and within law schools and jurisdictions; around pedagogies and resources, values and aims, policies and politics. However, were the University of Rutland to wish to begin on this journey immediately, there are already some models of good practice it could look to and draw upon to begin this journey towards transformation. At the heart of these models is an awareness and understanding that emotions (and inter-related aspects of wellbeing and mental health) are vitally important to the law school's mission. They are not an irrelevance or even a simply pastoral issue. Instead, emotions are an integral part of the whole experience of studying law and therefore their role in each facet of legal education in every single law school needs to be examined and evaluated carefully. This may not be an immediate or easy discussion to navigate, but there are small initial, evidence-based steps that can be taken towards it.

To begin with (very aptly), there is evidence of the value of an induction programme which incorporates wellbeing (and, by extension, emotions), giving students the clear message that these are integral parts of legal education. This could encompass not only self-care techniques in relation to study and physical and mental wellbeing, but also the broader message that "thinking like a lawyer" should not (and cannot) involve simply switching off or ignoring emotions. For the more vocationally orientated law school, this could perhaps be via early references to the role of emotional competencies within lawyering, but by far the stronger approach is to foster a more nuanced approach, encouraging emotional awareness and self-reflection which begins with the induction and spans the whole of the law degree and its curriculum (Bannerjee et al., 2014). Part of this could also be around fostering collaborative ways of working, at a point where students are potentially keen to make new acquaintances and work with others. It could also involve challenging the academic competitiveness which pervades law and instead ask students to define what they perceive as success, bringing into the open and challenging some of the mythologies that pervade law schools (such as the need for a 2:1 classification).

As students move through the induction and on to the study of specific courses or modules, the activities that are provided, particularly at an early stage, are key to continuing to develop emotional awareness and reflection. If students are immediately introduced to a passage of case law or legislation to analyse and deconstruct, the first message they will absorb about law is around the primacy of a certain, rigid form of reason and rationality. If, instead, they are asked to reflect upon why that case or statute came into existence and what those involved feel about it, they are instantly being asked to accept a wider concept of law which is concerned with the people (and, by extension, the emotions) it envelopes. Similarly, if students are asked to take part in writing an analysis of a legal word or phrase, they are immediately accepting the need for an impersonal objectivity which may be unachievable and undesirable. If, instead, they are asked to begin by writing a narrative piece, as learners they are being asked to draw upon their own experience to develop their learning. Something that chimes well with the key tenets of constructivist and humanist styles of education.

Across the law degree, a range of pedagogic techniques could be used to encourage an awareness and understanding of the relevance of emotions within both the content and practice of law and the process of learning. This could involve, for example, the development, and reframing as necessary, of the role of personal tutors (Galloway and Bradshaw, 2010), the inclusion of narratives and storytelling (Watkins, 2011), the redesigning of the curriculum for core subjects (Baker, 2008) and the expansion of the role of clinical legal education and community legal engagement (Hall and Kerrigan, 2011). In short, approaches to teaching and learning which support students' emotional development and foster social connectedness could be embedded within and throughout the curriculum and across the law degree (Council of Australian Law Deans, 2013; Larcombe et al., 2013; Iijima, 1998). The more these become embedded within the "traditional" curriculum, the less they will be singled out by students as counter to legal study. Instead, the aim is for such emotional literacy to become accepted, even prized, as a key component of legal education.

For the academics involved, there will be a careful path to be navigated to avoid increasing the emotional labour involved in teaching and to ensure they are well-equipped to deliver such a holistic curriculum. To facilitiate this, appropriate training, a focus on mentoring and an emphasis on critical self-examination (Jones et al., 2013; Cownie, 2004) will all be valuable. It is also necessary for there to be an element of managerial and leadership buy-in to validate the notion of emotions as valuable. This may well be possible in an era where neo-liberalism has, to some extent at least, colonised the inner lives of both academics and students for the purposes of employability and productivity. At the same time, it is vital that these do not become the sole ends of the presence of emotion in the law school. They may be happy by-products, but the true value can be found within the lived experience of the law school for both the students and the legal academics involved.

Of course, when challenging the disregard and suppression of emotions within legal education there are likely to be difficulties along the way. Even assuming that the need for change is accepted at the both institutional and discipline-specific levels, issues may still arise such as that of academics lacking appropriate skills (Cownie, 2011), not to mention the difficulties in navigating the organisational confines in the way subjects are modularised and run (Guth, 2009; Twining, 1997b). Nevertheless, the myriad ways in which emotions form part of the theoretical and practical aspects of legal education, and the lived experience of the law school, all offer scope for a diverse and exciting range of ways in which to acknowledge and utilise their importance and value. For legal education to be fit for its purposes in the contemporary age, emotions must be an integral and holistic part of its lifeblood.

References

Abrams, K. (2009) "Barriers and Boundaries: Exploring Emotion in the Law of the Family", *Virginia Journal of Social Policy & the Law*, 16(2), 301–321.

Allen, J. and Baron, P. (2004) "Buttercup goes to Law School. Student Well-being in Stressed Law Schools", *Alternative Law Journal*, 29(6), 285–288.

Andrews, J. and Higson, H. (2008) "Graduate Employability, "Soft Skills" Versus "Hard" Business Knowledge: A European Study", *Higher Education in Europe*, 33(4), 411–422.

Averill, J. R. (2004) "A Tale of Two Snarks: Emotional Intelligence and Emotional Creativity", *Psychological Inquiry*, 15(3), 228–233.

Baker, G. (2008) "Rediscovering Therapeutic Jurisprudence in Overlooked Areas of the Law – How Exposing Its Presence in the Environmental Justice Movement Can Legitimize the Paradigm And Make the Case For Its Inclusion Into All Aspects of Legal Education and the Practice of Law", *Florida Coastal Law Review*, 9, 215–236.

Ball, M. (2009) "Learning, Labour and Employability", *Studies in the Education of Adults*, 41(1), 39–52.

Ball, S. J. (2003) "The Teacher's Soul and the Terrors of Performativity", *Journal of Education Policy*, 18(2), 215–228.

Bandes, S. A. and Blumenthal, J. A. (2012) "Emotion and the Law", *Annual Review of Law and Social Science*, 8(1), 161–181.

Bannerjee, R., Weare, K. and Farr, W. (2014) "Working with "Social and Emotional Aspects of Learning" (SEAL): Associations with School Ethos, Pupil Social Experiences, Attendance and Attainment", *British Educational Research Journal*, 40(4), 718–742.

Bartie, S. (2010) "The Lingering Core of Legal Scholarship", *Legal Studies*, 30(3), 345–369.

Beard, C., Clegg, S. and Smith, K. (2007) "Acknowledging the Affective in Higher Education", *British Educational Research Journal*, 33(2), 235–252.

Bellas, M. L. (1999) "Emotional Labor in Academia: The Case of Professors", *The Annals of the American Academy of Political and Social Science*, 561, 96–110.

Bergin, A. and Pakenham, K. (2015) "Law Student Stress: Relationships Between Academic Demands, Social Isolation, Career Pressure, Study/Life Imbalance and Adjustment Outcomes in Law Students", *Psychiatry, Psychology and Law*, 22(3), 388–406.

Bessant, S. E. F., Robinson, Z. P. and Ormerod, R. M. (2015) "Neoliberalism, New Public Management and the Sustainable Development Agenda of Higher Education: History, Contradictions and Synergies", *Environmental Education Research*, 21(3), 417–432.

Blalock, C. (2014) "Neoliberalism and the Crisis of Liberal Theory", *Law and Contemporary Problems*, 77, 71–103.

Boghossian, P. (2006) "Behaviorism, Constructivism, and Socratic Pedagogy", *Educational Philosophy and Theory*, 38(6), 713–722.

Bradney, A. (1995) "Raising the Drawbridge: Defending University Law Schools", *Web Journal of Current Legal Issues*, 1.

Bradney, A. (1998) "Law as a Parasitic Discipline", *Journal of Law and Society*, 25(1), 71–84.

Bradney, A. (2003) *Conversations Choices and Chances the Liberal Law School in the Twenty-First Century*, Oxford and Portland, Oregon, Hart Publishing.

Bradney, A. (2011) "English University Law Schools, the Age of Austerity and Human Flourishing", *International Journal of the Legal Profession*, 18(1–2), 59–71.

Bredo, E. (1997) "The Social Construction of Learning", in Pyhe, G. D. (ed), *Handbook of Academic Learning*, London, Academic Press Ltd, 3–45.

Bromberger, N. (2010) "Enhancing Law Student Learning – the Nurturing Teacher", *Legal Education Review*, 20(1–2), 45–57.

Brownsword, R. (1999) "Law Schools for Lawyers, Citizens and People", in Cownie, F. (ed), *The Law School: Global Issues, Local Questions*, Aldershot, Ashgate Publishing.

Burke, P. J. (2015) "Re/imagining Higher Education Pedagogies: Gender, Emotion and Difference", *Teaching in Higher Education*, 20(4), 388–401.

Burridge, R. and Webb, J. (2007) "The Values of Common Law Legal Education: Rethinking Rules, Responsibilities, Relationships and Roles in the Law School", *Legal Ethics*, 10(1), 72–97.

Burridge, R. and Webb, J. (2009) "The Values of Common Law Legal Education Reprised", *The Law Teacher*, 43(2), 263–269.

Burrows, R. (2012) "Living with the h-index: Metric Assemblages in the Contemporary Academy", *Sociological Review*, 60(2), 355–372.

Chamorro-Premuzic, T., Arteche, A., Bremner, A. J., Greven, C. and Furnham, A. (2010) "Soft Skills in Higher Education: Importance and Improvement Ratings as a Function of Individual Differences and Academic Performance", *Educational Psychology: An International Journal of Experimental Educational Psychology*, 30(2), 221–241.

Clegg, S. and David, M. (2006) "Passion, Pedagogies and the Project of the Personal in Higher Education", *Twenty-First Century Society*, 1(2), 149–165.

Collier, R. (2004) "'We're All Socio-Legal Now?' Legal Education, Scholarship and the "Global Knowledge Economy" – Reflections on the UK Experience", *Sydney Law Review*, 26(4), 503–536.

Conoghan, J. (2013) *Law and Gender*, Oxford, Oxford University Press.

Coplan, A. (2010) "Feeling without Thinking: Lessons from the Ancients on Emotions and Virtue-Acquisition", *Metaphilosophy*, 41(1–2), 132–151.

Cotterrell, R. (2002) "Subverting Orthodoxy, Making Law Central: A View of Socio-legal Studies", *Journal of Law and Society*, 29(4), 632–644.

Council of Australian Law Deans (2013) *Promoting Law-Student Well-being. Good Practice Guidelines for Law Schools*, www.cald.asn.au/assets/lists/Resources/Promoting%20Law%20Student%20Well-Being%20Good%20Practice%20Guidelines%20for%20Law%20Schools.pdf (accessed 7 January 2018).

Cownie, F. (2000) "The Importance of Theory in Law Teaching", *International Journal of the Legal Profession*, 7(3), 225–238.

Cownie, F. (2004) *Legal Academics Culture and Identities*, Oxford and Portland, Oregon, Hart Publishing.

Cownie, F. (2010) "Contextualising Stakeholders in the Law School", in Cownie, F. (ed), *Stakeholders in the Law School*, Oxford and Portland, Oregon, Hart Publishing Limited.

Cownie, F. (2011) "Twining, Teachers of Law and Law Teaching", *International Journal of the Legal Profession*, 18(1–2), 121–138.

Cownie, F. and Bradney, T. (2005) "Gothic Horror? A Response to Margaret Thornton", *Social & Legal Studies*, 14(2), 277–285.

Cullen, J., Hadjivassiliou, K., Hamilton, E., Kelleher, J., Sommerlad, E. and Stern, E. (2002) *Review of current pedagogic research and practice in the fields of post-compulsory education and lifelong learning. Final report for ESRC by the Tavistock Institute*, www.tlrp.org/pub/acadpub.html (accessed 6 October 2018).

Curzon, L. B. (2004) *Teaching in Further Education: An Outline of Principles and Practice*, 3rd edn, London and New York, Continuum.

Damasio, A. (2006) *"Descartes" Error*, London, Vintage.

D'Aoust, A.-M. (2014) "Ties that Bind? Engaging Emotions, Governmentality and Neoliberalism: Introduction to the Special Issue", *Global Society*, 28(3), 267–276.

Darwin, C. (Edited by Darwin, F.) (1890) *The Expression of the Emotions in Man and Animals*, 2nd edn, London, John Murray.

Davies, J. L. (1998) "The Shift from Teaching to Learning: Staff Recruitment and Career Development Policies Policies for the Universities of the Twenty First Century", *Higher Education in Europe*, XX111(3), 307–316.

Descartes, R. (Translator Voss, S. H.) (1989) *The Passions of the Soul*, Indianapolis, Hackett Publishing.

Ekman, P. (1992) "Are There Basic Emotions?", *Psychological Review*, 99(3), 550–553.

Ellsworth, P. C. (2013) "Appraisal Theory: Old and New Questions", *Emotion Review*, 5(2), 125–131.

Ertmer, P. A. and Timothy, J. N. (2013) "Behaviorism, Cognitivism, Constructivism: Comparing Critical Features from an Instrumental Design Perspective", *Performance Improvement Quarterly*, 26(2), 43–71.

Feldman Barrett, L. (2017) *How Emotions Are Made: The Secret Life of the Brain*, London, Macmillan.

Fish, S. (2008) *Save the World on Your Own Time*, New York, Oxford University Press.

Galloway, K. and Bradshaw, R. (2010) "Responding to Changed Parameters of the Law Student: A Reflection on Pastoral Care in the Law School", *Journal of the Australasian Law Teachers Association*, 3(1–2), 101–112.

Galloway, K., Bradshaw, R., Dunbar, N. and Fellows, J. (2011) "Approaches to Student Support in the First Year of Law School", *Legal Education Review*, 21(2), 235–249.

Garrison, J. (1998) "Toward a Pragmatic Social Constructivism", in Larochelle, M., Bednarz, N. and Garrison, J. (eds), *Constructivism and Education*, Cambridge, Cambridge University Press.

Gates, G. S. (2000) "The Socialization of Feelings in Undergraduate Education: A Study of Emotional Management", *College Student Journal*, 34(4), 485–504.

Gendron, M. and Feldman Barrett, L. (2009) "Reconstructing the Past: A Century of Ideas About Emotion in Psychology", *Emotion Review*, 1(4), 316–339.

Goleman, D. (1996) *Emotional Intelligence*, London, Bloomsbury.

Goodrich, P. (1996) "Of Blackstone's Tower: Metaphors of Distance and Histories of the English Law School", in Birks, P. (ed), *Pressing Problems in the Law Volume 2 What Are Law Schools for?* Oxford, Oxford University Press.

Green, K. and Lim, H. (1987) "A Lib-Lib Pact: Silences in Legal Education", *The Law Teacher*, 21(3), 256–262.

Gregory, J. (2006) "Experiential Learning", in Jarvis, P., Holford, J. and Griffin, C. (eds), *The Theory and Practice of Teaching*, 2nd edn, Abingdon and New York, Routledge, 114–129.

Grossi, R. (2015) "Understanding Law and Emotion", *Emotion Review*, 7(1), 55–60.

Grover, S. (2008) "Personal Integration and Outsider Status as Factors in Law Student Well-Being", *Washburn Law Journal*, 47, 419–452.

Grummell, B., Devine, D. and Lynch, K. (2009) "The Care-less Manager: Gender, Care and New Managerialism in Higher Education", *Gender and Education*, 21(2), 191–208.

Guth, J. (2009) "The Case for Time Turners – The Practicalities of Being a New Law Lecturer", *The Law Teacher*, 43(2), 185–199.

Hall, J. and Kerrigan, K. (2011) "Clinic and the Wider Law Curriculum", *International Journal of Clinical Legal Education*, 16, 25–37.

Hall, K. (2009) "Do We Really Want to Know? Recognising the Importance of Student Psychological Wellbeing in Australian Law Schools", *Queensland University of Technology, Law and Justice Journal*, 9(1), 1–12.

Hargreaves, A. (1998) "The Emotional Practice of Teaching", *Teaching and Teacher Education*, 14(8), 835–854.

Harris, D. R. (1983) "The Development of Socio-Legal Studies in the United Kingdom", *Legal Studies*, 3(3), 315–333.

Harris, P. and Beinart, S. (2005) "A Survey of Law Schools in the United Kingdom, 2005", *The Law Teacher*, 39(3), 299–366.

Heath, M., Galloway, K., Skead, N., Steel, A. and Israel, M. (2017) "Learning to Feel Like a Lawyer: Law Teachers, Sessional Teaching and Emotional Labour in Legal Education", *Griffith Law Review*, 26(3), 430–457.

Hepple, B. (1996) "The Renewal of the Liberal Law Degree", *Cambridge Law Journal*, 55(3), 470–487.

Hey, V. and Leathwood, C. (2009) "Passionate Attachments: Higher Education, Policy, Knowledge, Emotion and Social Justice", *Higher Education Policy*, 22(1), 101–118.

Hutchinson, T. and Duncan, N. (2012) "Defining and Describing What We Do: Doctrinal Legal Research", *Deakin Law Review*, 17(1), 83–119.

Hyland, T. (2014) "Mindfulness-based Interventions and the Affective Domain of Education", *Educational Studies*, 40(3), 277–291.

Iijima, A. (1998) "Lessons Learned: Legal Education and Law Student Dysfunction", *Journal of Legal Education*, 48(4), 524–538.

Illeris, K. (2009) "Introduction", in Illeris, K. (ed), *Contemporary Theories of Learning*, Abingdon, Routledge.

Immordio-Yang, M. H. and Damasio, A. (2011) "We Feel, Therefore We Learn: The Relevance of Affective and Social Neuroscience to Education", *Learning Landscapes*, 5(1), 115–131.

James, C. (2008) ""Lawyers" Well-being and Professional Legal Education", *The Law Teacher*, 42(1), 85–97.

James, W. (1884) "What is an Emotion?", *Mind*, 9, 188–205.

Johnstone, G. (1999) "Liberal Ideals and Vocational Aims in University Legal Education", Web *Journal of Current Legal Issues*, 3.

Jolly-Ryan, J. (2009) "Promoting Mental Health in Law School: What Law Schools Can Do for Law Students to Help Them Become Happy, Mentally Healthy Lawyers", *University of Louisville Law Review*, 48(1), 95–137.

Jones, E., Samra, R. and Lucassen, M. (2018) "The World at Their Fingertips? The Mental Wellbeing of Online Distance Learning Students", *The Law Teacher*, [early online access].

Jones, S. M., Bouffard, S. M. and Weissbourd, R. (2013) "Educators' Social and Emotional Skills Vital to Learning", *Kappan Magazine*, 94(8), 62–65.

Kennedy, D. (1982) "Legal Education and the Reproduction of Hierarchy", *Journal of Legal Education*, 32(4), 591–615.

Kinman, G. and Wray, S. (2013) *Higher Stress. A Survey of Stress and Well-being Among Staff in Higher Education*, University and College Union, www.ucu.org.uk/media/5911/Higher-stress-a-survey-of-stress-and-well-being-among-staff-in-higher-education-Jul-13/pdf/HE_stress_report_July_2013.pdf (accessed 12 October 2018).

Kiersey, N. J. (2014) ""Retail Therapy in the Dragon's Den": Neoliberalism and Affective Labour in the Popular Culture of Ireland's Financial Crisis", *Global Society*, 28(3), 356–374.

Knowles, M. (1984) *The Modern Practice of Adult Education: From Pedagogy to Andragogy*, Engelwood Cliffs, Cambridge Adult Education.

Kotzee, B. (2010) "Seven Posers in the Constructivist Classroom", *London Review of Education*, 8(2), 177–187.

Krannitch, J. M., Holbrook, J. R. and McAdams, J. J. (2009) ""Beyond "Thinking Like a Lawyer" and the Traditional Legal Paradigm: Towards a Comprehensive View of Legal Education", *Denver University Law Review*, 86(2), 381–404.

Krieger, L. S. (2002) "Psychological Insights: Why Our Students and Graduates Suffer and What We Might Do About It", *Journal of the Association of Legal Writing Directors*, 1(1), 258–265.

Krieger, L. S. (2008) "Human Nature as a New Guiding Philosophy for Legal Education and the Profession", *Washburn Law Journal*, 47(2), 247–312.

Larcombe, W., Tumbaga, L., Malkin, I., Nicholson, P. and Tokatlidis, O. (2013) "Does am Improved Experience of Law School Protect Students against Depression, Anxiety and Stress? An Empirical Study of Wellbeing and the Law School Experience of LLB and JD Students", *Sydney Law Review*, 35(2), 407–432.

Lazarus, R. S. (1984) "On the Primacy of Cognition", *American Psychologist*, 39(2), 124–129.

Lynch, K. (2006) "Neoliberalism and Marketisation: The Implications for Higher Education", *European Education Research Journal*, 5(1), 1–12.

Lynch, K. (2010) "Carelessness: A Hidden Doxa in Higher Education", *Arts & Humanities in Higher Education*, 9(1), 54–67.

MacLean, P. D. (1949) "Psychosomatic Disease and the "Visceral Brain" Recent Developments Bearing on the Papez Theory of Emotion", *Psychomatic Medicine*, 11, 338–353.

Maharg, P. (2000) "Rogers, Constructivism and Jurisprudence: Educational Critique and The Legal Curriculum", *International Journal of the Legal Profession*, 7(3), 189–203.

Maharg, P. and Maughan, C. (2011) "Introduction", in Maharg, P. and Maughan, C. (eds), *Affect and Legal Education. Emotion in Learning and Teaching the Law*, Aldershot, Ashgate Publishing, 1–10.

Maroney, T. A. (2006) "Law and Emotion: A Proposed Taxonomy of an Emerging Field", *Law and Human Behaviour*, 13(2), 119–142.

McArthur, J. (2011) "Reconsidering the Social and Economic Purposes of Higher Education", *Higher Education Research & Development*, 30(6), 737–749.

McCosker, H., Barnard, A. and Gerber, R. (2001) "Undertaking Sensitive Research: Issues and Strategies for Meeting the Safety Needs of all Participants", *Qualitative Social Research*, 2(1), Art. 22, www.qualitative-research.net/index.php/fqs/article/view/983/2142 (accessed 14 October 2018).

McCrudden, C. (2006) "Legal Research and the Social Sciences", *Law Quarterly Review*, 122, 632–650.

McIntosh, A. (2010) "Humanist Learning Theories", in McKintosh-Scott, A., Gidman, J. and Mason-Whitehead, E. (eds), *Key Concepts in Healthcare Education*, London, Sage Publications Ltd.

Menkel-Meadow, C. (1988) "Feminist Legal Theory, Critical Legal Studies, and Legal Education or "The Fem-Crits Go to Law School"", *Journal of Legal Education*, 38, 61–85.

Moors, A. (2014) "Flavours of Appraisal Theories of Emotion", *Emotion Review*, 6(4), 303–307.

Murphy, K. A. and Sideman, L. (2006) "The Two EIs", in Murphy, K. A. (ed), *A Critique of Emotional Intelligence. What Are the Problems and How Can They Be Fixed?* London, Lawrence Erlbaum Associates.

Naffine, N. (1990) *Law and the Sexes Explorations in Feminist Jurisprudence*, London, Allen & Unwin.

Nias, J. (1996) "Thinking about Feeling: The Emotions of Teaching", *Cambridge Journal of Education*, 26(3), 293–306.

Newman, J. H. (1994) *The Idea of a University Defined & Illustrated I. In nine discourses delivered to the Catholics of Dublin II. In occasional lectures and essays addressed to the members of the Catholic University*, London, Routledge.

Nussbaum, M. (1997) *Cultivating Humanity: A Classical Defense of Reform in Liberal Education*, Cambridge, Massachusetts, Harvard University Press.

Nussbaum, M. (2001) *Upheavals of Thought: The Intelligence of Emotions*, Cambridge, Cambridge University Press.

Oatley, K., Keltner, D. and Jenkins, J. M. (2006) *Understanding Emotions*, 2nd edn, London: Blackwell Publishing.

O'Connor, K. E. (2008) ""You Choose to Care": Teachers, Emotions and Professional Identity", *Teaching and Teacher Education*, 24(1), 117–126.

Pekrun, R. and Linnenbrink-Garcia, L. (2014) "Introduction to Emotions in Education", in Pekrun, R. and Linnenbrink-Garcia, L. (eds), *International Handbook of Emotions in Education*, London and New York, Routledge.

Pertegel-Felices, M. L., Castejon-Costa, J. L. and Jimeno-Morenilla, A. (2014) "Differences Between the Personal, Social and Emotional Profiles of Teaching and Computer Engineering Professionals and Students", *Studies in Higher Education*, 39(7), 1185–1201.

Pons, F., de Rosnay, M and Cuisinier, F. (2011) "Cognition and Emotion", in Aukrust, V. G. (ed), *Learning and Cognition in Education*, Oxford, Elsevier Limited.

Rhode, D. L. (1993) "Missing Questions: Feminist Perspectives on Legal Education", *Stanford Law Review*, 45(6), 1547–1566.

Rogers, C. (1957) "Personal Thoughts on Teaching and Learning", *Merrill-Palmer Quarterly*, 3, 241–243.

Rowland, S. (2008) "Collegiality and Intellectual Love", *British Journal of Sociology of Education*, 29(3), 353–360.

Sanders, A. (2015) "Poor Thinking, Poor Outcome? The Future of the Law Degree after the Legal Education and Training Review and the Case for Socio-Legalism", in Sommerlad, H., Harris-Short, S., Vaughan, S. and Young, R. (eds), *The Futures of Legal Education and the Legal Profession*, Oxford and Portland, Hart Publishing.

Sheldon, K. M. and Krieger, L. S. (2004) "Does Legal Education Have Undermining Effects on Law Students? Examining Changes in Motivation, Values, and Well-being", *Behavioral Sciences and the Law*, 22(2), 261–286.

Sheldon, K. S. and Krieger, L. S. (2007) "Understanding the Negative Effects of Legal Education on Law Students: A Longitudinal Test of Self-Determination Theory", *Personality and Social Psychology Bulletin*, 33(6), 883–897.

Schutz, P., Cross, D. I., Hong, J. Y. and Osbon, J. N. (2007) "Teacher Identities, Beliefs and Goals Related to Emotions in the Classroom", in Schutz, P. and Pekrun, R. (eds), *Emotion in Education*, Burlington, San Diego and London, Elsevier.

Schutz, P., Hong, J. Y., Cross, D. I. and Osbon, J. N. (2006) "Reflections on Investigating Emotion in Educational Activity Settings", *Educational Psychology Review*, 18(4), 343–360.

Sherry, S. (1996) "The Sleep of Reason", *Georgetown Law Journal*, 84, 453–484.

Shore, C. and Davidson, M. (2014) "Beyond Collusion and Resistance. Academic-management Relations Within the Neoliberal University", *Teaching and Learning*, 7(1), 12–28.

Siems, M. M. and Mac Sithigh, D. (2012) "Mapping Legal Research", *Cambridge Law Journal*, 71(3), 651–676.

Silver, M. A. (1999) "Emotional Intelligence and Legal Education", *Psychology, Public Policy and Law*, 5(4), 1173–1203.

Skread, N. K. and Rogers, S. L. (2014) "Stress, Anxiety and Depression in Law Students: How Student Behaviours Affect Student Wellbeing", *Monash University Law Review*, 30(2), 564–587.

Solomon, R. C. (2000) "The Philosophy of Emotions", in Lewis, M. and Haviland-Jones, J. M. (eds), *Handbook of Emotions*, 2nd edn, New York and London, The Guilford Press.

Stanley, C. (1988) "Training for the Hierarchy? Reflections on the British Experience of Legal Education", *The Law Teacher*, 22(2), 78–86.

Stropus, R. K. (1996) "Mend It, Bend It, and Extend It: The Fate of Traditional Law School Methodology in the 21st Century", *Loyola University of Chicago Law Journal*, 27(3), 449–489.

Sturm, S. P. (1998) "From Gladiators to Problem-Solvers: Connecting Conversations about Women, the Academy and the Legal Profession", *Duke Journal of Gender Law and Policy*, 4, 119–147.

Sugarman, D. (1983) "The Legal Boundaries of Liberty: Dicey, Liberalism and Legal Science. The Rule of Law: Albert Venn Dicey, Victorian Jurist by Richard A. Cosgrove", *The Modern Law Review*, 46(1), 102–111.

Sugarman, D. (1986) "Legal Theory, the Common Law Mind and the Making of the Textbook Tradition", in Twining, W. (ed), *Legal Theory and Common Law*, Oxford, Basil Blackwell.

Tani, M. and Vines, P. (2009) ""Law Students" Attitudes to Education: Pointers to Depression in the Legal Academy and the Profession?", *Legal Education Review*, 19, 3–39.

Thornton, M. (2001) "Among the Ruins: Law in the Neo-Liberal Academy", *Windsor Yearbook of Access to Justice*, 20, 3–24.

Towness O'Brien, M., Tang, S. and Hall, K. (2011a) "No Time to Loose: Negative Impact on Law Student Wellbeing may Begin in Year One", *The International Journal of the First Year in Higher Education*, 2(2), 49–60.

Towness O'Brien, M., Tang, S. and Hall, K. (2011b) "Changing our Thinking: Empirical Research on Law Student Wellbeing, Thinking Styles and the Law Curriculum", *Legal Education Review*, 21(1–2), 149–182.

Twining, W. (1994) *Blackstone's Tower. The English Law School*, London, Stevens & Sons/Sweet & Maxwell.

Twining, W. (1997a) "Introduction", in Twining, W. (ed), *Law in Context Enlarging a Discipline*, Oxford, Oxford University Press.

Twining, W. (1997b) "Pericles and the Plumber", in Twining, W. (ed), *Law in Context: Enlarging a Discipline*, Oxford, Oxford University Press.

Twining, W. (1998) "Thinking about Law Schools: Rutland Reviewed", *Journal of Law and Society*, 25(1), 1–13.

Vanistendael, H. (2009) "Designing a Humanistic Legal Education", *European Journal of Legal Education*, 3(1), 59–73.

Watkins, D. (2011) "The Role of Narratives in Legal Education", *Liverpool Law Review*, 33, 113–133.

Watts, J. and Robertson, N. (2011) "Burnout in University Teaching Staff: A Systematic Literature Review", *Educational Research*, 53(1), 33–50.

Webb, J. (2006) "The "Ambitious Modesty" of Harold Arthur's Humane Professionalism", *Osgoode Hall Law Journal*, 44(1), 119–155.

Williams, S. H. (1993) "Feminist Legal Epistemology", *Berkeley Women's Law Journal*, 8, 63–105.

Wilson, J. C. and Strevens, C. (2018) "Perceptions of Psychological Well-being in UK Law Academics", *The Law Teacher*, [early online access].

Yilmaz, K. (2011) "The Cognitive Perspective on Learning: Its Theoretical Underpinnings and Implications for Classroom Practices", *The Clearing House: A Journal of Educational Strategies, Issues and Ideas*, 84(5), 204–212.

Zembylas, M. (2007) "Emotional Ecology: The Intersection of Emotional Knowledge and Pedagogical Content Knowledge in Teaching", *Teaching and Teacher Education*, 23, 355–367.

Index

academic pressure 130, 131
ACLEC statement 89–90
"active" learning 104
adaptationalist view 63–64
administration 154–155
adult learning theories 114
adversarialism 132–133
affect 44, 58–59, 70–71, 126, 149
affective dimension 96
affective domain 9–10, 18, 23, 114, 162
affective forecasting 49
Advisory Committee on Legal Education and Conduct 89–90
andragogy 114
anxiety 105, 126, 128–129, 135, 140–141, 155, 158
appraisal theory/theories 63–65, 69, 70, 80, 170
Aristotle 63
autonomy 131, 132, 134, 135

basic emotions theory 60–61, 62, 70, 73; and Cartesian dualism 170; and legal education traditional paradigms 63
behaviourism 109, 110
behaviourist theories 109–111
better person 27
black-letter law/approach 18, 20, 37
bodily changes 61, 70
bodily expressions 60, 61
bodily sensations 2, 59
brain: hierarchical structure 62, 66, 170; mechanisms of emotions 66
Bruner, Jerome 111

Cannon-Bard theory 61
"care-less" academic 156, 158, 162, 175
Cartesian dualism 2–3, 6, 16, 44, 59, 61, 62, 93, 109, 115; and appraisal theory 170; and basic emotions theory 170; and cognitive theories 113; and legal education paradigms 80, 168
Cartesianism 2, 12, 43, 44, 50
case method 18
central affective programmes 66
civil law, and emotions 14–15
classical behaviourist theories 109
cognition 59; different concepts of 69–71; and emotions 62, 63–67, 68, 69–70, 74, 95, 105–106, 167; intertwined/interrelated with emotion 66, 67, 69, 74, 112, 149, 169–171, 176
cognitive dissonance 134
cognitive learning theories 111–112
cognitive theory/theories 70, 71, 80, 173
cognitivism 111, 112
cognitivist theories 113, 173
competitiveness 130–131
comprehensive law 16, 52–53
conditioning 109, 110, 119n1
constructivist learning theories 112–114, 117, 118, 173
constructivism 67–69, 111, 112, 116
corporatisation 85
criminal law, and emotions 14
critical epistemology 44–45
critical legal studies 43–49; criticism of 46
culture, of legal education 4, 6, 23, 30, 46, 59, 126, 133, 134, 139, 140, 153, 154, 162

Darwin, Charles 60
decision-making 65, 66–67
deep acting 160
depression 127–130, 134, 135
Descartes, Rene 2–3
disengagement from studies 136–137

doctrinal tradition 16–17, 30, 37–39, 88, 167; and basic emotions theory 63; critique of 20–21, 23, 24–25; current characterization of 22–23; development of 17–19; and emotions 17, 18, 19–20, 23; redefining 22; and socio-legal studies 37–39; and vocational legal education 21–22
dualist approach 73–74; *see also* Cartesian dualism

educational theory,lack of interest 24, 117, 173
emotional awareness 8
emotional competence/competencies 72, 92, 94–95, 172
emotional harm 14–15
emotional intelligence 6, 53, 71–73, 81, 92, 94–95, 148, 171
emotional labour 158–161
emotional literacy 86, 109, 150, 177
emotional phenomenon approach 49
"emotions as reason" approach 74
emotion-centered approach 49
emotion/emotions: acknowledgment of 5; approaches to within literature 49–50; circumscribed display of 2; and cognition 62, 63–67, 68, 69–70, 74, 95, 105–106, 167; as "communications" 71; conceptualising within higher education 115–119, 173; and decision-making 65; defined 58–59; embodied character of 62; general conceptions about 59–63; and information processing 65; judicial lack of regard for 16; and the law 1–2, 49–52; and learning 104–107; physiological aspects of 61–62; and reason 1, 3, 63–67; and sentiment 157; socially constructed 68–69; suppression of 2, 12, 15, 17, 30, 46, 115; in teaching 148–154; three broad approaches to 73–74; transformative power of 5; *see also* emotional labour; emotions in legal education; reason and emotion
"emotions and reason" approach 74–75, 171
emotions in legal education: 3–7, 52, 73–75, 107, 167, 175–176; *see also* emotion/emotions
emotion-theory approach 49, 50
empathy 27, 93, 107, 150
employability 22, 80, 81, 84, 152

eudaimonia 13, 126
experiential learning 114
experiential thinking 133–134
extrinsic motivations 137
extrinsic values 132, 134, 137

family law, and emotions 15, 16
feeling 64
feminist and critical approaches 43, 52, 80
feminist legal epistemology 45
feminist legal studies/thought 46–49, 169–170
formalism 45, 46

generalized emotions theory 66
good citizenship 26–27, 88
good teacher 117
group work 131

Harvard 18, 19
higher education 80, 84, 85; conceptualising emotions within 115–118; "golden age" of 82; and measurable outcomes 86; new role of 81–83; and skills 92–94; 96; *see also* university/universities
holistic: approach to legal education 4, 9, 31, 139–140, 142, 154, 162, 167, 177–178; approach to legal practice 52; learning process 175; way of thinking 133
humanist learning theories 114–115, 118, 173

induction programme 176–177
integrative law 52–53
intelligence 72, 92–93; *see also* emotional intelligence
intentionality 70
intrinsic motivation 134, 137, 138–139; of legal academics 156; of teachers 151
intrinsic values 132, 135, 137

James-Lange theory 61
judgement, and emotions 58, 63, 69, 70, 74, 121
judicial oath 15
jury 15, 16

law and emotions scholarship 43, 49–52, 170; currents in 50–51
Law and Society 36; *see also* socio-legal studies
Law in the Real World 42

learning and emotions 104–107, 113, 119, 136, 172–174; in law schools 117
learning programmes, social and emotional 107–108
learning theories 108–109, 116–118, 172–173; behaviourist 109–111; cognitive 111–112; constructivist 112–114; and emotions 113–114, 116
legal academics 7, 161–162; the work of 147–148; emotional impact of research and administration on 154–158; factors impacting psychological wellbeing 158; and focus on performance 154–155, 156; intrinsic motivation of 156; and socio-legal studies 37; stifling of positive emotions 155–156
legal academy 3, 9, 25, 29, 38, 40, 43, 51, 54, 89, 96, 97, 147, 150, 153, 154, 161, 172, 175, 176
legal actors 12; and emotions 15–16
legal culture 4, 38
legal doctrine 13, 21, 46
Legal Education and Training Review (LETR) Report 95–96
legal education: definitions within 95–96; growth of 83; influence of neo-liberalism on 89; *see also* emotions in legal education
legal positivism 12, 13–14
legal research 22, 37, 39, 40, 42
legal-actor approach 50
liberal education 24–26, 28
liberal legal education 23–24, 25, 26–27; critiques of 28; and emotions 26, 27, 28, 29; and vocationalism 26
liberal tradition 23–29; and basic emotions theory 63
liberalism 28, 29
libertarianism 17
loss of control defence 1, 14

managerialism 85, 86
master and slave metaphor 3, 14
memory 136, 149

narrative imagination 27
natural law theory 12–13, 14
neo-behaviourist theories 109–110
neo-liberal ideology 81, 83–84; and law 88; and soft skills 94, 171–172; and emotions 93–94
neo-liberal law school 88–92
neo-liberalism 83–88, 141, 172; emotional components of 93; impact on society 84–85; impact on universities 85; and legal academics 154–157, and New Public Management theory 84; origins in the UK 84
New Public Management theory 84
non-cognitive theory/theories 69, 70
norms, within legal education 6, 23, 30, 69, 75, 128, 140, 152
Nuffield Inquiry 42–43

objectivism 45, 46
objectivity 13, 15, 17, 20, 28, 29, 47
Ormrod Report 82, 89
orientation 139, 153

pastoral care/support/work 136, 153; and women 154–155
pedagogic techniques 177
Piaget, Jean 111, 112
Plato 59
politics and policies: government policies 84; in academia/higher education 8, 80–81, 167, 176; in education 149, 152; neo-liberal 157
preventative law 16
"primary" appraisal 64
propositional attitude/thoughts 69, 70
psychological distress 126–130, 174; and lack of autonomy 132; and lack of social connectedness 135

Quality Assurance Agency (QAA) 90

rational thinking 133
rational-experiential inventory 133–134
rationality 2–3, 14, 16; in liberal legal education 28, 29
reason 44; supremacy of 30; *see also* reason and emotions; reason and rationality
reason and emotions 1, 3, 15, 19, 58; dichotomised 12–15; intertwined 63–67, 106–107; polarization of 30; *see also* cognition
reason and rationality 24, 27, 28, 29, 30, 73; *see also* rationality; reason and emotions
recognition current 50–51
reconnaissance current 50, 51
regulation current 51

research 154, 156, 157
resistance: dissipate 93; to neo-liberal policies 87, 96, 157, 172, 175; to the incorporation of emotion 23, 147
Robbins Report 81–83

SAFE principles 107–108
scaffolding 113, 139; emotional 148
science 13, 18, 19, 40, 50
"secondary" appraisal 64
SEAL programme 108
self-determination 132
self-determination theory 132, 158
self-efficacy 137
self-esteem 106
self-regulation 106
skills 81, 83, 84, 86–87, 89–91, 94, 95–96, 172; academic 89, 90; analytical 22; and attributes 92, 95–96; definitions of 92; vocational 89, 90, 91; *see also* soft skills
skills agenda, implementing 87, 96
Skinner, Burrhus Frederic 110
social and emotional learning programmes 107–108, 139–140
social connectedness 135, 139–140
social constructivism 112, 114
socialisation, of law students 6, 30
socio-legal studies 36–41, 66, 170; and basic emotions theory 80; development of 36–37; and doctrinal tradition 37–39; emotions in 41–43
Socratic method 18–19
soft skills 80–81, 85, 86, 92–95, 97n1, 137, 171–172; definitions of 92; and emotional competencies 92; emotions as a form of 85, 97
Solicitors Qualifying Examination (SQE) 41
somatic-marker hypothesis 65
stress 140–141; in academics 157; and disengagement from studies 136–137; and learning/academic performance 136; in legal academics 158; reduction 140; in students 126, 128, 129, 130, 138
student support 139, 148, 153
suicide 127, 129
suppression of emotions 2, 12, 15, 17, 30
surface acting 160

teaching: approach to 151; quality of 151; role of emotions in 148–154, 174; teachers' emotions 149; and training 153–154; *see also* emotional labour
teaching, social and cultural factors 151–152, 159
theory-of-law approach 50
therapeutic jurisprudence 53, 97
"thinking like a lawyer" 21, 30, 44, 69, 89, 132, 133, 134, 174
transformation 4–5, 7
transformative learning theory 4
tripartite soul 59
two factor theory 61–62

university/universities 81–83; corporatisation of 85; focus on useful knowledge 85–86; four themes in 85–86; and neo-liberalism 84–85; response to neo-liberalization 87–88

values 29, 132, 134, 147
victim impact statements 14
vocationalism 22, 26, 96, 97, 172
vocational legal education 21–22; *see also* vocationalism

wellbeing of law students 174; and competitiveness 130–131; and lack of social connectedness 135; and self-determination 132; and emotions 125–126; and student values 132; psychological distress 126–130, 132
whole school approach 108, 139
work-life balance 29, 158

For Product Safety Concerns and Information please contact our EU
representative GPSR@taylorandfrancis.com
Taylor & Francis Verlag GmbH, Kaufingerstraße 24, 80331 München, Germany

www.ingramcontent.com/pod-product-compliance
Ingram Content Group UK Ltd.
Pitfield, Milton Keynes, MK11 3LW, UK
UKHW011014180926
475701UK00004B/730
* 9 7 8 1 0 3 2 2 4 0 5 1 0 *